Congress Against the President

Proceedings of
The Academy of
Political Science

Volume 32
Number 1

Edited by Harvey C. Mansfield, Sr.

New York, 1975

Congress Against the President

Contents

Preface

The relations between Congress and the president at any given time are a simultaneous and shifting mixture of cooperation, comity, and conflict. This volume brings together thirteen studies of facets of these relations as they appeared in the opening session of the Ninety-fourth Congress, in 1975, when the tides of conflict, though subsiding after the resignation of President Nixon, were still strong and prominent. The short-run effects of that event, moreover, were mingled with longer term influences previously under way that are profoundly altering the operation of congressional institutions, and thereby the capacity of Congress to prevail against the president. The basic theme of this volume is a test of the continuing truth of Madison's observation (*The Federalist*, No. 49), "that the tendency of republican governments is to an aggrandizement of the legislative at the expense of the other departments."

Some of the essays in this book were discussed at a conference sponsored by the Academy of Political Science on June 2, 1975, at the Center for Continuing Education, Columbia University. The Academy is deeply grateful to Harvey C. Mansfield, Sr., Ruggles Professor Emeritus of Public Law and Government in Columbia University, who organized the conference and edited this volume. Professor Mansfield's scholarly studies of Congress and the presidency are well known to all students of American government.

The Academy serves as a forum for the dissemination of informed opinion on public questions, but it makes no recommendations on political issues. The views expressed in this volume do not necessarily reflect those of the Academy, the editor, or the institutions with which the authors are affiliated.

74070

ROBERT H. CONNERY
President of the Academy

Contributors

MARGUERITE ROSS BARNETT is Assistant Professor, Department of Politics, and James Madison Bicentennial Preceptor, Princeton University. In 1974–75, she was Guest Scholar, Brookings Institution.

ROBERT G. DIXON, JR., who has served as an Assistant Attorney General, is Daniel Noyes Kirby Professor of Law, Washington University, St. Louis.

HARRISON W. FOX, JR., is Director of Legislation and Research, Office of Senator William Brock. He is coauthor, with Susan Webb Hammond, of a forthcoming book titled *Congressional Staffs*.

SUSAN WEBB HAMMOND is Assistant Professor of Political Science, The American University.

RALPH K. HUITT, Executive Director of the National Association of State Universities and Land-Grant Colleges, is on leave from the University of Wisconsin, Madison, where he is Professor of Political Science. He is coauthor of *Congress: Two Decades of Analysis*.

MAX M. KAMPELMAN is Senior Partner in the Washington law firm, Fried, Frank, Harris, Shriver & Kampelman. A former counsel to Senator Hubert Humphrey, he is the author of *Legislative Control of the Bureaucracy*. He was the first moderator of the public television program "Washington Week in Review."

SUSAN B. KING is the Founder, Vice President, and Executive Director, Center for Public Financing of Elections. She is the former Washington Director, National Committee for an Effective Congress.

EDWARD A. KOLODZIEJ is Professor and Head, Department of Political Science, University of Illinois, Urbana-Champaign.

HARVEY C. MANSFIELD, SR., is Ruggles Professor Emeritus of Public Law and Government, Columbia University. He was managing editor of the *American Political Science Review*, 1956–65, and has held government and consulting positions.

RONALD C. MOE is Senior Analyst, Government Division, Congressional Research Service, Library of Congress.

ROBERT L. PEABODY, Professor of Political Science, Johns Hopkins University, is coauthor of *To Enact a Law: Congress and Campaign Finance*, and, since 1965, Associate Director, American Political Science Association Study of Congress.

RICHARD M. PIOUS, Assistant Professor of Political Science at Barnard College, is writing a book on the presidency .

HARRY HOWE RANSOM, Professor of Political Science and former Chancellor, Vanderbilt University, is the author of *Central Intelligence and National Security*.

ALLEN SCHICK, who has served as Consultant, U.S. Bureau of the Budget, is Senior Specialist, Congressional Research Service. He is the author of *Budget Innovation in the States*.

JOHN G. STEWART, who served in Hubert Humphrey's office as Legislative Assistant to the Vice President, is Executive Director of the Democratic Advisory Council of Elected Officials.

The Dispersion of Authority in Congress

HARVEY C. MANSFIELD, SR.

Three long-term phenomena seem directly pertinent to the dispersion of authority in Congress. One is institutional—the transition, spread over a generation, in the outlooks, attitudes, and roles of members of Congress consequent on their becoming, so many of them, full-time rather than part-time legislators. The bulk of the present essay is devoted to tracing the source and some immediate ramifications of this change, in the direction of the further dispersion of authority in Congress. One of these is the growth of professional staff, the subject of a separate study by Harrison W. Fox, Jr., and Susan Webb Hammond. The dispersion itself furnishes incentives for the emergence of informal, policy-oriented groupings. Marguerite Ross Barnett examines the ambivalences in one of these, the Congressional Black Caucus. The dispersion also raises afresh the larger problem of creating stable central policy organs in Congress and the role of party organization in that regard. John Stewart reviews developments along that line, including the revival of the caucus. Dispersion raises again the perennial issues over the origins of domestic policy initiatives and the urgent need for recognized and dependable channels of communication from the White House to the Hill if cooperation is to loom larger than conflict in the mix of relationships. Richard M. Pious and Ralph K. Huitt consider these issues from very different vantage points.

A second and more far-reaching change in the political system, post-World War II, is the rise and ubiquity of the media—the flowering of investigative reporting, the dominance of television selections and presentations of demonstrations and other crowd events, as well as of news and opinion, and the intensified demands for more "sunlight"—disclosure—and less privacy for the conduct of governmental business. Congressional committees had their days of glory exploiting the media in 1973 and 1974, when the Ervin committee of senators and the Rodino committee of House Judiciary members held the nation's fascinated attention as they probed malfeasance in the White House. But usually the advantage of access to the media lies with the president. Max Kampelman's essay questions whether their power is sufficiently matched with responsibility.

In the Ninety-third Congress, as the conflict with President Nixon heightened toward its climax, the Senate gained the cooperation of the House in extending the coverage of its power of confirmation of executive appointments. Ronald C. Moe reviews the fruits of this tactic. Both chambers engaged also in pushing perennial boundary disputes with the executive over issues of shared administration, legislative vetoes, classified access to documents, and assertions of executive privilege—the subject of Robert G. Dixon's essay.

Congress was not content with tactical moves, however. There was a cyclical character, combining short-run opportunities with long-run needs, marking two major institutional reforms that were driven through to the statute books, on the budget and on presidential campaign finance. Three times in this century the Congress, controlled by one of the major parties, has ridden high on electoral success, or the smell of it, while the presidency, controlled by the other party, sank to a political nadir. Confrontation ensued on each occasion, not only over specific policies but, transcending these, also over the continuing relationships between the two branches, as Congress tried to nail down the advantage it had gained. A firmer grasp on federal finances was a principle objective.

In 1918-20 a triumphant Republican Congress stopped Woodrow Wilson's drive toward United States membership in the League of Nations, and went on in quest of "normalcy" to enact the Budget and Accounting Act of 1921 and to restore to the appropriations committees their lost monopoly jurisdiction over expenditures. Ironically, that act proved in practice to be the initial step in the direction of the later creation of the Executive Office at the President—the institutionalized presidency.

In 1946-48 a Republican Congress went along with President Truman in a bipartisan foreign policy but fought him to a standstill over domestic affairs, such as housing, and passed the Taft-Hartley Act over his veto. A permanent institutional residue, the Legislative Reorganization Act of 1946—also a bipartisan effort—was a landmark on the way to recognition of the need for legislative staffing. It greatly strengthened committee operations, but its ambitious attempt to erect a Joint Budget Committee in comprehensive control of expenditures proved stillborn. Ironically, the committee realignments presently secured the dominance of an oligarchy of mostly conservative committee chairmen selected by strict seniority. Under such a regime the president and his agents could often outweigh or outwit the nominal congressional leadership.

In 1973-74 a Democratic Congress, challenged by the appropriation impoundments, budget ceilings, and assertions of fiscal virtue by a Republican president, passed the Congressional Budget and Impoundment Control Act. President Nixon signed it, among the last of his official acts before resigning. Allen Schick's analysis herein makes it plain that this will not put an end to budget battles.

A different cyclical span of years marks the intervals between scandals that have precipitated legislative regulations of campaign finances. The prohibition against corporate and national bank contributions goes back to Theodore Roosevelt's time. The Corrupt Practices Act of 1925, after Teapot Dome, fashioned a broader screen that turned out rather to be a sieve. The Hatch Act of 1939 and the Taft-Hartley restraint on union donations had anti-New Deal overtones. Accident, in part, then, and in part a response to the growing sense that the escalation of media costs in a television culture required a fresh approach, as well as the events of the 1972 campaign conjoined to bring about the passage of the Federal Election Campaign Act Amendments of 1974. The Congress here prescribed medicine for presidential campaigns that it was not ready to accept for itself. As Susan King and Robert Peabody show, this may nevertheless introduce the most durable and significant of all the institutional changes in executive-congressional relations attributable to the Watergate era.

Finally, a third fundamental change in the post-World War II domestic political system, is the necessity of adapting to a permanent large-scale military establishment and global diplomacy. After all previous wars the military were packed off home and ignored until the next time. But ever since the Korean war, the Defense Department, the Central Intelligence Agency, other security agencies, the atomic energy agencies, and all their related and advanced technology industries have been maintained at high levels of strength and development. Congress accordingly has had to deal in peacetime—or at any rate in the absence of any pervasive sense of domestic danger or emergency—with civil-military and foreign policy issues, problems of congressional control over secret operations, the use of forces abroad, foreign military and economic aid, and the like, that in 1973-74 strained and ultimately burst the ordinary limits of executive-legislative cooperation. Harry Howe Ransom and Edward A. Kolodziej focus in their essays on the inherent tensions and ensuing conflicts in these areas, culminating in such events as the War Powers Act and the exposure of the CIA.

It is pertinent now to return to the initial theme, the subtle redistribution of influence that has been taking place within the national legislature and affecting its capacity to confront the executive. An underlying question accordingly is whether—paraphrasing a celebrated remark about

General Motors—what is good for the member is good for the Congress.

The fragmented nature of congressional authority in Congress is a familiar theme. Woodrow Wilson remarked on it in 1885 while pointing to tyrannies in committee chairmanships and in the speaker's office. It was a target in debates on the Legislative Reorganization Acts of 1946 and 1970. To some degree it is inherent in a structural arrangement of separate powers that locates the executive, not within the legislative branch, as in a parliamentary government, but outside it, and makes the legislature bicameral as well. But one need only look at some state legislatures, such as New York's or Ohio's, where party discipline is firmly maintained, to realize that the separation of powers is not by itself a sufficient explanation.

Nor does the erosion of party discipline fully explain the fragmentation. At a time when their sanctions were far more formidable, James Bryce described the congressional parties as "headless." Their enfeeblement is a general and long-run trend in this country, traceable back to the early years of this century, and affecting many other institutions and political processes besides the Congress. The decline of partisanship has not prevented the emergence of formal and informal concentrations of authority in Congress in recent decades over such immensely important fields as atomic energy policy and tax policy—concentrations only lately appearing to be in some stage of disintegration. In the 1950s and 1960s, first Pat McCarran and then Lyndon Johnson in the Senate and Wilbur Mills in the House forged personal networks of influence not seen in Congress since.

But the dispersion of authority so evident in the Ninety-third and Ninety-fourth Congresses in 1974 and 1975 is a very different matter from what Woodrow Wilson observed. Dispersion has been on the increase, irregularly but irreversibly, since the end of World War II. It has increased in spite of certain provisions of the Legislative Reorganization Acts that pointed in the opposite direction and notwithstanding a good deal of preaching—not only from academic sources—about the need for party responsibility and its advantages. A movement that potent, that important to the workings of Congress, calls for further explanation. It could hardly have been planned.

Without claiming to offer a single-cause diagnosis of a complex condition, the first thesis of this essay argues that unanticipated side effects of the Twentieth Amendment have been influential and overlooked factors in bringing about the present outcome, by providing a set of incentives to which members of Congress have individually responded on a wide scale, without plan or conspiracy, and in the name of civic virtue. A second thesis is that the resulting institutionalization and professionalization, especially of the House, are transforming the nature of the legislative regime, and thereby of its processes and of its resources and motives for coping with the executive branch. More particularly, the changes seem to accentuate the familiar paradox of participation. In Harlan Cleveland's words, "How do you get everybody in on the act and still get some action?"

The Twentieth Amendment

The so-called Lame Duck Amendment was the culmination of a decade of persistent efforts by Senator George W. Norris of Nebraska. As he tells the story in his autobiography, he became outraged at the passage of the ship subsidy bill in December 1922, in the short session following the congressional elections, with the crucial votes of a number of members who had been defeated for reelection the month before when that bill was a prominent issue. Lame ducks, beyond accountability to the voters, were easy targets for corrupting influences, from the executive branch or from outside the government.

The biennial short session with its fixed terminus at noon of March 4 also put a premium on holdup tactics by filibusterers, especially in the Senate. Senator Norris himself had taken active leadership in the famous filibuster in the spring of 1917 (not during a lame-duck session) against President Wilson's proposal to arm merchant ships. But he justified this exception by the gravity of the issue—"the issue of war," as he saw it—and regarded the filibuster generally as "often a national disgrace" and in any event "a legislative weapon to be employed sparingly if at all."[1] Shifting the inaugural date back from March 4 and the beginning of congressional terms and sessions forward, to January dates, was therefore a stone to kill two birds. It would also set the newly elected Congress to work within sixty days, discontinuing the customary thirteen-month wait unless a special session were called.

The Norris resolution proposing the amendment passed the Senate easily in February 1923 (after being stripped of a provision that would also have abolished the electoral college in favor of a direct popular vote for the president and vice president), but in the House it was buried in committee. In succeeding Congresses it passed the Senate five more times, in alternate years until the climax in 1932. It had once reached a floor vote in the House, in March 1928, a reform presidential year, but passed by a majority short of the needed two-thirds. In the last days of February 1931—with a touch of irony, in the lame-duck session following the marginal Democratic victory the previous November—it was the victim of a conference deadlock over a House amendment that would have retained the March 4 closing. In the opening weeks of the long session the

---

[1] George W. Norris, *Fighting Liberal: The Autobiography of George W. Norris* (New York: Macmillan Co., 1946), p. 175. Chapter 19 recounts the tactics of the 1917 filibuster. Chapter 31 gives his account of the lame-duck amendment.

next year, January 1932, with both chambers then Democratic by an edge, it was adopted by overwhelming bipartisan majorities. Ratification proceeded swiftly and was completed in January 1933.

The obstruction that had delayed matters for ten years was Speaker Longworth; plainly, he felt a vested interest in the status quo. In a lame-duck session, particularly toward its end, his influence was greatly enhanced by the discretionary authority of the presiding chair to recognize or fail to recognize members clamoring for brief access to the floor for action on their bills or amendments before the constitutional guillotine descended at noon, March 4. With his demise as speaker, the resistance collapsed. The merits of doing away with the lame-duck session were taken for granted. Much of the brief floor debate was devoted to exposition of another feature of the amendment, irrelevant here and also non-controversial, that was designed to fill a constitutional void—to provide for the succession in the several contingencies that might arise if a presidential or vice presidential candidate should have died or failed to qualify at the commencement of his term.

The Twentieth Amendment took effect with the Congress following the midterm elections of 1934; the first session of the Seventy-fourth Congress opened on January 3, 1935. As for the president, it took effect after the 1936 election, shortening Roosevelt's first term by some six weeks. It also eliminated the need for brief special sessions of the Senate alone in March or April, a regular quadrennial feature in previous history, to act on presidential nominations that required immediate senatorial confirmation; the last of these occurred over the weekend March 4-6, 1933. Unnoticed, new incentives for members came into play.

Continuous Sessions

With every annual session since January 1935 open-ended, the average length of sessions forthwith increased. Regular sessions have adjourned as early as the third week in June only twice (1936 and 1938); only twice more (1952 and 1956), as early as July; and eight times in August but two of these (1937 and 1939) were followed by special sessions in the fall. The regular sessions have not adjourned as early as August since 1958, Eisenhower's second midterm. From January 1940 through 1974, seventeen sessions—nearly half the total—lasted to adjournment dates in December or even into the first days of January. Practically speaking, and apart from short recesses for Lincoln's birthday and Jackson Day functions, nominating conventions, elections, and Christmas, Congress has been in virtually continuous session since January 1939—upwards of thirty-five years, longer than the service of any senator still in office in 1975 and longer than the service of all but four or five veterans in the House in 1975.

Table 1 shows how sharp the contrast is between current and historical experience. During the 112 years from Jefferson's time—when the government settled in its new capital in Washington—through Taft's, the regular sessions ran scarcely a dozen times through the summer to adjournment dates in September or later. The figures exclude special sessions, on the premise that members did not base their long-term career expec-

TABLE 1

Duration of Annual Regular Sessions of Congress,
1801–1974, by Selected Periods

	Session length, in days					
	Under 100	100–150	150–200	200–250	250–300	Over 300
Period 1801–1912, sessions commencing usually in early December:						
Odd-numbered years	0	6	16	21	9	4
Even-numbered years	50	5	1	0	0	0
Period 1913–33, sessions commencing usually in early December:						
Odd-numbered years	0	0	3	3	2	2
Even-numbered years	10	0	0	0	0	0
Period 1934–39, sessions commencing in January:	0	0	3	3	0	0
Period 1940–74, sessions commencing in January:	0	0	1	8	9	17
Totals:	60	11	24	35	20	23

Source: *Congressional Directory*, 93d Cong., 1st sess. (Washington: GPO, 1973), pp. 394–400.

tations or calculations on these unpredictable occurrences. But even so, table 2 shows that in the whole of the nineteenth century, special sessions adding more than two months were held only five times. Only once, from March 4, 1867, to March 3, 1869, was there a nearly continuous span, in the contest with Andrew Johnson. Lengthy special sessions, of ninety-nine days or more, became more frequent in the twentieth century, always in odd-numbered years: two in Taft's administration, three in Wilson's, and one each in Harding's, Hoover's, and Franklin Roosevelt's.

The immediate effect of the Twentieth Amendment was to lengthen the short sessions, not the long ones. From 1934 through 1939 the pattern of regular sessions alternated between adjournments in June in even (election) years and in August in odd years. So there may be something to David Brinkley's comment, broadcast over NBC on June 20, 1974. The

TABLE 2
Duration of Special Sessions of Congress, 1801–1974

Nineteenth Century		Twentieth Century	
Year	No. of days	Year	No. of days
1801–08	None		
1809	38	1903	29
1813	71	1909	144
1837	43	1911	141
1861	34	1913	239
1867	274	1917	188
1869	38	1919	185
1871	48	1921	227
1877	50	1922	15
1879	106	1929	222
1893	89	1933	99
1897	131	1937	37
		1939	44

Source: Same as for table 1.
Note: No special session in years not listed.

introduction of air-conditioning equipment into members' offices in the late 1930s, he lamented, made summertime work in Washington tolerable, and so was responsible for the regular year-round sessions—to the detriment of the Treasury and the taxpayers. But very few government offices were air-conditioned during World War II when the new pattern of annual sessions running at least into the autumn took permanent hold. The Twentieth Amendment had an enabling effect; it or its equivalent was a necessary though not a sufficient condition for the wholesale change in the career outlooks of congressmen that has underlain the dispersion of authority. Adaptations to the changed outlooks have spread across a generation and more and are not yet complete. Part-time legislators are likely also to be short-term legislators; in any event they need another source of livelihood. Full-time legislators, unless independently wealthy, must find their livelihoods in office.

Tenure and Turnover in the House

The figures on the duration of sessions therefore need to be read in conjunction with the dramatic changes in the tenure and turnover of seats that have also taken place since the nineteenth century, particularly in the House. James Bryce had that earlier experience in mind when he remarked, "Uneasy lies the head of an ambitious congressman, for the chances are almost even that he will lose his seat at the next election."[2] Stability is the modern rule.

[2] James Bryce, The American Commonwealth, rev. ed., vol. 1 (New York: Macmillan Co., 1920), p. 150.

A decade ago two perceptive academic observers directed attention to the phenomenon of growing professionalization and institutionalization in the House. A considerable body of scholarly literature on the subject has extended and refined their work.[3] On turnover, the record shows that the percentage of first-term members at the opening of each Congress, from the beginning through the entire nineteenth century, fell below thirty-five only once (1827); it rose above sixty twice (1843 and 1853). After the Civil War the trend turned downward irregularly, and after 1883 the percentage never again topped fifty; after 1895, never above forty. The twentieth century story is different. The percentage of first-termers dipped below twenty in 1909 and 1917 and again in the Coolidge-Hoover era, but stayed consistently so low only after 1949. It broke above that ceiling, barely, in 1965, but in 1969 for the first time dropped below ten, also just barely. So when the 1974 elections once more returned newcomers to a fifth of the House seats, that result in itself was extraordinary only in comparison with the experience of the previous two decades. The current norm, in the approximate range between 12 and 18 percent, dates from 1951. Price attributed the great shift from the nineteenth century turnover pattern mainly to the party realignments of 1894 and 1896, which made many more seats safe. This shift could not account, however, for the far higher degree of stability in membership prevailing since World War II, when the practice of continuous sessions became permanently established.

As to tenure, the average terms of service of the incumbent members of the House, again for each Congress from the beginning through the nineteenth century, fluctuated only by fractions above and below 2.0 terms, though after 1875 no longer below. It moved above 3.0 for the first time in 1901. It crept up gradually to a peak of 4.48 terms in 1931 —matching the reduction in turnover in the late 1920s—but dropped back during the depression decade. It returned to 4.24 in 1941, to stay above 4.0. In 1955 it pushed past the ten-year average mark with a figure of 5.19, and has remained somewhat above that ever since: 5.65 in 1973 and 5.3 in 1975.

[3] H. Douglas Price, "The Congressional Career—Then and Now," originally a working paper for the American Assembly in 1964, reprinted in *Congressional Behavior,* ed. Nelson W. Polsby (New York: Random House, 1971), pp. 14–27; see also his "Congress and the Evolution of Legislative 'Professionalism,' " in *Congress in Change,* ed. Norman J. Ornstein (New York: Praeger Publishers, 1975), pp. 2–23, and in that same volume, Morris P. Fiorina, David W. Rohde, and Peter Wissel, "Historical Change in House Turnover," pp. 24–57; Polsby, "The Institutionalization of the U.S. House of Representatives," *American Political Science Review* 62 (March 1968), 144–168; Charles S. Bullock, III, "House Careerists: Changing Patterns of Longevity and Attrition," *APSR* 66 (December 1972), 1295–1300. Data on turnover and tenure in the text herein have been taken from these sources, chiefly the last three.

Seniority as Incentive

The start of inflexible deference to seniority as the basis for advancement within the committee structure of the House is shrouded in the obscurity and distractions of the World War I years. It was not in place in 1911, when the Democrats organized the House after the demise of Speaker Cannon's authority the year before, nor was it installed in 1913 when Wilson had a legislative program. Average tenure at that time appeared stable within a narrow range: from 3.48 terms in 1905 to 3.44 in 1915, from a bulge at 3.84 in 1909 to another of 3.83 in 1917. Seniority is a means of supporting and administering oligarchy while minimizing hard feelings. It is a form of rationing a limited supply of authority by queuing, in the dimension of time. The seniority rule, starting in the late 1930s, after the Twentieth Amendment and when continuous sessions also began to be the rule, came to operate in a generation of rising tenure expectations. Departures from rigid adherence to it in recent years, prior to 1975, cannot be laid to any decline in these anticipations. On the contrary, they rather appear to be concessions to dissatisfaction with its arbitrary consequences in certain limited cases.

The unprecedented unhorsing of three veteran House committee chairmen in the organization of the Ninety-fourth Congress in 1975 coincided, to be sure, with a dip in average tenure occasioned by an unusually large retirement of seniors and influx of freshmen in 1974, by the shadow of Watergate, and by the fortuitous eclipse of Wilbur Mills. These were short-term factors. The longer-term truth, it seems fair to surmise, is that with the spread as well as the lengthening of tenure the seniority rule is becoming dysfunctional, or at any rate uncongenial, to the preferred life-styles of too large a proportion of the membership to be retained without substantial modification. Career incentives, once satisfied by the rewards it dangled for a patient and fortunate few, have come increasingly to run against it. There are not enough chairmanships to go around.

Career Expectations

Technical difficulties in measures of turnover and tenure may have helped to obscure a timely recognition of powerful influences on emerging changes in the internal organization of the House. Whenever a new seat is created, for instance, its first incumbent is necessarily a newcomer, though no one has been ousted. This happened often in irregular lumps as the admission of new states intermittently enlarged the House from sixty-five in 1789 to its 435-member size in 1917, and temporarily again in a small way in 1959 and 1960 when Alaska and Hawaii were admitted. It happened in the course of reapportionments and redistrictings after decennial censuses and, in the 1960s after court orders. Polsby, counting only first-term members without prior service, included all such cases. This swelling of the concept of "turnover" was more than offset, on the other hand, by his excluding members in their first terms for purposes of the seniority rule though they had returned indeed after interruptions from prior service. These were numerous in the nineteenth century, less so in recent years. Six of them—more than usual—made their way back in the 1974 elections. An index of actual replacements, new or shopworn, accordingly runs generally somewhat higher than Polsby's turnover.

Prior service is particularly significant for its effect on the distribution of influence. The typical portrayal of freshmen members pictures them as bewildered and fumbling, not knowing their way around, and spending their first terms in a process of "socialization." Books have been written to guide their apprenticeship. But Hubert Humphrey, returning to the Senate in 1971 after his vice presidency was not the novice one might suppose from his 1975 ranking in an eight-way tie for fortieth place. In 1974 at least two of the half-dozen successful brides-but-not-virgins, James H. Scheuer and Richard L. Ottinger, both New York Democrats, were active leaders in transforming the House freshmen of the Ninety-fourth Congress into an organized bloc with a program for change, something that previous newcomers had never achieved. With experience and independent means these two were able to reinforce incumbent reformers in the Democratic Study Group (DSG) by promoting a presession caucus of freshmen to formulate demands, coordinate tactics, and confront the House leadership and committee chairmen with a unified voting strength too large to be deflected and focused on modifying seniority in the selection of committee chairmen and the method of making subcommittee assignments.

Economic and geographic factors also affect turnover rates. Temporary but marked jumps in turnover occurred in the elections of 1874, 1894, 1932, 1958, and 1974, dates all associated with economic distress. Geographic differences have been more durable. Turnover in southern states districts has always been consistently less frequent than in eastern districts—over the four decades from 1937 to 1970 by a margin of some seven percentage points. This differential may be in process of dissolution. Seats held as elements in the patronage of big city machines have also been relatively immune to the tides of party competition. Presumably an incoming member forms an estimate of future prospects and tenure, makes career calculations and commitments accordingly, and alters these with accumulating experience and the march of events, all with respect to a particular district. The surrounding political landscape and atmosphere are secondary elements to be taken into account, along with pure chance.

Tenure averages and turnover rates are obviously related phenomena but not the same. Polsby's tenure averages, calculated simply by dividing the number of representatives in a given session into the total number of terms they had by then served, tell nothing of the range and frequency distribution of long and short careers in office. And as with turnover, until a newly created district has been in existence at least as long as the tenure average, that average is necessarily depressed by including such an incumbent's tenure in the computation. Nonpolitical factors also enter. Life expectancy in the population as a whole has roughly doubled since 1900, so it would be surprising if representatives did not live longer too, and thereby raise tenure averages. Representatives elected in their early thirties presumably have a much better chance of raising the tenure averages than those who were nearing fifty when they entered. Finally, the average is a temporal cross-section—the view a member gets as he looks around the chamber at his or her colleagues on a particular day, not as a longer perspective might give. The ultimate average of members' years of service can only be reckoned after they have died or retired, i. e., for Congresses thirty years or more in the past.

For present purposes, more is to be learned from the numbers and percentages of House members elected to, say, ten or more Congresses, with service records, that is, of upwards of twenty years. In 1911 there were just eleven such, 2.8 percent of the whole body. By 1941 there were 39 (9.0 percent), and 48 (11.0 percent) in 1943. A decade of stability followed, but in 1955 and 1957, as the New Deal generation matured, the numbers rose again, to 54 (12.4 percent) and 71 (16.3 percent), respectively. In 1971 there was a peak at 87 (20.0 percent), though in 1975 a sharp drop to 61 (14.0 percent)—one in seven, a ratio still larger than any prior to 1957.

What brings a termination to these seniors' service? Of 176 who reached the twenty-year mark or beyond and who vacated their seats between 1941 and 1970, the largest proportion, 39.2 percent, retired; 27.8 percent died in office; and 7.4 percent left to seek other offices. Only the remaining quarter lost out in efforts to stay on, 13.1 percent beaten in a primary and 12.5 in a general election. The mean age of those who retired was 69.7 years at retirement.

The six- or seven-fold increase in the number of such veterans, from scarcely a dozen in 1911, and their doubling since full time sessions became the rule, offer vivid testimony to the transformation in career outlook that has occurred. It is not necessary here to settle how far this means that it has become easier to get reelected or that the satisfactions of staying on have grown. No doubt both influences have been at work.

It would be a mistake, moreover, to suppose that the approximately five out of six who do not make it for as long as twenty years do not share a career view of their functions. The median length of service for all House members in 1973 was five terms, and in 1975 it was four terms. A *New York Times* story on April 14, 1975, reported that of 103 members of the Ninety-third Congress who did not survive into the Ninety-fourth, about half were still working in Washington. Many of them were lobbyists; some Republican lame ducks had found employment in the executive branch. The old adage that "they never go back to Pocatello" is commonly thought to be grounded in the social attractions of life in the capital. But for those not yet ready to retire it also means that a congressional stint has equipped many departing members with skills, resources, and contacts suitable for continuing a familiar way of life—extensions of their public careers, in substance.

Incentives, Rewards, and Requirements

Members of Congress who take a professional view of their jobs and future prospects share the aspirations and respond to the incentives common to other professions—law, medicine, architecture, accounting, or whatever. They want their occupations to be rewarding, comfortable, congenial, and constructive. To that end much has happened to the perquisites of congressional office since full-time sessions became the regular order. The Legislative Reorganization Act of 1946 initiated the improvements. Congressional Quarterly's *Guide to Congress* conveniently collected many of the specifics, as they were in 1970. The Legislative Reorganization Act of that year and further measures culminating in the Congressional Budget and Impoundment Control Act of 1974 have materially liberalized the provisions since then. Additional benefits in 1975 required no floor votes. It is not necessary to recite them in detail; for the present argument, a summary of the categories is enough.

The first is direct compensation. Beginning with the 1946 act, the salaries of members have more than quadrupled, from the previous level of $10,000 to $42,500 in 1969, the latest increase. A contributory pension plan makes members eligible on retirement after age sixty-two and a minimum of six years' service—one term for a senator, three for a representative—for benefits calculated at 2.5 percent of the best three-year salary average times the number of years served. Similar benefits were opened to staff employees.

The next category is staff help, the subject of another essay in this volume. Prior to World War II the clerk of the House Appropriations Committee, Marcellus Shields, and the chief of staff of the Joint Committee on Internal Revenue Taxation, Colin Stam, built durable and legendary reputations around the Hill on the basis of nonpartisan and personal integrity, indefatigable labors, and professional competence in indispensable staff functions. These exceptions apart, the meager clerk hire allotted to a member typically procured a low-paid political assistant or in a good many cases a family member. Committee clerks were patronage of the chairmen. Again the Legislative Reorganization Act of 1946 paved the way for far-reaching change. For each of the newly reconstituted standing committees, it authorized professional assistants, directed to be selected on standards of merit. Administrative assistants for senators followed shortly afterward. At the time, House and Senate committee staffs together totaled about four hundred. By 1974 the number exceeded two thousand, and the number of individual members' staff assistants was approaching nine thousand. Relatively, the legislative branch had for two decades become the fastest-growing part of the federal civilian establishment. Salaries and fringe benefits for them improved, too— everything except security against arbitrary firings. A large proportion of the committee and subcommittee assistants are hired on a project basis rather than in permanently designated positions.

Staff people, like members, want comfortable and constructive lives. Beyond satisfying their employers in assigned tasks, they have built-in and continuing incentives to find and cultivate new and longer-lasting projects that will engage their members' interest and favor. Alertness toward jurisdictional encroachment from another committee quarter, or an opportunity to establish a rival beachhead, is one way. Explorations of promising issues, contacts with other congressional staff and agency employees, and reconnaissance among potential witnesses for future hearings are others. Inherently, professional assistants are a self-generating source of more things to do, as Parkinson's law asserts.

Swelling the informational, investigative, and research capabilities of the staffs of committees and members are the great institutional service resources comprised in the legislative branch: the General Accounting Office (not until 1968 funded in the annual Legislative Appropriations Acts), the Congressional Research Service, the more recently established Office of Technology Assessment, and, the newest of all (1975), the Congressional Budget Office, not to mention the traditional drafting services in the Office of the Legislative Counsel for each chamber. All of these have benefitted greatly from the postwar era of staff expansion.

The third factor is work space. The first House Office Building was opened for occupancy in 1908; until then only committees—and so in practice their chairmen—and not individual members had space assignments in the rabbit-warren corridors and basement bowels of the Capitol. By 1975 the House had three office buildings and the Senate two; the former Congressional Hotel and an old Government Printing Office building were converted to annexes, and covetous eyes were being cast on more real estate. Members had suites of a half-dozen rooms. Committees had hearing rooms as well as offices. A symbiotic relation has existed between staff and space: an increment of either creates an additional demand for the other.

The fourth category is logistic support and subsidized conveniences. Under this heading come the greatly increased special allowances for travel, office equipment, stationery, and supplies; postage in addition to franking privileges; telephone toll calls and other wire services; fees for consultants and for the attendance of witnesses at hearings; facilities for printing, duplicating, large-scale mailings, and broadcasting; reprints from the *Congressional Record*; rent and other expenses of maintaining separate offices in home districts; space for press galleries and ticket offices; medical services in military hospitals; flowers from the Botanic Garden; support of low prices in the Capitol restaurants and barber shops; and access for staff assistants to many of these auxiliaries. Members' annual travel allowances were increased in 1975 from twelve to twenty round trips to their homes, and typically half of them also manage a trip abroad in the course of a year. As William Safire observed, "An overseas tour by a Congressman is described by him as a *fact-finding trip*, and as a *junket* by his opponents." Self-conscious wrangles over abuses of these various perquisites surface occasionally in floor debates and more often in press commentaries. Taking them together, however, they have unquestionably and vastly extended the reach of members, of committees, and of like-minded voting blocs during the quarter-century since the congressional resurgence got under way. For a crude and composite measure of the extent of the expansion, consider these comparisons across a twenty-year span: for the fiscal year 1951, the appropriation for the Senate amounted to $12,259,136; for the House, to $21,574,735; and for joint items to $288,715; a total of $34,122,586. For FY 1971 the corresponding amounts were, for the Senate, $60,929,464; for the House, $110,526,455; and for joint items, $14,558,775; a total of $186,014,694, more than a sevenfold aggregate increase.

The fifth and final category is "turf"—that is, jurisdiction over a subject matter area, within which the member can expect presently to acquire a tolerable mastery of detailed knowledge and over which he or she can by sustained application, gain a discernible influence, perhaps even construct a durable monument to his or her career. Preferably, the jurisdiction should be legitimate and recognized as such, but it may also be a product of claim-jumping or of assignment by higher authority. The subject area may come by choice or by chance. If choice is operative, Fenno's categories indicate that an issue-oriented legislator will seek something in foreign or domestic policy; one who prefers to gain influence among colleagues will reach for, say, the House Administration Committee or Public Works; and one whose anxiety is over reelection will look for leverage over constituency services, as in the Postal Service, Interior, or Small Business committees.[4] In the House, the search for a congenial and available jurisdictional preserve inevitably entails further specialization. Just from the Ninety-first Congress to the Ninety-fourth,

---

[4] Richard Fenno, *Congressmen in Committees* (Boston: Little, Brown & Co., 1973).

the Nixon years, the number of legislative subcommittees increased from 108 to 142. A senator has more room for moving into and out of one subject after another.

The combined impact of the five factors that have been sketched here has potentially momentous consequences for the organization of the two chambers and for the manner of their internal governance and, in turn, for their capacities for coping with the president and with the executive branch. Plainly, these trends of the decades since the Twentieth Amendment took effect do not favor a restoration of dominant power in the speaker of the House, let alone in a titular leader of the Senate. They do not seem to foster the imposition of an effective central party discipline, along the lines of a parliamentary model, as a means of compelling adherence to legislative programs. They have eroded the oligarchy implicit in the structural arrangements adopted in the name of reform by the Legislative Reorganization Act of 1946—a dozen and a half committees in control of all legislation and controlled themselves by chairmen owing their places to seniority. In spite of the renewed effort in the 1970 reorganization to rationalize committee coverage, these forces have instead produced a splintering of overlapping jurisdictions among scores of subcommittees that afford a multitude of potential points of access for almost any proposal. They have also promoted an equalitarian dispersion of authority among members so that each can run an office more or less on the model of a substantial and autonomous law firm. Rayburn's rule— to get along, go along—has lost some of its compulsion.

Table 3 shows the extent of the proliferation of subcommittees of the standing committees in the Ninety-fourth Congress, little changed from the Ninety-third. No longer ago than in the Kennedy administration the *Congressional Directory* did not bother to list subcommittees at all. The directories for 1973 and 1975 list them, but with the names of two and only two members of each, the chairman and ranking minority member. Without going beyond these posts the Senate had enough places for an average of nearly two apiece for the majority members and four apiece for the greatly outnumbered minority. Its Judiciary Committee could even spare one—a harmless one, to be sure, on Federal Charters, Holidays and Celebrations—to be chaired by a Republican, the venerable Roman L. Hruska of Nebraska. In the House there were enough so that virtually every other Democrat could be a chairman, and every Republican a ranking minority member. How much further can equalitarian principles be carried?

Evidence for the dispersion of authority is to be found in the popularity, especially among junior members, of a series of changes, hailed as reforms, in committee and floor procedures, tending toward greater ventilation and disclosure of deliberations and impeding the ability of chairmen to control outcomes by parliamentary manipulations. The 1946 act made a start along these lines. The 1970 act went further in requiring

TABLE 3

Distribution of Subcommittees, Ninety-fourth Congress (1975)

House		Senate	
Agriculture	10	Aeronautical and Space Sciences	0
Appropriations	13	Agriculture and Forestry	6
Armed Services	7	Appropriations	13
Banking, Currency and Housing	9	Armed Services	9
Budget	0	Banking, Housing and Urban Affairs	8
District of Columbia	6	Budget	0
Education and Labor	8	Commerce	13
International Relations	10	District of Columbia	0
Government Operations	7	Finance	11
House Administration	11	Foreign Relations	9
Interior and Insular Affairs	7	Government Operations	5
Interstate and Foreign Commerce	6	Interior and Insular Affairs	7
Judiciary	7	Judiciary	16
Merchant Marine and Fisheries	5	Labor and Public Welfare	11
Post Office and Civil Service	6	Post Office and Civil Service	4
Public Works and Transportation	6	Public Works	8
Rules	0	Rules and Administration	7
Science and Technology	7	Veterans Affairs	4
Small Business	6		131
Standards of Official Conduct	0		
Veterans Affairs	5		
Ways and Means	6		
	142		

Source: *Congressional Directory*, 94th Cong., 1st sess. (Washington: GPO, 1975), pp. 252–67; 281–304.

advance notice of meetings and hearings, allowing a committee majority to call a meeting when the chairman fails to do so on request, allowing the minority to call their own witnesses at hearings, prohibiting the use of general proxies, requiring the publication of record votes, and so on. Through the work of the Hansen committee a so-called "subcommittee bill of rights" was adopted in 1973; it defined jurisdictions, set limits on multiple chairmanships, provided them with separate staff assistants, and the like. If nearly everyone becomes a chairman, is he or she then likely to see more virtue in seniority and the status quo?[5] Congressman John Moss, an otherwise liberal Democrat, who lost one of his chairmanly hats in the process, resisted this "reform" all the way.

What of It?

The recent equalitarian dispersion is not a formula for legislative anarchy, though it may sometimes convey that impression. There is no

[5] Norman J. Ornstein, "Causes and Consequences of Congressional Change: Subcommittee Reforms in the House of Representatives, 1970–1973," in his *Congress in Change*, cited above, note 3, pp. 88–114.

evidence that individual members in their lately enhanced capacities are less open to reason and compromise than the handful of oligarchical chairmen once were. On democratic premises it must also be counted a great gain for the responsiveness of the system that so many channels of access have been opened. It has become far more difficult for a hostile chairman to foreclose for years, even decades, the serious consideration of unwelcome changes, such as repeal of the oil depletion allowance, in matters within his committee's province. For another example, it was a reorganization plan handled by friendly subcommittees of the Government Operations Committees in 1967 that broke up the previous monopoly of the District of Columbia Committee chairmen and transformed local government in the capital city. It was a subcommittee of the Senate Judiciary Committee, not the appropriations committees, that took up the cudgels against the Nixon administration on the subject of impoundments.

Dispersion, on the other hand, is not a formula for producing disciplined troops, capable of being marshalled in serried ranks to vote—as in the state assemblies in Albany, say, or Columbus, Ohio—at the cue of the speaker to support his collective bargaining with the other chamber and with the governor. Despite all his troubles, President Nixon was overridden on only one of nine vetoes in his second term, the War Powers Act of 1973. President Ford in 1975 was rebuffed on impoundments, which required only an adverse majority vote in either chamber, but he had a surprisingly successful record on vetoes; although easily overridden on food stamps, he prevailed in contests over farm price supports, publicly financed jobs, strip mining restrictions, and home building subsidies—all Democratic campaign issues.

Dispersion is a formula for producing and encouraging a cadre of miners and sappers like Senator Proxmire and Congressman Les Aspin, skilled in tunneling and penetrating hidden recesses and placing explosive charges in the executive branch—the military-industrial complex, the CIA, Watergate, and domestic surveillance; missionaries like Congressman Drinan seeking converts to their causes; entrepreneurs and brokers putting together the elements of a conglomerate bill that can pass; broken-field runners and players to the grandstand; and, in the Senate, aspirants to the presidency.

Dispersion poses acutely the paradox of participation. One facet of it is apparently procedural, the orderly regulation of participation itself—what Bertrand de Jouvenel once described as the chairman's problem: how to parcel out time and recognition—access—in an assembly when time is limited and everyone wants the floor. Reforms in congressional procedure introduced from 1970 to 1973 were largely addressed to this problem, by way of restrictions on the freedom of action (and inaction) of chairmen.

The other facet is substantive and political. As stated earlier, it is how to get everyone in on the act and still get anything done. Chairman Russell Long gave it classic statement, in the course of driving a Senate Finance Committee session through its revision of the House version of the 1975 tax reduction bill in time to meet a Democratic caucus decision to get final action on it before the Easter recess just ahead. To a member's complaint about haste in the proceedings he said: "If every man insists on knowing what he's voting for before he votes, we're not going to get a bill reported before Monday."

Because effective action is usually group action, a number of more or less durable though loosely knit blocs have emerged in Congress. The anti-New Deal coalition of southern Democrats and midwest Republicans that formed in 1938 and was operative through the Truman, Eisenhower, and Kennedy administrations had negative goals and disintegrated in defeat in the 1960s. More lately the Democratic Study Group, the Congressional Black Caucus, the Women's Caucus, the District of Columbia regional caucus, even—shades of bygone days that it should be thought needed—the Congressional Rural Caucus, have embodied efforts to consolidate strength for the advancement of positive, if perhaps parochial, goals. These are claimants, not governors. The logical end of their multiplication is the Polish veto. The nominal House leadership, the speaker and majority floor leader, and the lately revived Democratic Caucus with its steering and policy committee seem to be, in principle, rivals for hegemony. Do they provide the makings of an effective and legitimate instrument of governance for the House majority? In 1975 the caucus had some substantial achievements to record, but its future prospects were still problematical as the 1976 campaign approached.

The implementation and "dry run" of the fiscal processes mandated in the Congressional Budget and Impoundment Act of 1974 marked a further attempt to organize consensus where opinions have been sharply at variance and the stakes high. But it is not at all clear that a sufficient number of individual members, enjoying their present resource bases, will be willing to subordinate their freedom of action for the benefits of collective strength. The disarray in coping with the energy crisis in 1975 underlined the inherent difficulties.

As for Congress against the president, it must be concluded that Congress has not yet managed even by working full time to organize a dependable method—short of impeachment—of transcending the constitutional separation of powers. As against the executive departments and agencies the record suggests that Congress, by splintering its own authority and turning its members loose, has devised an ingenious, formidable, and undependable array of methods for giving the agencies a run for their money.

Central Policy Organs in Congress

JOHN G. STEWART

Flailing Congress for its many shortcomings is a recognized part of American life. Editorial writers and academics perennially relish the outrages waiting to be corrected. Private groups such as Common Cause recruit hundreds of thousands of members in the name of saving Congress from itself. The public can be counted on to award Congress dismally low marks whenever a pollster inquires as to how the national legislature is doing. And members of Congress themselves are frequently among the harshest critics. "Just send me back for another term," the incumbent pleads, "and maybe I can bring some small measure of sanity to the proceedings."

Less predictable is the reaction that occurs when Congress actually "reforms" its rules. Most citizens, to be sure, have only dim notions of how Congress operates or what it is. (According to a recent nationwide survey conducted for the Senate, 60 percent thought Congress was composed of just the House of Representatives or just the Senate or that the Supreme Court was part of Congress.) But even better informed persons, including the institution's most outspoken critics, are less successful in grasping the meaning of congressional change than they are at pointing out what should happen next. As a result, most people are ignorant of the institution's capacity to adjust its operations to changing political climates in the country when, in fact, a plausible case can be made that Congress is among the political institutions most sensitive to public demands.

The presidency has been subjected to intense public scrutiny since the mid-1960s. Rising opposition to the Vietnam war, racial upheavals, and Watergate have driven two presidents from office and produced a flood of proposals for cutting the imperial presidency down to size. Although the personalities in the Oval Office have been shuttled in and out, it is not readily apparent how the presidency itself has changed in any significant way. But on Capitol Hill the story is different. Subject to the same political pressures that have bedeviled Presidents Kennedy, Johnson, Nixon, and Ford, Congress has responded by radically shifting the locus of power internally and, as a consequence, changing in a fundamental way the process by which legislative decisions are made. This is not to say that congressional decisions now will necessarily be "better" than they used to be; that will continue to be a matter of opinion. But in this period of considerable public cynicism about the responsiveness of popularly elected bodies, it seems appropriate to examine what has happened in Congress and to speculate about what the future may hold.

What follows is primarily a Democratic story, not because Republicans have refused to make many of the changes that Democrats have made (in some instances Republicans have gone further), but because Congress has been and for the foreseeable future will be a Democratic institution. Democrats have the job of organizing and running Congress. Their decisions necessarily affect the institution's character and behavior to a far greater degree than Republican decisions.

The Inheritance of the Ninety-fourth Congress

President Ford devoted his first State of the Union message to laying out a comprehensive energy-economic recovery program that most Democrats promptly opposed. For once the Democratic opposition had some basis for a response other than instinctive rhetoric and press releases. Five weeks before Ford's appearance, Speaker Carl Albert had appointed a task force of the Democratic Steering and Policy Committee and charged it to design a Democratic economic program. On January 13, just hours before Ford's scheduled evening television speech, Albert announced the outlines of the Democratic program and assigned its various parts to appropriate House committees for more detailed attention. He also laid down a ninety-day limit for committee action.

On the Senate side of the Capitol, Majority Leader Mike Mansfield appointed an ad hoc subcommittee, chaired by Senator John Pastore (Rhode Island), of the Majority Policy Committee to develop a Democratic alternative to Ford's energy-economic recovery program. The staff of the Policy Committee convened the principal Senate committee aides in the areas of energy and the economy and went to work. Then Speaker Albert asked his economic task force, chaired by Representative James C. Wright, Jr. (Texas), to tackle the energy issue on behalf of House Democrats.

By mid-February, the respective House and Senate task forces were meeting jointly to see if a common Democratic program could be hammered out. By the end of February, the Senate Majority Policy Committee and the House Steering and Policy Committee had agreed upon a Democratic alternative. Then, just before President Ford imposed a second $1 tariff on imported crude oil, members of the House and Senate policy bodies packed up their alternatives and trouped to the White House to confer directly with Ford. On the basis of this presentation, the president postponed the second $1 tariff and announced his willingness to work with the congressional Democratic leadership in finding a compromise energy package.

News reports of the White House meeting focused on a number of short range economic and political considerations. Could Ford and the new Democratic Congress avoid a major showdown over energy policy? Would Ford call off his frontal attack on Congress for its alleged ineffective behavior? Was compromise possible? No one mentioned, or probably even recognized, that the Democratic congressional leadership and the Republican president had just carried out, for the first time, one of the more controversial but now forgotten recommendations of the Joint Committee on the Organization of the Congress—the LaFollette-Monroney committee—that released its report on congressional reorganization fully twenty-nine years earlier.

In a recommendation that Congress never implemented, the LaFollette-Monroney committee had urged "that the Majority policy committees of the Senate and House serve as a formal council to meet regularly with the Executive, to facilitate the formulation and carrying out of national policy, and to improve relationships between the executive and legislative branches of Government." Of course, the ad hoc process pieced together by Mansfield and Albert hardly comprised the "formal council" that the LaFollette-Monroney committee envisioned meeting regularly with the president. Nor could it be said that the Democratic alternative developed by the policy groups and presented to the president represented the last word among Democrats in Congress. Indeed, Representative Al Ullman (Oregon), newly elected chairman of the Ways and Means Committee, let it be known publicly that he disagreed with many of the Democratic recommendations and that Ways and Means was developing alternatives to the alternative.

Moreover, the process had been handled differently in the two Houses. The ad hoc Pastore group had met with all standing committee chairmen and many other senators who had responsibility for writing the actual legislation. The full Senate Democratic conference had unanimously approved the final product of the Pastore task force. On the House side, however, only the Democratic Steering and Policy Committee, not standing committee chairmen and not the Democratic caucus, had signed off on the proposals of the Wright group.

Under these conditions, it would be distinctly premature to jump to the conclusion that Congress had finally adopted the centralized policy-making model long touted by "responsible party" advocates and contained in the LaFollette-Monroney report. Nonetheless, it would be equally short-sighted to ignore the fact that the policy deliberations surrounding the alternative Democratic program were of a piece with a fundamental shift of power in Congress that had been under way for about fifteen years. Slowly but inexorably the power of standing committee chairmen to control crucial legislative decisions had been slipping away, particularly in the House, and the power of party-based bodies—the Democratic caucus in the House and the Democratic conference in the Senate—had been growing. While a considerable amount of discretion remained with committees, it was now clearly established that this discretion could not be exercised in ways that flouted the majority opinion among Democrats. And this much was certain: Lyndon Johnson and Sam Rayburn would have looked upon the leadership-sponsored process of producing a Democratic energy-economic recovery program as from another planet.

By the time that the Ninety-fourth Congress had completed its organizational decisions, even a casual observer must have suspected that unusual things were happening on Capitol Hill. Incumbent chairmen of the Agriculture, Armed Services, and Banking and Currency committees were rejected by the House Democratic caucus and replaced with less senior members. The Democratic members of the Ways and Means Committee were relieved of their power-laden job of assigning Democratic colleagues to standing committees and nominating committee chairmen. It was handed over to the Democratic Steering and Policy Committee, dominated by the speaker and majority leader. In a further dilution of the Ways and Means power base, the committee was enlarged from twenty-five to thirty-seven members in order that the full Democratic House membership could be represented more adequately. (These changes were in process before the unfavorable publicity suffered by Wilbur Mills, the former chairman of Ways and Means, although that ensured the election of a new chairman.) Speaker Albert was given authority to nominate the chairman and Democratic members of the Rules Committee—the final act in the drama that began with the 1961 battle against Judge Howard W. Smith to bring this vital committee under control of the party leadership. Chairmen of the Appropriations Committee subcommittees were made subject to approval of the full Democratic caucus. Chairmen of other standing committees were deprived of their arbitrary power to make subcommittee assignments; these were now to be decisions of the full Democratic membership on each committee. Other changes were also adopted by the Democratic caucus, all in the spirit of bringing committee operations under the general control of the full Democratic membership.

Preparations and tactics for these several moves had been worked out a month in advance when, in another innovation, House Democrats had met in early December for an initial and unofficial week–long organizing session.

The press dramatized the role of freshmen Democratic members, an upstart band that summoned incumbent committee chairmen for inquisitorial sessions prior to caucus action on their nominations. Since the freshmen voted almost as a bloc, their presence was decisive in some cases. But it would be a serious misreading to attribute the decisions of the House Democratic caucus solely to the freshmen. Since the early 1960s, but especially in the years following the election of Richard Nixon as president, House Democrats had been chipping away at the prerogatives and power that the committee-based structure had sustained. Barely noticed or taken seriously at first, this quiet revolution reached its climax coincidentally with the arrival of seventy-five new faces in the Democratic caucus.

Similar though less precedent-shattering changes were taking place on the Senate side. The Democratic conference there approved a rule requiring an automatic and secret ballot in the conference on the nominations of committee chairmen made by a Steering Committee that now represented the full Senate Democratic membership. Even though no chairmen were challenged in 1975, the shotgun had been loaded and left within easy reach. For the prior six years, moreover, Majority Leader Mansfield had been encouraging a steady expansion of the policy roles played by the Democratic conference and the Majority Policy Committee —a sharp reversal of Lyndon Johnson's practice of never permitting policy issues to come before either body. By 1975, the notion of the Policy Committee and the conference devising a general Democratic strategy on energy and economic recovery struck no one as revolutionary.

To sum up: As the Ninety-fourth Congress organized itself in January 1975, the proposition had already been accepted that an enlarged policy role for party-based institutions was an appropriate counterweight to the decentralizing tendencies of the committee system. Or, to look at the other side of the equation, it was already beyond debate that the moderate-to-liberal majority among House and Senate Democrats would no longer allow standing committees or their chairmen arbitrary control over the congressional agenda. The majority of Democrats had a right to be heard and to have their proposals acted upon. Obstacles to the exercise of that right should be removed. That was the inheritance waiting to be claimed as the Ninety-fourth Congress got down to work.

Origins of Change

The notion that Congress should respond to its majority party is at least as old as Woodrow Wilson who had a program for congressional enactment in 1913. It was spelled out explicitly in the 1946 report of the LaFollette-Monroney committee: "Under the American party system, there are always two main groups, each checking the other and offering the choice of alternative courses of action. Around these two groups Congressmen can rally and express themselves." The report noted further that "if party accountability for policies and pledges is to be achieved, stronger and more formal mechanisms are necessary." The Senate accepted the committee's recommendation that majority and minority policy committees be created. But the House rejected the proposal ("I am the Policy Committee," Speaker Rayburn reportedly declared), and policy committees were stricken from the final version of the Legislative Reorganization Act of 1946. In 1947, the Senate set them up anyway through the Legislative Branch Appropriations Act. No comparable body existed in the House until a steering committee was established in 1962.

Academic documents such as the 1950 report of the Committee on Political Parties of the American Political Science Association and books such as *The Deadlock of Democracy* (1963) by James MacGregor Burns developed the responsible party argument. In the late 1950s, a frustrated Democratic national chairman, Paul Butler, had tried to circumvent what he perceived as insufficiently partisan Democratic leadership in Congress by propounding national policies through a Democratic Advisory Council of his creation (1956-60). He invited Majority Leader Johnson and Speaker Rayburn to join the advisory council, but they flatly refused and roundly attacked Butler, who was only too glad to reciprocate.

The problem confronted by those Democrats who wanted Congress to enact policies of the national party was both organizational and electoral. Even though Democrats organized Congress (usually by narrow majorities) most of the time, the working majority on Capitol Hill was comprised of a conservative coalition of southern and border-state Democrats and Republicans. Their views on public policy, especially on economic and social issues, were at considerable variance from the positions expressed in national Democratic platforms and enunciated by Democratic presidents and standard-bearers. James MacGregor Burns described the southern Democratic-Republican coalition as the "congressional" party and he juxtaposed it and the more liberal, activist politicians whom he enrolled in the "presidential" party as antagonists. But breaking this "deadlock of democracy" was going to require far more than creating central policy organs in Congress as vehicles for the "presidential" party to propound its views. Above all, it would depend on electoral constituencies that supported the legislative goals of the "presidential" party and that were ready to express this support at the ballot box.

The outrage voiced by responsible party advocates was not generally shared by the public at large during most of the 1950s. President Eisenhower's legislative expectations were limited and, more often than not, he used his presidential leverage in behalf of the "congressional" party. A highly skilled legislative operator like Lyndon Johnson could maneuver the system in ways that produced a few moderate achievements, such as the Civil Rights Act of 1957, but more far-reaching changes had to await the kind of political pressure that only elections could produce. Academic reports, learned books, and fiery floor speeches in Congress just did not carry the clout.

Time after time the southern Democratic-Republican coalition had the votes on critical issues, or it kept issues from coming to a vote. The conservative coalition was also better organized and more adept at using parliamentary rules and practices to advantage. Senior Democrats and Republicans usually came from one-party states or districts and lacked the perspective that tends to be a product of vigorous political competition. The tradition of seniority (it was never an established rule) gave them virtual control over committee activity, the hub of the legislative process.

Critics of the committee-based congressional system argued that such an arrangement was not etched in the Constitution. Congress had not always been run in such a decentralized and fragmented way, nor had Congress always been oblivious, if not hostile, to concerns of the national party. In 1912, for example, in the aftermath of Woodrow Wilson's presidential victory, progressive Senate Democrats revolted against the established party leadership, ousted the incumbent majority leader, Thomas S. Martin (Virginia), and elected one of their own, John Worth Kern (Indiana). Standing committees were reorganized to ensure favorable action on legislative proposals to be submitted by Wilson. Finally, the caucus was empowered to establish a binding party position on major bills. Similar discipline was invoked by Democrats in the House of Representatives. Earlier, in 1890, Speaker Thomas B. Reed (Republican of Maine) forced through a major revision of House rules that permitted the majority he controlled to work its will. In both instances, however, the internal congressional changes had been preceded by electoral decisions at the ballot box that highlighted the need for legislative reform. Yet these centralizing measures did not last. The dominance of Republican speakers ended when Joseph Cannon was unhorsed in 1910. The caucus lost its binding power after World War I and fell into disuse as an instrument of policy.

The 1958 congressional election stands as the moment when the outgunned forces for change in Congress began to acquire the political muscle that eventually produced the revolution of the 1970s. Forty-seven new House Democrats and fifteen new Senate Democrats took the oath of office in January 1959. This influx of Democrats dramatically altered the balance of power, or at least appeared to do so. The Democratic majority in the House had been thirty-three votes, and it now stood at 129.

In the Senate, a narrow two vote margin had been transformed into a solid thirty-two seat majority. Equally important, the new arrivals were almost solidly "presidential" in outlook—to use Burns's typology—supporting the federal government's intervention in a host of domestic problems. The country was deeply mired in an economic slump, unemployment was high, the Russians were embarrassing the United States in outer space, civil rights pressures were continuing to build, and President Eisenhower and Treasury Secretary George Humphrey were inveighing against the evils of government spending. But the Democrats, at long last, seemed to have the means to mount a congressional response.

Twenty months later, the heady enthusiasm of January 1959 had vanished, leaving even higher levels of frustration and bitterness. With the agenda still crammed with priority bills, Johnson and Rayburn, with the concurrence of Democratic presidential nominee John F. Kennedy, recalled members from their 1960 convention recess to an August session in hopes of passing such legislation as federal aid to education, minimum wage, and medicare before the November election. It was not to be. The southern Democratic-Republican coalition effectively blocked the Democrats at every turn. Judge Howard Smith, chairman of the House Rules Committee, refused to let his committee send the education bill to conference. Other bills were blocked in conference or defeated on the floor. Kennedy, pinned down in Washington and unable to campaign, finally gave up in disgust. Congress adjourned on September 1.

The experience of the Eighty-sixth Congress (1959-60) dramatized an important lesson: given existing rules and traditions, a minority of skillful legislators determined on inaction could frustrate the new liberal majority that desired to act. Moreover, the majority lacked weapons to attack the web of committee-based power that served the minority so effectively. The conservative coalition controlled such power centers as the House Rules Committee, Ways and Means (both in considering substantive legislation and in making Democratic committee assignments), House and Senate Appropriations, the Democratic Steering Committee that made committee assignments in the Senate, the Majority Policy Committee, and most of the major Senate standing committees. The "presidential" Democrats were scattered, disorganized, and lacked access to the levers of power.

In early 1959, Speaker Rayburn had personally assured a delegation of House liberals that all major Democratic bills would move through the Rules Committee without undue delay. Rayburn had conferred with Judge Smith, and he reported that things would work out satisfactorily. When they did not, Rayburn knew that he could no longer postpone the confrontation he had hoped to avoid. President-elect Kennedy, still smarting from the end-of-the-session debacle, was ready to make the fight. In a bitter, hard-fought struggle, administration Democrats in the

House managed to win a narrow five vote victory (217-212) to enlarge the Rules Committee from twelve to fifteen members. Kennedy then had a slim one vote majority on the Rules Committee for the priority items in his legislative program. The revolution was under way.

As befits a bicameral legislature, the House and Senate were to follow different, although broadly parallel, paths over the next fifteen years. The House required a more organized, intense effort, and more specific changes were made than in the Senate; but the House was always much more precise about its rules. Also, in the Senate it was more a problem of *using* the party-based instrumentalities that existed—the Democratic conference, the Majority Policy Committee, and the Steering Committee— but that rarely functioned in behalf of the majority. And Democrats in both chambers faced the common problem of making committee operations and decisions ultimately subject to majority approval.

If that was the challenge, Kennedy and Johnson approached it with great caution. For the balance of the 1960s, it was more a matter of tinkering with the existing system rather than mounting a frontal assault to change it. Democrats had lost seats to the GOP in 1960, and Kennedy concluded, perhaps correctly, that this reduced majority permitted no encores to his all-out battle against Judge Smith, lest he jeopardize further his beleaguered legislative program.

When the Johnson landslide of 1964 brought two-to-one Democratic majorities back to the House and Senate, Democratic liberals in the House resurrected the twenty-one day rule that permitted the speaker, with majority approval, to call up for floor action any bill that the Rules Committee had not acted on for a period of twenty-one days. The rule had existed in one prior Congress—the Eighty-first (1949-50)—only to be repealed in the next. But in the Eighty-ninth (1965-66) it was used on eight occasions to move Johnson legislation to the House floor. (When the Democratic majority was trimmed in 1966, the southern Democratic-Republican coalition promptly abolished it again.) In 1965 the House also authorized the speaker, with majority approval, to send a bill to conference without clearance by the Rules Committee.

In the Senate, the southern Democratic-Republican coalition suffered a crushing defeat when a pro-civil rights coalition managed to invoke cloture and stop the filibuster that was blocking majority action on the Civil Rights Act of 1964. Although the Senate rules were not changed by this struggle, the conservative, committee-based forces had been outorganized and outmaneuvered for the first time. It was the first solid evidence that the old coalition was beginning to crumble.

Majority Leader Mansfield, who succeeded Lyndon Johnson in 1961, approached his job as Senate leader in a distinctly different way. Johnson accumulated every available scrap of personal influence and power—from personally assigning rooms in the Capitol to holding bills on the calendar—in order to execute his elaborate legislative strategems. Mansfield, on the other hand, sought to disperse power among individual senators. He placed the burden of legislating on the entire Senate. Freshmen senators quickly became full-fledged legislators instead of waiting quietly on the sidelines for the customary two or four years. Under Mansfield, the Democratic conference and the Majority Policy Committee were convened with greater frequency. Slowly the Steering Committee's membership was made more representative of the Democratic majority.

In one sense, these trends under Mansfield might suggest a weakening of the power of the party leadership that had been built up during Johnson's years as leader. This, in turn, might produce a strengthening of committee-based authority. But such a conclusion would overlook another and more significant facet of Mansfield's style: the great expansion of influence accorded individual senators in comparison to the restricted roles that were possible under Johnson. This trend, once set in motion, led inexorably to an enlarged role for the party conference—the place where individual senators could be heard—together with the evolution of the Majority Policy Committee as the executive committee of the conference. It also encouraged majority rule in the operations of most committees, a step that necessarily reduced or eliminated the arbitrary power of the chairman.

Momentum of Change

The pace of the revolution quickened perceptibly with the election of Richard Nixon in 1968. The Democratic Study Group (DSG) had been organized in 1959 by moderate-to-liberal House members as a catalyst in their common struggle to mount a more activist Democratic program. By 1969, the DSG had grown in numbers and importance with the arrival of more issue-oriented members during the Kennedy-Johnson years. Leaders of the DSG assumed that Nixon would do everything possible to revive the old southern Democratic-Republican coalition. White House leverage that had helped Democratic congressional leaders maneuver bills through (or around) inhospitable committees would now be used against them. But the DSG leadership decided that a strengthened Democratic caucus might successfully counter this effort. What had been a process of tinkering with the existing system through most of the 1960s was transformed into a systematic, step-by-step restructuring of the power relationships in Congress.

But, as before, caution and patience were necessary. In 1969, the DSG was satisfied to achieve its initial goal of regular monthly meetings of the Democratic caucus (instead of the annual caucus to elect party leaders) and the right of individual members to place items on the caucus agenda. Caucus decisions, if attained, were persuasive, but imposed no binding obligation on participants to vote accordingly. The caucus also agreed to approve formally committee assignments made by the Democratic members of the Ways and Means Committee. The chipping away continued. In 1970, the caucus created the Hansen committee to study the seniority system in relation to the caucus and House procedures. In 1971, the caucus moved further by declaring explicitly that nominations for committee chairmen need not follow seniority and that ten members could demand a separate roll call vote on any chairmanship. And, in 1973, this provision was amended, as already noted, to provide for an automatic vote, by secret ballot, on each nominee for committee chairmen. This set the stage for the defeat of three incumbent chairmen in 1975.

In these years many specific changes were made. They achieved four broad objectives: strengthening the Democratic caucus as a vehicle for changing party procedures and setting party policy; breaking the stranglehold of seniority in selecting committee chairmen; increasing the power of subcommittees by reducing the unrestrained power of full committee chairmen and by ensuring the participation of all members; and changing House rules to strip away secrecy and to open operations of the House and its committees to public view.

The net result was clearly evident in the first months of the Ninety-fourth Congress. But as early as April 1972 the Democratic caucus in the House had instructed the Democratic majority on the Foreign Affairs Committee to report legislation setting a date certain for the end of United States military involvement in Indochina—the first time in fifty years that the caucus had instructed a standing committee of the House. Although the resolution did not finally win House passage until May 1973 (and did not take effect until August of that year), the impetus provided by the caucus proved to be a major factor in the final decision by Congress to end United States participation in the war. The expanded role of the Democratic caucus in the business of the House is indirectly suggested by this comparison: in 1969, the rules of the caucus were set forth in 450 words; by 1975, the caucus was governed by a body of rules that ran to 6,200 words.

Senate Democrats never attempted such a wholesale transformation of their legislative environment. In 1971, Mansfield pledged that the Democratic conference would be convened upon the request of a single senator. He continued efforts to place younger senators in positions of responsibility and to secure balanced representation on the Majority Policy Committee and the Steering Committee. He also brought policy matters before the Policy Committee and the conference with increasing regularity. In the post-1969 period, issues such as standby wage-price controls, tax reform, a freeze on deployment of new offensive and defensive weapons systems, the eighteen-year-old vote, social security benefits, postal rates, and campaign expenditure limitations were acted on formally by the Policy Committee. In addition to its traditional role in scheduling legislation, it could function as executive committee for the Democratic conference. In this capacity it pronounced the Senate's Democratic alternative to President Ford's energy-economic recovery program.

Irony of Change

By 1975, the visible trappings of a responsible congressional party system were in place. While committees would continue to do most of the work, their life-and-death power over bills had been taken away. In both the House and Senate, the reality (and threat) that entrenched chairmen could safely ignore the wishes of the Democratic majority had been eliminated. And majority sentiment on policy could be expressed by the caucus (or conference) and by the Majority Policy Committee in the Senate and the Steering and Policy Committee in the House.

But were things as they appeared? While the activities and powers of the caucus had grown enormously, many of these activities and powers were remedial in nature—directed at eliminating abuses of power by committees—rather than perfecting the processes of policy development. The policy role of the caucus was still emerging. For example, the Steering and Policy Committee had yet to assume the role of executive committee of the House Democratic caucus. Issues, such as the 1975 resolution opposing military aid to Cambodia, could be considered without the participation, much less the control, of the speaker or majority leader. As a result, there was growing concern among some Democrats that the caucus might blunder into policy areas that more properly should be developed by party leaders working with standing committees prior to caucus action. In both House and Senate, the policy role of central party organs was still very much part of an ad hoc process—one that was usually invoked in response to short-term pressures—rather than a routinized, well-staffed process for the long-term, coherent development of policy.

It was also curious that the strengthening of party-based institutions in Congress had occurred in a period of declining party identification and growing fragmentation within the two national parties. And if a Democrat should win the presidency in 1976, it was an even-money bet that he would encounter a Congress at least as concerned with preserving its newfound independence as in cooperating with a Democratic White House. What could one say then about the emergence of a "more responsible two party system"?

This irony reflects the fact that the evolution of the caucus and conference as instruments of Democratic policy making has taken place concurrently with an extraordinary growth of the prerogatives of individual members to speak their minds and act accordingly. The larger role now played by party *institutions* in Congress has not necessarily heightened the sense of obligation to *party* or party leaders. This is not surprising, given the political ferment that has gripped America for the past fifteen years. What "responsible party" advocate writing in the 1950s or early 1960s could have imagined the political impact of the Vietnam war or Watergate, much less legislative reapportionment, the decline of one-party districts, the growth of citizen action groups, the increasingly independent voting (or nonvoting) behavior of the electorate, and the growing importance of women and minorities in American politics? While these developments were critically important in building the momentum for change in Congress, they also contributed to the fragmentation of political parties outside of Congress. And they brought a new kind of Democrat to Washington.

It is more than a cliché to observe that Congress is not the place it used to be. Eighty-one percent of the 1975 House (and 75 percent of the Democrats) were not holding office when John F. Kennedy won the presidency. Seventy percent of the Senate (and 65 percent of the Democrats) have also arrived since 1960. Such a turnover is not high by historical standards, but it obviously bears on the importance of seniority; relatively few members have a personal stake in protecting the past, though many are interested in fruitful careers. Present members are also more attuned to issues, perhaps more likely to come from competitive districts, and more interested in achieving issue-related results. After 1968, these new and different Democrats saw their personal political interests served by pushing Congress into overt opposition to the policies and actions of the Nixon administration. The more frequent use of party institutions in the House and Senate to express this opposition did not, however, automatically bring with it a deepened commitment to party, as such, or to the party's elected leadership. Members were no less ready than before to act independently if their political survival required it.

These conditions among congressional Democrats reflected the unsettled state of American politics generally. It is not easy to weigh the relative influence of short- and long-term factors. What happens next in Congress will be determined in large measure by what happens in the 1976 presidential election. If the Democrats win with an attractive candidate who unifies the party, and with issues that generate enthusiasm among the voters, a Democratic victory could lead to new steps in the direction of what has already taken place in Congress. In such a political environment, one might expect to see greater development and institutionalization of the ad hoc policy role now played by central party organs. In the House, for example, party leaders could be given greater control over policy matters coming before the caucus, at least to the degree of having such items acted on initially by the Steering and Policy Committee. In the Senate, it remains a matter of using the existing institutions and procedures on a more systematic and routinized basis. These moves could be made with relative ease since the traditional obstacles of oligarchic committees and committee chairmen have been largely eliminated.

But a Democratic presidential victory is only one of the possiblities. In any event, recent efforts in both Houses to develop a more rational scheme of committee jurisdictions are likely to continue. Party leaders must still devote a great deal of their time, energy, and limited influence to attempts to resolve conflicts that arise from overlapping and duplication of legislative authority among committees. And it is interesting to speculate on the legislative impact of an affirmative decision to open House and Senate floor sessions to broadcast coverage. Resolutions to do this were pending in both bodies in 1975. Daily television and radio coverage seem likely to strengthen the control of party leaders over floor debate and generate additional pressures in behalf of more orderly legislative procedures. It is arguable that a continuance of divided party control over the White House and the Capitol would work in that direction too.

It is safe to say that steps toward greater party responsibility in policy matters will occur, however, only if members of Congress perceive such action to be in their individual political interests. But if a new Democratic president is able to give direction and purpose to American political life, there is no reason to assume that Congress will be caught lagging behind.

In the early 1960s, Senator Joseph S. Clark (Pennsylvania) bitterly attacked the existing congressional establishment in a series of well-publicized floor speeches. Expanding this indictment in a book titled *Congress: The Sapless Branch* (1964), Clark described the committee-based power structure that ran Congress as "almost the antithesis of democracy. It is not selected by any due process. It appears to be quite unresponsive to the caucuses of the two parties, be they Democratic or Republican. It is what might be called a self-perpetuating oligarchy with mild, but only mild, overtones of plutocracy." Well, former Senator Clark must be surprised and pleased with recent events on Capitol Hill. There *is* life in the sapless branch. Congress has shown itself to be very much alive. But so is the capacity for continued change. What kind of change depends fundamentally on the future direction and shape of American politics.

The Congressional Black Caucus

MARGUERITE ROSS BARNETT

Since 1971, when the Congressional Black Caucus (CBC) formally emerged, numerous other legislative caucuses of black elected officials have developed. The existence of the CBC and the proliferation of racially based caucuses raises issues seldom examined in literature on the legislative process. Why have formalized racial caucuses been organized in legislative arenas in which primordial loyalties have been traditionally amorphous, covert, and diffuse rather than rationalized and specific? What are the purposes and functions of these caucuses, and how successful have they been in achieving their goals? What is their general political significance?

Historical and contemporary examination of the CBC is not only intrinsically important but illuminates this growing phenomenon. CBC origins can be traced to the late 1960s when Congressman Charles Diggs (Michigan) formed the Democratic Select Committee.[1] Although called the forerunner of the CBC, the Select Committee only met sporadically. Diggs conceived it as a way of bringing black Representatives William Dawson (Illinois) and Adam Clayton Powell (New York)—both since

---

[1] All past and present CBC members are Democrats. Republican Senator Edward Brooke, the only black member of the Senate, does not belong to the CBC. The *New York Times* reported on May 17, 1975, that Fourtney H. Stark, a white member of Congress, had applied for membership and on June 19, 1975, that his application was turned down.

This essay is part of a larger study of the Congressional Black Caucus. Funds for that study have been provided by a James Madison Bicentennial preceptorship from Princeton University and a travel and study grant from the Ford Foundation. While conducting this research, the author has been a guest scholar at the Brookings Institution. None of these sponsors is responsible for any views expressed here.

deceased—together. In 1969, black members of Congress began coordinating their efforts. One of their first actions was public opposition to the nomination of Clement Haynsworth of South Carolina to be an associate justice of the Supreme Court. Also during 1969 they conducted an unofficial public hearing in Chicago on the killing of members of the Chicago Black Panther party.

Both internal and external factors contributed to the decision to formalize the caucus. Two circumstances, however, stand out in bold relief: the emphasis of many key black political elites on electoral politics following passage of the 1965 Voting Rights Act and the political climate of the Nixon presidency. Indeed, a protracted confrontation between the black members of Congress and the president contributed to their sense of common purpose and identity.

The "Collective Stage"

In February 1970 the black representatives in Congress sent a letter to President Nixon requesting a conference on a wide range of issues concerning black and poor people in the United States. After an initial refusal, Nixon met *fourteen months* later with the then thirteen-member caucus—a number that gradually increased to seventeen in the Ninety-fourth Congress (1975). The meeting took place only after prolonged and well-publicized efforts by the black representatives. Finally, black congressmen staged a boycott of the president's State of the Union message in protest over his high-handed treatment.

When the caucus did meet with the president, sixty-one recommendations for governmental action on domestic and foreign issues were presented. In an opening statement, the caucus asserted itself as the representative of the nationwide black community: "Our concerns and obligations as members of Congress do not stop at the boundaries of our districts, our concerns are national and international in scope. We are petitioned daily by citizens living hundreds of miles from our districts who look on us as Congressmen-at-large for black people and poor people in the United States."[2] Substantively, the caucus statement went on to call for "equality of results" in the following areas:

• Eradication of racism within the United States and in its dealings with other nations.

• Earning of a decent living or the means to survive in dignity when work is not available.

• Decent housing for black families and equal access to the total housing market.

[2] U.S., Congress, Senate, *Congressional Record,* 92d Cong., 1st sess., March 30, 1971 (speech by Charles C. Diggs, Jr.).

• Fair and impartial justice and adequate protection against drug abuse and crime.

• Enforcement of civil rights and other constitutional guarantees through vigorous affirmative action by the government.

• A fair share of the public funds used to support business and community development and full participation in determining how tax dollars are spent in black communities.

• The federal government's guarantee of ample health care for all citizens.

• Protection of federal standards and guarantees in programs financed by federal funds.

• Full participation by members of black communities in the executive, judicial, and legislative branches of the government at every level.

This meeting with President Nixon marked a turning point for the caucus. In a short time its members were caught in a transformation from a small, relatively powerless, and ignored group of junior representatives to a national cynosure. The caucus's emergence as a nationally known organization occurred at a time when the civil rights movement was in a period of decline. Leaders like Malcolm X and Martin Luther King were dead, leaving a perceived leadership vacuum. Furthermore, the new emphasis was on electoral politics, and the caucus was seen as the epitome of black political accomplishment. These factors set the context for the caucus's transition from an episodic, informal protest group within Congress to a highly visible and durably organized group of spokesmen for the black community inside and outside of Congress.

During the first year (from mid-1971 to mid-1972) the CBC saw itself as "Congressmen at large for 20 million Black people." The functions that individual members perform for their constituents, the CBC would perform for black Americans generally. In carrying through this mandate the caucus staff attempted to provide casework services, gather and disseminate information, engage in administrative oversight, articulate the interests of specialized groups within the black community (such as business and labor), and develop legislative proposals.

Much of the CBC visibility that first year came from a series of hearings held around the country on health, education, black enterprise, the mass media, Africa, and racism in the military. Results of these hearings were to be incorporated in the CBC Black Agenda. The Black Agenda was to be used inside Congress as the basis for a caucus legislative agenda and outside Congress as a document to be presented to both Democratic and Republican presidential candidates. The idea, which later came to fruition in slightly altered form, was to use the Black Agenda as the criteria for determining which party and candidate blacks should support in 1972. Indeed, as 1972 approached, more and more energy of individual CBC members was consumed in efforts to fashion pragmatic personal or group strategies for the forthcoming conventions and elections. The Black Political Convention in March 1972 in Gary, Indiana, was part of that process.

Congressman Charles Diggs, then chairman of the CBC, had issued the "call" for a national black political convention at a caucus-sponsored conference of black locally elected officials held in Washington, D.C., in November 1971. Speaking as chairman of the CBC and in its name, Diggs called for a national black political convention to be held in April or early May of 1972 "for the purpose of developing a national Black Agenda and the crystallization of a national Black strategy for the 1972 election and beyond."[3]

This call created internal conflict. While Diggs had "touched base" with some of the more active members of the caucus on the convention idea, he had not cleared his announcement with the full caucus at a formal meeting. By the time the CBC met formally to discuss the matter, a majority voted to withdraw official CBC backing from the convention. Some caucus members were afraid the convention would leave the CBC with financial deficits. Others feared it would get out of hand and create bad publicity. However, individual CBC members remained active. Diggs was an official convener of the assembly, along with Mayor Richard Hatcher of Gary, Indiana, and black nationalist leader Imamu Baraka. Walter Fauntroy (District of Columbia) was chairman of the crucial platform committee. Almost all caucus members attended the convention, and Howard Robinson, the caucus executive director, played an important role in organizing and orchestrating its actions.

The Gary convention marked an important transition point in CBC history. Even though the caucus was not the official sponsor of the convention, the CBC name was publicly associated with it as a result both of Diggs's "call" in November and of the subsequent visible involvement of some CBC members. The CBC, therefore, was unhappily associated with the two controversial resolutions passed at the convention on busing and on Israel.

Not satisfied with repeated personal disclaimers, the caucus issued press releases on these topics immediately after the Gary convention. The release on Israel reaffirmed "its friendship with the State of Israel" and stated: "As the Black elected representatives to the U.S. Congress, we reaffirm our position that we fully respect the right of the Jewish people to have their own state in their historical National Homeland. We vigorously oppose the efforts of any group that would seek to weaken or undermine Israel's right to existence."[4] The CBC also issued a press release in support of busing. Thus the caucus openly challenged

³ CBC Press Release, November 20, 1971, from the Congressional Black Caucus/Black Elected Officials Conference, Sheraton Park Hotel, Washington, D.C.

⁴ CBC Press Release, March 21, 1972.

the Gary convention's ongoing legislative body, the Black Assembly, less than a month after the convention. Further, the CBC issued a Black Declaration of Independence and a Black Bill of Rights before the Black Political Agenda produced by the Gary convention appeared publicly in final form. This behavior reflects inescapable facts of black political life.

The Black Political Convention, while well attended and representative of a broad cross-section of black America, had offended powerful black civil rights interests and powerful white liberal, Jewish, and labor interests. These groups formed the backbone of financial support for individual members and lobbying support for the group as a whole. Whatever their individual feelings, it was important for a majority of the caucus to dissociate themselves decisively from the convention because it was a political liability to them in their central arenas—Congress and national politics.

The Gary convention also revealed the extent of internal caucus conflict. While Fauntroy (D.C.), Diggs (Michigan), and Dellums (California) were active in the Gary convention, Shirley Chisholm (New York) viewed the convention as a personal rebuff to her. Indeed, the unenthusiastic, and at times hostile, response of some caucus members to her presidential candidacy created an enormous rift in the caucus and almost destroyed it.[5] By mid-1972 the caucus no longer seemed a "united voice for Black America." Never actually a monolith, even the myths of unity were punctured by the events surrounding the Gary convention and the 1972 Democratic Convention. The caucus's "collective stage" had come to an end.

"Collective stage" is a term used advisedly to describe the first year of the caucus, when it was depicting itself as a single, unified group representing a political construct called the "national Black community." While far from nationalistic, this conception rests both on an assumption of a commonality of black political interests and on a further assumption that black representatives can jointly represent that black collectivity. Central to this collective stage was a visible CBC role outside Congress.

While the collective CBC stage was often confusing for outsiders and hectic for the congressmen, some accomplishments mark that period. First, a staff nucleus was appointed; it performed a wide range of important activities and laid the groundwork for later caucus staff development. Second, a method of financing the caucus was institutionalized through the annual $100 a plate dinner. In fiscal year 1973 the caucus grossed $218,082 from the annual dinner, netting $96,384. The 1974 dinner was accompanied by a recorded benefit concert, which had

---

[5] Shirley Chisholm, *The Good Fight* (New York: Harper & Row, 1973) is a discussion of Congresswoman Chisholm's controversial presidential candidacy. It provides some indication of the level of conflict her efforts engendered.

netted the caucus $50,000 by February 1975. Third, an internal structure was established consisting of a chairman, executive committee, and policy oriented subcommittees. While some subcommittees were moribund from birth, others, such as the subcommittee on small business chaired by Parren Mitchell (Maryland), have been a tremendous success. Finally, the caucus gained support from many blacks around the country who perceived it as a group working for their benefit. (This expectation led to large numbers of casework requests from blacks going to the caucus staff and to offices of most caucus members.) Also the model of the caucus as an entity greater than the sum of its parts—an institution committed to the provision of services for black people by combining congressional and other resources—emerged in embryonic form. In short, the achievements of the collective period were the establishment of the caucus and the development of a firm institutional foundation for its continued existence.

The viability of the caucus was quickly tested by the events surrounding the Gary convention and the 1972 Democratic National convention. While the CBC survived, it changed drastically. Administrative changes included the election of Representative Louis Stokes (Ohio) as chairman and the replacement of the first executive director (who resigned to return to his position as a high ranking foreign service officer) by a new executive director, recruited from academia. However, the most dramatic change was in the caucus's self-perception, its conception of a relevant constituency, and its goals.

The "Ethnic Stage"

Stokes was quite explicit about the change in direction: "At first we were unclear about our proper role. Therefore, in the past year, we had to analyze what our resources were, what we should be doing, and how best to do it. And our conclusion was this: if we were to be effective, if we were going to make the meaningful contribution to minority citizens in this country, then it must be as legislators. This is the area in which we possess expertise—and it is within the halls of Congress that we must make this expertise felt."[6] By mid-1972, members of the caucus had turned away from the turbulence of visible national collective leadership to define themselves as "just" legislators—representatives of individual constituencies.

From mid-1972 to the end of 1974 the CBC entered what is best termed an "ethnic stage." Ethnic, because defining the role of black congressmen as identical to that of white congressmen implies a structural verisimilitude between blacks (and their problems) and whites. This suggests a parallel between the political assimilation of blacks and the

[6] Speech by Louis Stokes, July 1973.

political assimilation of white ethnic groups. The collective stage, in contrast, was implicitly based on an assumption that black congressmen had special responsibilities and had to play a role that responded to the unique problems of black Americans.

Evaluation of the caucus's ethnic stage presents special problems because it coincided with the deepening crisis of the Nixon administration. Indeed, during 1974 much of the energies of Charles Rangel (New York), who replaced Louis Stokes as CBC chairman in 1973, Barbara Jordan (Texas), and John Conyers (Michigan) was absorbed by their tenure on the House Judiciary Committee during the impeachment process. Furthermore, the entire Congress was caught up in the historical drama surrounding the tangled web of Watergate.

During this period the CBC undertook two major unified efforts, extension of OEO programs under the Economic Opportunity Act of 1964 and countering fund impoundments by President Nixon. These two efforts comprised the dynamics of CBC operation during its ethnic stage. All members of the CBC introduced or cosponsored legislation on impoundment and OEO. In addition, the caucus staff organized a nationwide lobbying effort on these issues. As part of this effort, a national strategy session was called. Over two hundred representatives of community organizations and other key representatives met to hear Senator Humphrey, Speaker Albert, Congressman Mahon, Congressman Hawkins, lobbyist Clarence Mitchell, and the Rev. Jesse Jackson, among others, discuss the problem of impoundment. This session served also as a rally to accompany an extensive lobbying, educational, and research effort spearheaded by the caucus and crucially involving powerful national organizations like the Leadership Conference on Civil Rights, the Southern Christian Leadership Conference, PUSH, Coalition for Human Needs and Budget Priorities, the National Urban Coalition, Movement for Economic Justice, Common Cause, the Urban League, and the League of Women Voters.

Although the caucus's efforts on OEO and impoundment were only partially successful, the process contributed to its development. By the time of his resignation in September 1974, Augustus Adair, the executive director, had worked out effective relationships with key organizations such as those mentioned above and many others. Unquestionably the caucus was further institutionalized during the ethnic stage. Its support base was widened and informal networks that were personal and specific to the Robinson regime during the earlier period became more formal and organized as a result of these mobilization efforts.

Reflection on this period, however, raises a serious question. Was a formally organized caucus and the staff and operating costs it entailed necessary? No doubt there were significant legislative achievements during the ethnic period—most notably the District of Columbia home rule bill—but those were individually achieved. The caucus countered presidential conservatism in many ways—for instance, by issuing its own state of the union message, "The True State of the Union"—but it could have united for those purposes without a formally organized caucus.

Similarly the OEO and impoundment efforts could have been coordinated through the offices of individual members. The caucus staff attempted to develop a research capacity that reflected the black perspective, through caucus legislative alerts. But since neither the caucus members nor staff had defined what constitutes a black public policy perspective, the alerts were often imitations of Democratic Study Group (DSG) efforts. Even when legislative alerts were of particular relevance, many caucus members did not use them or even read them, according to the candid assessment of Adair. In fact, it is difficult to think of many activities during the ethnic stage that necessitated an ongoing, formally organized CBC. The point is not that the caucus as an institutionalized entity with staff capacity was or is useless. Rather, it is that when black representatives define their role in the narrowest terms they may enhance their collective bargaining power, but they obscure the other reasons for taking the unusual step of institutionalizing a racially based political caucus and thus undermine their own legitimacy.

By the end of 1974, caucus members, the CBC staff, and outside supporters and observers of the caucus were becoming increasingly uneasy. There was an *impression* among many black elites that despite the individual capablity of some caucus members, the caucus as a whole was ineffective and floundering. Accurate or not, this criticism and other internal problems among the members led to a CBC retreat and self-evaluation in December 1974 and January 1975. Some administrative decisions were made. Charles Rangel was unanimously reelected CBC chairman, and Augustus Adair, who resigned as executive director to return to teaching, was replaced by Barbara Williams, a young lawyer who had previously served as Ronald Dellums's (California) administrative assistant. More significantly, an innovative legislative strategy was adopted for the Ninety-fourth Congress.

Caucus Strategy for the Ninety-fourth Congress

As a result of the CBC retreat, three significant changes were made that helped shape caucus strategy for the Ninety-fourth Congress. First, the caucus worked out more effective methods of exchanging information and discussing legislation so they would display more unity in legislative and political matters. The assumption was that often caucus differences resulted from lack of proper exchange of information rather than deep, internal ideological cleavages.

This was partially in response to outside criticism of caucus disunity. Whatever the justification for this criticism as an evaluation of caucus capacity to exert political leadership on a wide variety of issues, analysis of key House votes in 1974 shows that out of sixteen key votes in 1974 all members of the caucus voted the same way on eleven.[7] On two more votes—campaign reform (H.R. 16090, Federal Elections Campaign Act) and an increase in the 1974 fiscal authorization ceiling on United States military aid to South Vietnam (H.R. 12565, Defense Supplemental Authorization, fiscal 1974)—all caucus members were united except Congressman Nix. On one vote (H.R. 10294, Land Use Planning) all caucus members were agreed except Congresswoman Collins. Thus only two key votes severely split the caucus: one was the Sugar Act amendments, and the other was the Rockefeller nomination. On both issues there were intensive cross-pressures and side issues that obscured clear definition of both the "liberal" position and black self-interest.

The second change that grew out of the caucus self-evaluation was acceptance of the "Fauntroy strategy" employed in achieving home rule for the District of Columbia as a general legislative strategy for the CBC. The "Fauntroy strategy" was based on a series of studies done by the Joint Center for Political Studies showing that blacks compose 25 percent or more of the population of fifty-eight congressional districts and that in fifty-one of these districts the black population of voting age was approximately two or three times the margin of victory for the winning candidate in the 1972 congressional elections, indicating that a heavy turnout of black voters in those districts could be very influential if other factors remained constant.

Fauntroy had singled out the southern constituencies with 25 percent or more black population. Letters were mailed to black elected officials and a few other prominent people in those districts requesting them to contact their congressman and ask him to vote for H.R. 9682, the District of Columbia home rule bill. Fauntroy then contacted the congressmen from those districts and asked support for the bill. Thus the strategy involved a coordinated lobbying and peer approach to southern congressmen from the target districts.

Subsequently, a modified version of the Fauntroy strategy was also

[7] The sixteen key votes were H.R. 12435, Minimum Wage Increase; H.R. 69, Elementary and Secondary Education Act Amendments; H.R. 12565, Defense Supplemental Authorization; H.R. 14368, Energy Supply and Coordination; H.R. 13834, Stanley Energy Emergency Authority; H.R. 14747, Sugar Act amendments; H.R. 10294, Land Use Planning; H.R. 7130, Congressional Budget Reform; H.R. 16090, Federal Elections Campaign Act; S. 3066, Housing and Community Development Act; H.R. 12859, Urban Mass Transit; H. Res. 1333, Impeachment Report; H.J. Res. 1131, Continuing Appropriations Fiscal 1975; H.R. 16900, Supplemental Appropriations Fiscal 1975; H.R. 16596, Public Service Jobs; and the Rockefeller nomination. Key votes chosen by CQ Weekly Report 33 (January 11, 1975) pp. 77, 78.

used in the 1973 mobilization for extension of OEO. In both the District of Columbia home rule and OEO examples, other complicating factors prevent a precise assessment of the part played by the Fauntroy strategy in the final outcome. Certainly, in both cases there were large differences between what black lobbyists and other organized interest groups wanted and the legislation finally passed. One important fact did emerge from these efforts—the willingness of black elected officials and local black influentials to cooperate with the CBC. As a caucus strategy, the Fauntroy plan is expected to be elaborated by the creation of nationwide congressional district caucuses in districts of high black voting age population. These district caucuses are to consist of black elected officials and local black influentials and are to form the basis of a CBC "whip system."

The third change that resulted from the CBC retreat was the adoption of an approach developed by Parren Mitchell. Called the "Mitchell Model," it involves approximately three hundred advisers (called "brainstormers") from around the country who discuss current public policy issues and congressional legislation. Because of Mitchell's particular interest in black business enterprise, his "brainstormers" are heavily weighted toward businessmen, bankers, economists, and lawyers. As adapted for caucus use, the Mitchell Model would mean creation of a much larger group of "brainstormers" with broader professional representation.

Through this legislative strategy the caucus hoped to move from reacting to crises to shaping events and decisions. Also, through the Mitchell Model and the district caucuses, caucus members hoped to develop a nationwide system of support and expertise. The total strategy was aimed at increasing effectiveness of the CBC Ninety-fourth Congress legislative agenda.

The caucus has produced legislative agendas before. Usually conglomerations of unpassable legislative proposals woven together by press release rhetoric, they were soon forgotten. The CBC agenda for the Ninety-fourth Congress differed in two ways: first, there was a specific strategy aimed to increase the possibilities that a portion of the agenda would be passed. Second, from among the many laudable items included in the agenda for symbolic purposes, the CBC chose one measure for particular attention—H.R. 50, the equal opportunity and full employment bill. This legislation, introduced by Augustus Hawkins (California), cosponsored by the entire caucus and sixty-nine other representatives, would create a job guarantee office and a standby job corps, as well as require the president to develop a national full employment and production program. Full employment would be achieved through both private and public employers.

Largely shaped by Leon Keyserling, chairman of the Truman administration Council of Economic Advisers, H.R. 50 embodies an economic policy that rejects the idea of a tolerable level of unemployment. CBC focus on this legislation reflected the disastrous effect of the 1974-75 recession on black people. The Hawkins full employment bill became a priority not only of the CBC, but also of many national black organizations. Meeting in September 1974 at a black economic summit, over a hundred representatives from the organizations articulated their support for the measure.

All this is not to say that major black organizations have no problems with the bill. Many labor unions have been generally unenthusiastic about the Hawkins measure, and most civil rights organizations have been too dependent on labor support to ignore their wishes on this crucial issue. Nevertheless, the Hawkins bill came closer to receiving enthusiastic majority support among black influentials than almost any measure since the Voting Rights Act of 1965. Moreover, it placed the CBC in a posture of confrontation with the president and the domestic policy advisers of his administration.

Other important priorities on the 1975 caucus legislative agenda included extension of the 1965 Voting Rights Act; tax reform; passage of a universal voter registration law, such as postcard registration; and amendment and modification of the Revenue Sharing Act and the Higher Education Act, both of which were scheduled to expire in 1975.

The CBC approach to the Ninety-fourth Congress integrated collective strategic elements into an essentially ethnic posture. Both the Mitchell Model and the Fauntroy plan involve CBC mobilization of elite segments of the black community in support of their legislative agenda. Once the caucus seeks support from this nationwide network, it must again define itself as something more than a collection of representatives who happen to be black. Collective support implies a collective entity to support. Comparison of the CBC with other unofficial groups in the House illuminates collective elements in caucus strategy and helps define the unique aspects of CBC structure and function.

The CBC was one of nine unofficial groups in the House in 1975. The others were: The New England Caucus (a bipartisan group of twenty-five congressmen from the Northeast); the Wednesday Group (thirty liberal to moderate Republicans); the Congressional Rural Caucus (a bipartisan group of fifty congressmen); the Republican Study Committee (sixty conservative Republicans); the Democratic Research Organization (seventy-five conservative, mostly southern, Democrats); the Democratic Freshman Class (in the process of being organized among the seventy-five freshman Democrats); United Democrats of Congress (one hundred "moderate" or "middle-of-the-road" Democrats); and the powerful and liberal Democratic Study Group composed of 218 Democratic members. Members of Congress for Peace through Law (MCPL) is a bicameral group of 150 House and Senate members, mostly liberals, interested in foreign affairs.[8] Two additional groups have been discussed but as of May 1975 were not officially launched—an environmental caucus and a radical caucus. A group of congresswomen meet sporadically when the occasion arises but have not yet instituted a formal organization. Acorns, SOS, and the Chowder and Marching Society are discussion groups composed of conservative and moderate Republicans.

While the CBC is the smallest of the unofficial groups (seventeen members in the Ninety-fourth Congress), its staff of seven (including four professionals) is the third largest, next after the Republican Study Committee staff of fourteen and the DSG staff of twelve. The MCPL with 150 members has a staff of only five. The CBC is also one of the best financed groups.

Most of the unofficial groups in the House finance their activities through a combination of dues from congressional members and portions of their allotments for clerk hire donated for use by the group in hiring staff. Only the MCPL has been completely privately financed. Their major fund raiser nets about $85,000 annually, which is supplemented by contributions and small fund raisers throughout the year. The CBC supplemented funds from its annual fund raiser with benefits, contributions, and limited use of clerk hire.

In the Ninety-fourth Congress the CBC was one of the most ambitious and highly organized groups. In this respect unofficial groups fall roughly into two categories. Those like the United Democrats of Congress are the most informal. Meeting only to hold briefings for members, they do not provide legislative alerts or analyses. Staffing is part-time and consists of people from the offices of the chairman or executive committee members. On the other end of the spectrum are the well-organized DSG, Republican Study Committee, and MCPL. These organizations have sophisticated research capacities, weekly legislative alerts, and at times whip calls. The new CBC staff has a multitude of complex functions to perform for members. It publishes a newsletter, produces legislative alerts and larger research reports, holds briefings, and must oversee realization of the caucus strategy. The district caucuses (the "whip system"), the legislative agenda, and the elaborate Mitchell Model go well beyond what most unofficial groups undertake. Needless to say, the collective stage in caucus history is unparalleled in the experiences of other unofficial House groups.

The CBC as a group does not have formal ties with any other unofficial group in the House. However, all four black congresswomen (Shirley Chisholm [New York], Yvonne Burke [California], Barbara Jordan [Texas], and Cardiss Collins [Illinois]) participate in the informal

---

[8] Members of the House often belong to more than one informal group.

discussions of the women's "caucus." All members of the CBC belong to the DSG, and many are very active members or officers. In an interview, the DSG executive director, Richard Conlon, described DSG as a "union" for House Democrats, particularly those lowest in seniority. Total CBC membership in DSG reflects both caucus liberalism and caucus need for a "union." Until recently caucus members were low in seniority and not often recipients of choice committee assignments.

CBC ability to demand and get better committee assignments has been one of the few clear achievements of black representatives organizing as a caucus. Three reasons account for their improved assignments in the Ninety-fourth Congress: negotiations conducted with the House leadership by Charles Rangel, CBC chairman; CBC lobbying for better committee assignments through their network of colleagues in the DSG and in their state delegations; and the greater opportunity for committee mobility in the Ninety-fourth Congress because of the large number (103) of representatives who lost in the 1974 elections. Table 1 shows CBC committee assignments and seniority rankings. Caucus members in 1975 accordingly were represented on the three most powerful House committees: Appropriations, Ways and Means, and Rules. In addition there was representation on Foreign Affairs (Robert N.C. Nix [Pennsylvania] chaired the International Economic Policy Subcommittee and Charles C. Diggs chaired the International Resources, Food and Energy Subcommittee); Education and Labor (Augustus Hawkins [California] chaired the Equal Opportunities Subcommittee); Budget; and Banking, Currency and Housing.

A few caucus members have even penetrated the House leadership. Barbara Jordan (Texas) and Ralph Metcalfe (Illinois) became part of the new twenty-four member Democratic Steering and Policy Committee, which was granted committee assignment power for all House Democrats by the Democratic party caucus. Also, Shirley Chisholm was assistant secretary of the Democratic caucus and Cardiss Collins an at-large Democratic whip.

Three days after Ford succeeded to the presidency he moved to initiate a meeting with the CBC. The public relations benefits to Ford were enormous because of the caucus's past history with Nixon. With one stroke and without making any commitments, Ford projected an image of accessibility. Furthermore, once the invitation was extended, caucus refusal became politically difficult.

The caucus prepared a statement for the president that emphasized many of the same issues discussed in the 1971 meeting with Nixon. However, the focus was on the related problems of inflation, recession, and unemployment. Congressman Augustus Hawkins outlined the provisions of his full employment bill, and the caucus sought support for it. The caucus also requested appointment of more blacks in high echelon positions in the Ford administration. After the meeting, the black

TABLE 1

Ninety-fourth Congress Caucus Committee Assignments and Seniority

Member	Committees	Seniority
Charles Diggs (Michigan)	D.C. Committee (chairman) Foreign Affairs	20
Robert Nix (Pennsylvania)	Foreign Affairs Post Office and Civil Service	25
Augustus Hawkins (California)	Education and Labor House Administration	36
John Conyers (Michigan)	Judiciary Government Operations	43
Shirley Chisholm (New York)	Education and Labor	49
William Clay (Missouri)	Education and Labor Post Office and Civil Service	49
Louis Stokes (Ohio)	Appropriations Budget	49
Ronald Dellums (California)	Armed Services D.C. Committee Select Intelligence	58
Ralph Metcalfe (Illinois)	Merchant Marine and Fisheries Interstate and Foreign Commerce	58
Parren Mitchell[a] (Maryland)	Budget Banking, Currency and Housing Small Business	58
Charles Rangel (New York)	Ways and Means	63
Yvonne Burke (California)	Appropriations	63
Barbara Jordan (Texas)	Judiciary Government Operations	63
Andrew Young (Georgia)	Rules	63
Cardiss Collins (Illinois)	Government Operations Foreign Affairs	65
Harold Ford (Tennessee)	Banking, Currency and Housing Veterans Affairs Select Aging	73
Walter Fauntroy[b] (D.C.)	Banking, Currency and Housing D.C. Committee	

Source: *Congressional Quarterly* 33 (January 18, 1975), p. 148, (February 8, 1975), p. 295; *List of Standing Committees and Select Committees of the House of Representatives of the United States, 94th Congress,* compiled by W. Pat Jennings, clerk of the House of Representatives, March 14, 1975.

[a]Parren Mitchell has taken a leave of absence from the small-business committee.

[b]As delegate from the District of Columbia, Walter Fauntroy can serve on committees and introduce legislation but may not vote.

special assistant to the president, Stanley Scott, was appointed as liaison between the caucus and the White House. The caucus had requested this appointment, and Scott was the logical choice.

Ford's subsequent pardoning of Richard Nixon and his pursuit of other policies with which the caucus disagreed chilled the relationship. Nevertheless, in 1974 most CBC members, in contrast to most other members of Congress, gave Ford somewhat greater voting support than Nixon. Differences between CBC and House support for Nixon reflected caucus liberalism as well as a more specific confrontation with the Nixon administration's "politics of benign neglect." The short caucus honeymoon with Ford soon ended. Table 2 shows caucus support for and opposition to Presidents Nixon and Ford in 1974.

Formation of the CBC was, at least partially, a response stimulated by the Nixon administration's deliberate "politics of benign neglect." This helps to locate the CBC theoretically and illuminates the growing phenomenon of racial legislative caucuses. As a phrase, "benign neglect" summarized a national political climate in which the crystallized majority reaction to the civil rights reforms of the late 1950s and 1960s often took a thinly disguised antiblack form. Thus, the CBC did not introduce primordial politics into the congressional process but simply organized around a primordial bond—race—that had already become politicized.

In the initial stages, organization took a collective form, rooted in an ideology in which the national black community was viewed as an at least partially autonomous, holistic entity, a coherent social subsystem represented politically by the CBC. The contradiction between the demands of a collective ideology and the pressures of the highly fragmented politics of the individual members eventually produced the strains and conflicts that resulted in a drastic change in direction.

The next period, the ethnic stage, was marked by CBC ideological self-perception in individualistic terms, as individual representatives representing their specific constituencies. Passing references were still made to a broader constituency of 25 million black people, but the precise relationship that should exist between black representatives and 25 million black people was never clarified. Indeed, rhetoric masked the central contradiction of the ethnic stage, when the CBC invoked the symbols of universality to legitimize its racially based organization—and to raise large sums of money for it—yet failed to act effectively in collective ways for collective ends. Changes in CBC strategy for the Ninety-fourth Congress involved an integration of elements from the collective and ethnic eras in order to achieve certain limited legislative ends.

It is tempting, but premature, to place the collective and ethnic stages on an evolutionary vector that culminates in a happy synthesis—a sort of CBC nirvana in the Ninety-fourth Congress. Instead, the collective

TABLE 2

C B C Presidential Support and Opposition — 1974

Congress-persons	Nixon Support Score 1974 %	Ford Support Score 1974 %	Nixon Opposition Score 1974 %	Ford Opposition Score 1974 %
Dellums	32	35	57	61
Hawkins	28	26	34	33
Burke	26	37	49	50
Young	30	41	57	28
Metcalfe	25	39	53	44
Collins	28	41	51	57
Conyers	26	24	53	56
Diggs	21	26	30	39
Clay	32	33	45	54
Chisholm	19	41	64	54
Rangel	26	37	66	56
Stokes	34	41	49	52
Nix	26	39	51	54
Jordan	45	46	53	50
Mitchell	26	33	55	52
Caucus Average	26	34	48	46
House Average	54	45	35	41
Difference	28	13	11	5

Source: *Congressional Quarterly* 33 (January 18, 1975), p. 148.
Note: Congressman Fauntroy does not vote as D.C. delegate, and Congressman Harold Ford was not present in the Ninety-third Congress. Scores for President Nixon are based on votes taken between January 20 and August 8. Scores for President Ford are based on votes taken between August 9 and December 20.

and ethnic stages may be no more than oscillations reflecting a shifting balance in contextual forces as they impinge differentially on CBC members. As long as being black remains a powerful ascriptive category, subject to provocative and emotional politicization, collective action through racial legislative caucuses remains a plausible strategy. But continued collective action flounders on the failure to define a black legislative perspective, determine what political action it entails, and delineate a level of responsibility and accountability. Black legislators avoid these issues and even the question of long-range goals and direction because they (and blacks in general) are unclear as to whether blacks are ethnics, destined to follow the assimilation route of white ethnic groups, or are an unassimilable residue whose special problems demand unique solutions and entail new forms of political action.[9]

[9] For a further discussion of ethnic and collective orientations in black politics, see Marguerite Ross Barnett, "A Theoretical Perspective On Racial Public Policy," in *Public Policy Strategies for Black People in the Coming Decades*, eds. Marguerite Ross Barnett and James A. Hefner (Port Washington, N.Y.: Alfred Press), forthcoming.

Black legislators are in a double bind. Caught between pressures to represent blacks collectively as a holistic unit and constraints dictated by their individual political circumstances, they can neither act solely as a unit nor solely as individuals. Oscillations between ethnic and collective group styles are replicated in the behavior of individual congressmen as they seek to mediate these contradictions. Of course, no period or individual is ever completely ethnic or collective; rather, one ideological motif encompasses the other in more or less complete and effective ways. Thus, while the CBC and other racial legislative caucuses will be features of the near future, their long-range viability is shrouded by the larger unresolved issues of the nature of American racism and the construction of any form of group organization in an individualistic ideological context.

The Battle of the Budget

ALLEN SCHICK

In one of his last major acts as president, Richard Nixon signed the Congressional Budget and Impoundment Control Act into law on July 12, 1974. Less than one month later, he was gone from the national scene, leaving to his successor not only the litter of Watergate but also executive-legislative confrontation in many areas of American politics. This essay considers the new congressional budget process in the context of conflict between the two branches, particularly the strife that merges out of the budgetary role of the federal government.

The budget is a perennial battleground of American politics. Everybody fights. Agencies strive for more money, budget offices for more control over spending. The president announces one set of budget priorities; Congress enacts another. Within Congress, it is House versus Senate, authorizing versus appropriations committees, and spenders versus savers.

It could hardly be otherwise. With tens of billions of dollars at issue every year and with vital interests and policies hinging on the outcomes, the budget has virtually boundless potential for conflict. The budget could be a routine, settled affair only if disadvantaged interests were suppressed or if the United States possessed sufficient resources to satisfy all legitimate claimants. Because neither condition prevails, conflict is a ubiquitous aspect of budgeting.

Yet in American budgeting, almost everything gets settled. Despite the potential for open and protracted strife, the federal budget is decided each year, sometimes after little more than ritualistic disagreement, sometimes after great struggle. There are signs that budgetary warfare—in particular, conflict between the president and Congress—has escalated in recent years, and the prospect is for more tension in the future than was customary in the past. The problem is much more than the division of legislative and executive power between the Democratic and Republican parties; it wells out of significant changes in budgeting and the larger political process it serves.

Some indicators of heightened conflict are the impoundment battles between the White House and Congress, enactment of a confirmation requirement for the director and deputy director of the president's Office of Management and Budget, counterbudget pressures from interest groups and research organizations, increased use of continuing resolutions to fund federal agencies and programs, and, most significantly, establishment of a new congressional budget process and the Congressional Budget Office. In order to appraise these developments, it is appropriate to consider the resources available for containing budget conflict and the reasons why discord has become much more widespread.

How Budgetary Conflict Is Managed and Why It Is Spreading

Settling the budget is too important to leave to chance or to only a single method of resolution. Among the factors working to abate budgetary conflict are the one-year-at-a-time approach, concentrating on inputs rather than on outcomes or results, avoiding direct determination of budget priorities, and tolerating second best—or worse—programs. All of these have been attenuated by efforts to promote "rational" long-range planning, Planning-Programming-Budgeting Systems (PPBS), and cost-benefit analysis. But two factors merit special attention because they manifest far-reaching changes in national politics. These are the opening up of federal budgeting to previously excluded groups and the loss of a fiscal increment for mitigating budget disputes.

The budget ordinarily is peacefully negotiated because the price of extended disagreement is unacceptably high to the major participants. A budget in deadlock threatens payless paydays for public employees, federal activities grinding to a halt, favored programs aborted, and new ones discarded. Almost everyone enters the budget process expecting to reach agreement, committed not to push a view beyond the point of prudent dispute. Budget makers are schooled in the necessities of accommodation. They reach agreement because they have been socialized to believe that protracted disagreement is improper. Reinforcing this attitude are the visible risks of being blamed for holding up a settlement: a bad press, pressure from affected interests, and banishment from the political mainstreams.

Of course there are exceptions. Senator Proxmire blocked transportation appropriations until the SST project was abandoned. Foreign assistance programs have been stalled in recent years because of intense divisions over America's Indochina policy. President Nixon waged a broad impoundment war in an effort to force a retreat from statutory commitments. These cases attest to the vulnerability of the budget process to discord, but they also suggest the abnormality of prolonged deadlock.

As long as the cast of budget participants was limited to presidential officials and congressional appropriators, budgetary peace was comparatively easy to attain. The chosen few had stable roles and relationships. They understood that for the budget to be settled, the number of issues must be limited. They knew that old sores must not be reopened. They ruled out radical alternatives. They were comfortable with the pace of incremental change and willing to ignore big questions of national objectives and priorities.

In recent times the number and variety of budget participants has steadily expanded as the number of issues that must be confronted has increased. While it would be misleading to speak of a completely open federal budget process, the trend has been markedly in the direction of more varied participation. Three illustrations show what has happened. One is drawn from executive practice, the second from the legislative arena, and the third from outside groups.

(1) Relying on its interpretation of the Budget and Accounting Act of 1921, the Office of Management and Budget (and its predecessor, the Bureau of the Budget) long resisted congressional demands for agency budget estimates. This policy did not disadvantage the appropriations committees, because they were able to obtain the data in the course of their hearings on agency requests.[1] The effect, therefore, was to exclude other sectors of Congress as well as public groups, thereby permitting the insiders to maintain their privileged relationships. But during the past few years, perhaps taking a cue from the privileged position of the Joint Committee on Atomic Energy, Congress has chipped away at this wall of executive secrecy by requiring certain agencies such as the Consumer Product Safety Commission to submit their raw estimates directly to Congress at the same time that they are given to OMB. During the Ninety-third Congress, bills were introduced (S. 704 and S. 1214) to extend this requirement to all federal agencies or at least to regulatory commissions. The new Congressional Budget Office has broad powers to obtain budget data from executive agencies, and the General Accounting Office is newly authorized to establish accessible data files. In addition, a regular procedure now operates for reporting impoundment actions. In a more specialized area, pressure is building up for publication of CIA budget figures and for information on how intelligence funds are spent. Such moves entitle outsiders to timely budget data and enable them to become effective participants in the budget process.

(2) As late as the end of World War II, the House and Senate appro-

---

[1] The OMB policy is based on Section 206 of the Budget and Accounting Act of 1921 and is set forth in OMB Circular A-10.

priations committees had virtual monopolies on the consideration of spending legislation in Congress. Most agencies and programs operated under permanent authorizations with the result that they were not subject to annual or periodic review by the legislative committees. Backdoor spending—financing authorized outside the appropriations process— was limited in scope and applied to only a specialized portion of the federal budget.

But, during the past twenty years, a pronounced trend to annual and short-term authorizations had grown up so that an increasing number of federal agencies must go before authorizing committees (prior to and in addition to the Appropriations Committee) in order to secure funds from Congress. The programs operating under annual authorization include military procurement, construction, and research and development; foreign assistance; the Maritime Administration; NASA; and the National Science Foundation. In 1972, the State Department became the first cabinet department to be subjected to this procedure. In addition, many domestic programs, especially those providing assistance to state and local governments, have limited authorizations of two to five years' duration. By means of limited authorizations, virtually every House and Senate committee has gained some jurisdiction over budget policy.

Authorizing committees have two distinct motives for seeking annual authorizations. One is to enhance congressional (and their own) oversight of executive agencies; the other is to enable them to bolster the spending claims of a particular agency or program. The first reason invites heightened conflict between Congress and the executive branch; the second brings conflict between the authorizing and appropriating committees. A significant yardstick of this intracongressional conflict is the authorization-appropriations gap, the difference between the amount of money authorized and the amount appropriated. This gap certainly exceeds $10 billion annually for federal domestic programs.[2]

Although they have been able to muscle into the budget process, the authorizing committees are at a disadvantage *vis-à-vis* their appropriating counterparts because standard authorizations cannot be spent unless funds have been actually appropriated. To redress this imbalance a number of authorizing committees have devised backdoor spending methods that authorize agencies to use funds prior to or outside the regular appropriations process. One popular type of backdoor is contract authority which permits an agency to obligate funds in advance of appropriations. The matter comes before the appropriations committees only when money is needed to liquidate the obligation, too late for them to exercise any meaningful control. Contract authority is used to finance

---

[2] See U.S. Advisory Commission on Intergovernmental Relations, *The Gap Between Federal Aid Authorization and Appropriations: Fiscal Year 1966-1970* (Washington: GPO, June 1970).

the interstate highway system, the multibillion dollar water pollution control program, and a number of smaller programs.

Another backdoor strategy is to authorize agencies to borrow funds from the Treasury or from the public. Borrowing authority in excess of $150 billion—most of it outside the appropriations process—has been authorized since this backdoor was opened in 1932. Generally this form of backdoor is utilized for commercial type programs.

The third and most prevalent form of backdoor is a mandatory entitlement of specified payments to eligible beneficiaries. Most entitlements are open-ended: their cost depends on the varying number of claimants and amounts allowable to each, rather than on current legislative decisions. Most entitlements are also in the form of permanent appropriations that bypass the appropriations committees altogether. Even when the entitlements go through the regular appropriations process (as is the case with public assistance and veterans' benefits) the appropriations committees have no real say over the amounts that are to be spent.

Enlarging the number of budget participants through limited-term authorizations and backdoor spending has helped to intensify budget conflict. The points of access to budgetary power have multiplied and rendered it much more difficult for the traditional participants (OMB and the appropriations committees) to thwart pressures for more money. As a consequence, the federal government no longer is assured of unencumbered resources for new programs.

(3) The closure of the budget process to outside scrutiny has been abetted by its inherent complexity, the needless obscurantism of budget documents, the impenetrability of the tax laws, and the unwillingness of affected interests to invest in budget research and data. There is much truth in the observation that the House Appropriations Committee gained budgetary power by dint of long hours of hard work and expertise over the details of expenditure. On the tax side, the advantaged status of the House Ways and Means Committee was gained through a monolithic committee structure (no subcommittees), the insistence on closed rules for floor consideration of tax measures, and exclusive access to expert staffs.

For most outsiders, the budget was an intimidating document, a curtain of numbers that inhibited them from knowing what was going on. The privileged few did little to improve the understandability of the basic documents. After all, the ignorance of others augmented their own budget power. It would not be difficult to design a more informative federal budget—most states have simpler and more straightforward documents—but there was little incentive to substitute vital statistics for accounting detail. Instead, the outsiders had to settle for easy-to-read "budgets in brief" whose size was scaled down to the meager power they exercised.

All this has been changed by the recent publication of readable and intelligent analyses of the federal budget. One milestone was the issuance of *Counterbudget* by the National Urban Coalition in 1971; another, the annual *Setting National Priorities* series of the Brookings Institution. These publications have inspired numerous interest organizations to issue budget studies of their own each year. Shortly after the president's budget goes to Congress, the mayors, governors, county officials, and many interest groups release analyses of what the budget means for them or their clients. The various publications that offer alternatives to the president's budget have affected both the quality of budget debate and the range of participation.

Change has been even more dramatic with regard to tax policy. Stanley Surrey's political breakthrough in defining "tax expenditures" has focused public attention on the provisions of the Internal Revenue Code that benefit special interests. The Congressional Budget Act requires the president to publish tax expenditure data in his annual budget, and the 1976 budget included them. With expansion of the membership of the House Ways and Means Committee, its establishment of subcommittees, and relaxation of the closed rule, wider participation can be anticipated in the future.

In his 1960 study, *The Semisovereign People*, E. E. Schattschneider conceived of politics as a tension between the privatization and the socialization of conflict. Socialization—expansion—of the scope of conflict, he said, affects its outcome: "The first proposition is that the outcome of every conflict is determined by the *extent* to which the audience becomes involved in it. That is, the outcome of all conflict is determined by the *scope* of its contagion. The number of people involved in any conflict determines what happens." The socialization of budgetary conflict is contagious and difficult to reverse. Any increase in the number of participants is apt to mean an increase as well in the claims on the budget. Whether these pressures are in the form of demands for tax breaks, cash subsidies, or favored programs, they can be satisfied only at the expense of some group in society (if the total is thought to be fixed) or by means of "free," unencumbered resources available to the federal government (if the pie to be cut can be enlarged). If satisfaction is to come at the expense of others, budgetary conflict will rise unless the disadvantaged groups are too weak to protest or have been duped to believe that they will gain from the outcome. But with the expansion of budgetary participation, it is not likely that significant resources can be claimed without a fight.

This leads to the second important reason why budgetary conflict has escalated: the traditional means for cooling budgetary conflict no longer is conveniently available. The standard budget solution of applying incremental resources to new budget claims cannot work when the increment has already been encumbered by past commitments.

The classical method for containing budget conflict is the now familiar incremental policy described by Aaron Wildavsky in *The Politics of the Budgetary Process*. He discerned different decisional rules for the "base" and the "increment." The base consists of the continuing costs of existing programs; the increment, funds for new and expanded programs. The base tends to be a conflict-free zone. Once a program has been established, it is generally continued in future budgets. Because past decisions are not reviewed annually, it is possible to quarantine budget conflict to the increment that deals with proposed program additions. The process of budgeting comes to be "whose ox is to be fattened," a much more pleasant task than deciding "whose ox is to be gored."

The budget increment can be spent in a way that mitigates conflict and encourages the participants to accommodate their claims to one another. If $1 billion of unencumbered funds are available, budget makers can curb conflict by spreading the money among a large number of new programs rather than by allocating the increment to a single use. Moreover, the satisfaction of conflicting claims can be managed in a way that promises more ample funds in future years. Thus, many programs are funded at low start-up cost, with additional funds built into future budgets.

A *sine qua non* for this incremental budget strategy is an increment available for future use. Otherwise, new claims could be satisfied only by invading the base, by taking from agencies and programs funded in previous budgets. In federal budgeting, increments derive from three sources: economic growth, new taxes, and deficit financing. Only the first of these permits a conflict-free resolution of the annual budget process.

A major explanation for the recent escalation in budget conflict is that increments are no longer available in sufficient amounts to cover both the built-in increase in the budget and claims for new programs. Nowadays, much of the budget battle revolves around future increments. Inasmuch as the current increment is already claimed by past commitments, the various interests maneuver to gain an advance commitment of future increments. This means that when next year arrives, its normal increment has already been encumbered by past decisions, and it is necessary to buy budget peace by claiming another year's share. The predicament thus becomes self-perpetuating.

The decade since Wildavsky's book first appeared has experienced zig-zagging economic fortunes. During the mid-1960s, many economists projected a rosy future in which the federal government would have a "fiscal dividend" to devote to its Great Society innovations. Spurred by the instant success of the New Economics, they anticipated a future in which the normal growth of federal revenues would outstrip incremental growth in program costs. The tax cuts of 1964 had indeed produced billions of dollars in additional revenues, with personal and corporate income tax collections in 1967 almost $25 billion higher than they had been before the rates were lowered. The economy was operating at full employment, and economists were confident that they possessed "fine tuning" skills to maintain it on a productive growth path.

The dividend vanished with the Vietnam war. The Johnson administration straddled a "guns and butter" policy that tolerated high military and domestic spending. But this was regarded as a temporary aberration that would be corrected once the Vietnam war ended and the "peace dividend" was realized. However, Vietnam did not conform to this expectation or to the pattern of any previous American war. Without exception, every previous war produced a steep rise in federal spending followed by a sharp decline, though to a trough well above the prewar level. This pattern is displayed in table 1. Had it been adhered to in Viet-

TABLE 1

Effects of War on Federal Expenditures
(in thousands of dollars)

War	Prewar Level	Wartime Peak	Postwar Low
War of 1812	$ 8,058	$ 34,721	$ 15,000
Mexican War	27,767	57,281	39,543
Civil War	66,547	1,297,555	241,334
Spanish War	365,774	605,072	485,234
World War I	734,056	18,514,880	2,974,030
World War II	9,062,032	98,416,220	33,068,709
Korean war	39,617,003	74,274,257	64,569,973
Vietnam war	118,584,000	184,548,000	196,588,000

Source: Department of Commerce, *Historical Statistics of the United States* for all wars other than Vietnam. Data for the Vietnam war were drawn from *The Budget of the United States Government, Fiscal Year 1974.*

nam, there might have been a peace dividend. However, in no post-Vietnam year has spending been lower than in the peak war year. In other words, the trend has been uninterruptedly upward. The wind-down in Vietnam did not even yield a one-year drop in spending.

This phenomenon cannot be explained by blaming it on continuing high levels of defense spending. Between fiscal year 1964 (the last full pre-Vietnam year) and fiscal 1969, defense expenditures rose from $53.6 billion to $81.2 billion, an increase of almost $28 billion. Even if military spending had dropped to its pre-Vietnam level (in current, not real dollars), budget outlays would have continued to rise. Thus, 1971 expenditures were $27 billion above the 1969 level; 1973 spending was $25 billion higher than the 1971 amount; and 1975 spending will be at least $65 billion above the 1973 total.

This pattern is due to the advance commitment of future budget increments. Between 1971 and 1975, nearly three-fourths of the total growth in the federal budget has been devoted to human resource programs. Many of these are mandatory entitlements over which Congress has little current control. The amounts spent for a particular benefit program are determined by exogenous factors, such as the number of people on social security, receiving public assistance, or applying for unemployment compensation. During the 1970s, there has been a steady rise in the number receiving benefits in major entitlement programs, as shown in table 2, accounting for much of the growth in federal expenditures. As the

TABLE 2

Number of Beneficiaries in Major Entitlement Programs
(in thousands of persons)

Program	1970	1975 (estimated)
Unemployment insurance	5,780	14,121
Public service employment	5	284
Public assistance (AFDC)	7,258	10,995
Old-Age Survivors Insurance	22,889	28,302
Disability insurance	2,495	3,962
Supplementary security income (aged, blind, disabled)	3,034	4,465
Veterans' benefits	5,975	7,420
Food stamps	6,470	15,800
Military and civil service retirement	1,712	2,448
Disabled coal miners	—	507

Source: Congressional Research Service, *Overview of the 1976 Budget.*

beneficiary populations increase, they generate automatic rises in federal payments. Moreover, many of these programs are indexed, i.e., the level of benefits is adjusted periodically as the cost of living rises. Federal civilian and military pay is adjusted annually to maintain comparability with private salaries. Civilian and military retirement is linked to the consumer price index (CPI). Beginning in 1975, automatic increases in social security benefits are tied to the CPI. Railroad retirement, benefits for disabled coal miners, supplemental security income, food stamps, and child nutrition programs also are indexed.

As a consequence of the mandatory entitlement programs, the uncontrollable percentage of the federal budget has climbed since 1967 from 59.2 percent to an estimated 74.7 percent in the 1976 budget. During these years, total budget outlays have soared from $158 billion to a projected $349 billion, an increase of $191 billion. But more than 85 percent of this increase—$161 billion—has been accounted for by rises in uncontrollable spending. As itemized in table 3, it is apparent that most of these increases have been in mandatory entitlements.

TABLE 3

Uncontrollable Budget Outlays, Selected Fiscal Years 1967-76

(in billions of dollars)

	1967	1970	1973	1976 (estimated)
Payments for individuals	$41.8	$ 62.2	$ 99.6	$165.1
Net interest	10.3	14.4	17.4	26.1
Prior-year obligations	37.0	41.5	39.6	54.0
Other uncontrollables	4.7	7.6	16.5	15.6
Total uncontrollable	$93.7	$125.7	$173.0	$260.7
Percent uncontrollable	59.2	64.0	70.2	74.7

Source: *The Budget of the United States Government, Fiscal Year 1976.*

These figures show how future budget increments are consumed before Congress has an opportunity to make current budget decisions. The result is that budgetary conflict cannot be contained merely by tapping the incremental resources of the federal government. The sluggish performance of the economy has complicated the problem in partly offsetting ways. The progressivity of the tax structure produced fiscal 1975 revenues as much as $15 billion higher because of double digit inflation in the United States. However, high unemployment costs the budget more. Fiscal 1976 revenues are projected at $55 billion below their estimated level at full employment, while increases in entitlement claims raise federal outlays.

Periodic reductions in federal tax rates have contributed to the loss of a fiscal dividend. Since 1964, cumulative reductions in taxes have produced an annual revenue loss well in excess of $50 billion, prior to the tax reductions enacted in March 1975 for antirecession purposes. The combination of spiraling expenditures, lowered tax rates, and revenue shortfalls because of economic sluggishness has resulted in chronic budget deficits. Between 1970 and 1974, annual deficits averaged almost $15 billion; in 1975 and 1976, the budget deficits are expected to total more than $100 billion.

Deficit spending has been a "safety valve," making it possible to avoid or at any rate to postpone the harsh choice of program cutbacks or tax increases. Thus it is a convenient conflict abatement strategy provided that the main parties are willing to accept the political onus of high deficits. Acceptance of the "unified budget" form in 1968 made it possible to offset some of the red ink in the administrative budget with trust fund surpluses. Undoubtedly, the presidential switch to the full employment budget concept for fiscal 1972 was also intended to make the projected deficit more palatable. It was a short-term accommodation to budget realities rather than a genuine conversion to new economic doctrine. The Nixon administration never abandoned its unease over ballooning expenditures and high deficits. In 1972 and 1973 it took two actions that heated up the battle of the budget, provoked direct confrontation between the executive and legislative branches, and led to enactment of the Congressional Budget and Impoundment Control Act of 1974. One action was unilateral impoundment of funds appropriated by Congress; the other was to demand that Congress give the president discretion to hold fiscal 1973 spending to $250 billion.

The Impoundment War

The impoundment of funds by President Nixon was a reaction to the loss of normal budget increments and chronic budget deficits. The president saw his way to gain some increased financial elbow room for things he wanted by cutting into the base of many domestic programs that he did not favor.

Impoundment is not a new practice—some historians trace it as far back as 1803 when President Jefferson did not spend funds appropriated for gunboats—but until recent times, impoundments were generally used only for routine purposes or for defense-related reasons. The common ingredient of all impoundments is the failure of the executive branch to use funds appropriated by Congress. Many of them are noncontroversial, involve no deviation from legislative policy, and represent only the savings made possible by efficient operations or the prudent reservation of funds for contingencies. These routine impoundments are authorized by the Antideficiency Act, which was initially passed to deter federal agencies from spending at a rate that would compel deficiency appropriations.

In recent years, however, impoundments have become increasingly controversial because funds have been withheld in order to substitute executive policies for those established by Congress. Policy impoundments were first imposed on a large scale during World War II when President Roosevelt curtailed public works spending on the ground that the resources were needed for the war effort. During the 1950s and 1960s successive presidents refused to spend money appropriated by Congress for particular weapons systems. These executive-legislative confrontations involved the president's constitutional role as commander in chief and were limited to a narrow range of issues. During the Vietnam war, President Johnson introduced a broader use of impoundments when he ordered the deferral of billions of dollars of spending in an effort to restrain the overheating economy. Johnson's actions were taken in consultation with congressional leaders and did not provide a confrontation between the two branches.

Following the 1972 elections, President Nixon embarked on large-scale impoundments in programs that he wanted to terminate or curtail.

The impoundments—predominantly for policy purposes—totaled in excess of $18 billion, double the amount officially reported by the administration and far above the comparable action of any previous president. The justifications that he advanced centered on his responsibility to manage the economy and to abide by the statutory debt limit imposed by Congress. However, the impoundments were not applied across the board to all programs. Defense programs were spared all but routine reserves while dozens of domestic programs sustained deep cuts. Half of the $18 billion authorized by Congress for water treatment facilities was impounded. A moratorium was imposed on subsidized housing programs, disaster relief was abruptly curtailed, and rural and community development activities were suspended. Almost $2 billion appropriated for the Departments of Labor and HEW was withheld. Among the agriculture programs ticketed for elimination or curtailment were rural environmental assistance, rural electrification, water and sewer grants, emergency farm loans, and the water bank program.

Dozens of unprecedented court suits were brought during 1973 and 1974 to compel the release of impounded funds. Most were decided against the administration, but the decisions generally rested on particular statutory provisions without passing on the constitutional power of the president. On February 18, 1975, the U.S. Supreme Court issued its first rulings in impoundment suits. A unanimous Court in *Train* v. *City of New York* held that the Environmental Protection Agency had exceeded its authority in refusing to allot the full amounts authorized by Congress in the Federal Water Control Act Amendments of 1972. The Court's ruling was based entirely on its reading of the language of the 1972 act. Though it did not reach the constitutional issue, the decision is nevertheless bound to have an impact on executive-legislative relations.

While the impoundment litigation was proceeding through the courts, Congress was considering a number of anti-impoundment bills. In 1974 it passed the Impoundment Control Act, a compromise version, as part of the congressional budget reform enacted that year. This act established a procedure for detailed congressional review and control of impoundments. It also amended the Antideficiency Act to limit the purposes for which funds may be placed in reserve. Under the revised law, funds may be reserved only for contingencies or when they no longer are needed because of changed requirements or efficiency of operations.

The 1974 law divides impoundments into two categories—rescissions and deferrals—and applies different procedures to each. Rescissions may be proposed when the president does not anticipate any future need for the funds or when the withheld funds would lapse if not obligated before the end of the fiscal year. Deferrals are to be proposed when the president anticipates future but not current use of the funds. He may not propose the deferral of one-year money or of funds that would expire by the end of the fiscal year. Nor may he propose a deferral beyond the current fiscal year.

For both rescissions and deferrals, the president must transmit a special message to Congress, with a copy to the comptroller general, providing certain required information concerning his action. In the case of rescissions, the funds must be released unless Congress positively approves the action (by means of a rescission bill) within forty-five days of continuous sessions after the president's notification. In the case of deferrals, the withholding may continue unless it is disapproved by either the House or the Senate—the legislative veto technique. If either body adopts a disapproval resolution, the president must release the funds.

The new law gives the comptroller general responsibility for overseeing implementation of the impoundment controls. The comptroller general must inform Congress if the president has failed to report an impoundment or if an action has been improperly classified (for example, if a rescission has been listed as a deferral). In addition, the comptroller general is to review the facts, legal authority, and probable effect of each proposed rescission or deferral and submit his findings to Congress. Finally, the comptroller general is authorized to bring suit to enforce the new impoundment procedures.

In spite of this detailed routine for handling impoundment issues, it is unlikely that the new law will spell an end to conflict in this area. During the first months of experience under the law, several disputes erupted between Congress and the president and within the legislative branch. One issue was whether the new law applies to impoundments executed prior to July 12, 1974, the date of enactment. The administration's claim that only postenactment actions are covered is likely to be challenged in the courts. A second dispute was over the status of certain impoundments. The president reported the withholding of Section 235 housing funds as a deferral, but the comptroller general ruled that it should have been classified as a rescission. When the president persisted, the comptroller general in April 1975 sued before the federal district court for the District of Columbia to compel a reclassification. A third dispute related to jurisdiction over impoundment measures. A struggle between the Senate Appropriations and Budget committees was resolved only by establishing a complicated procedure giving each committee part of the action.

These procedural questions relate directly to issues of policy and the extent to which Congress will use the new controls to override presidential impoundments. The Impoundment Control Act has the capability to expand or curtail presidential power, depending on congressional disposition of rescission and deferred proposals. If Congress were to accede to presidential impoundment requests, the new law would have the effect of enlarging presidential control over spending. But if Congress were to reject most proposals, the net effect would be a contraction of the president's ability to impound funds.

The early returns strongly indicate a hard line by Congress, particularly insofar as rescissions are concerned. Between September 1974 and February 1975, President Ford proposed about eighty rescissions, totaling almost $2.5 billion. These were consolidated into three bills that rescinded less than 15 percent of the amounts the president had proposed. Most of the approved rescissions involved routine savings rather than policy issues. As of June 1975, Congress had rejected most presidential attempts to use impoundments as a means of cutting back domestic programs that Congress had established.

With regard to deferrals, the pattern is less clear because there is no time limit for congressional action. The 150 deferrals reported through April 1975 under the new law involve $25 billion in federal funds, but most of these are associated with water pollution programs ($9 billion) and highway assistance ($11 billion). The president unilaterally has released substantial sums for these two programs, and additional amounts are likely to be forthcoming because of court order and congressional action. During the first months of the Ninety-fourth Congress, resolutions disapproving certain policy deferrals advanced in the House and the Senate. As in the case of rescissions, Congress seemed hesitant to grant the president authority to impound for policy reasons.

If the impoundment route is restricted to routine business, a president who wants to confront Congress on budget policy will have to rely on his veto power. During his first months in office, President Ford made extensive use of vetoes, particularly on matters relating to federal expenditures. Rather than ending, the battle of the budget might only shift to a different stage.

The Congressional Budget Process

Future battles will be waged under a new set of ground rules adopted by Congress in the Congressional Budget Act of 1974.[3] This act establishes procedures designed to ensure congressional determination of national budget policies and priorities. The act does not eliminate any existing procedures for the authorization of programs and the appropriation of funds—a new congressional budget process is added to these—but it is likely to have a significant impact on the way Congress makes program and financial decisions. Nor does the legislation directly alter the executive budget process (except with regard to certain submissions and the budget timetable), but it is likely to generate major changes in legislative-executive fiscal relations.

[3] P.L. 93-344. Titles I-IX of the act are designated the Congressional Budget Act; Title X is the Impoundment Control Act.

The new law was born in conflict: first between the president and Congress, then between different interests within Congress. It all began on July 26, 1972, when President Nixon demanded that Congress impose a $250 billion limitation on outlays for the 1973 fiscal year which had just begun.[4] The president wanted unrestrained discretion to hold spending within that limit, and administration spokesmen refused to specify in advance which programs would be cut. The president castigated the "hoary and traditional procedure of the Congress, which now permits action on the various spending programs as if they were unrelated and independent actions." From the start, spending control was framed as a president versus Congress campaign issue.

Although the $250 billion ceiling was not very controversial—budget battles usually relate to the details rather than the aggregates—there was considerable disagreement over how it should be implemented. The House Ways and Means Committee reported a provision (as a rider to debt limit legislation) authorizing the president "notwithstanding the provisions of any other law" to reserve such amounts as may be necessary to maintain the $250 billion limit. But on the House floor, Chairman George Mahon of the Appropriations Committee deplored presidential discretion as a dangerous transfer "of legislative authority to the executive branch." He offered an amendment to direct the president to propose specific cuts which would take effect only if approved by Congress. Mahon's substitute was defeated by a vote of 167-216, and the House then passed the bill by a vote of 221-163.

The bill next moved to the Senate, where it again emerged from committee with full authority for the president to reduce spending in accord with his preferences. However, the Senate adopted a floor amendment requiring proportional reductions in programs and barring cuts of more than 10 percent in any activity or item. In conference, the requirement that program cuts be proportional was deleted, and the president was given authority to reduce indidivual programs by as much as 20 percent. The House approved the conference report on October 17, 1972, the day before adjournment for the elections, but on the same day the Senate rejected it by a vote of 39-27. After a second conference, with no time for deliberation, this phase of the battle of the budget was resolved by incorporating contradictory elements into the same law. One provision established a $250 billion ceiling for fiscal 1973; the next provided that one day after the bill became law, the spending limitation would cease to have effect and any action taken pursuant to the limitation would be null and void.

With Congress and the president deadlocked, the next phase in the perennial budget battle involved dissension within Congress. As part

[4] *Weekly Compilation of Presidential Documents* 8 (1972), p. 1176.

of the legislation containing the self-destructing limitation, Congress established the Joint Study Committee on Budget Control consisting of thirty-two members. Twenty-eight of the positions were allocated to House and Senate members of the appropriations and tax committees. The task of the joint committee was to devise new spending control procedures for Congress, and in April 1973 it issued a report recommending the creation of a congressional budget process. Anchoring this process would be new House and Senate budget committees, two-thirds of whose members plus the chairman would come from the Appropriations, House Ways and Means, and Senate Finance committees. This recommendation provoked protest in liberal quarters, such as the Democratic Study Group, which feared a conservative takeover of the congressional budget process. Controversy also raged over numerous features of the new process, such as the status of the congressional budget, floor procedures, and tax policy.

During fifteen months of consideration by two Senate committees, a House committee, and a conference committee, the budget reform legislation was revamped in numerous important details. Many of the changes were designed to open up the new process to broad congressional participation and to prevent any group within Congress from gaining one-sided advantage.

Budget committees have been established in the House and the Senate and are given jurisdiction over the congressional budget process. The committees are to report at least two budget resolutions each year—one in the spring prior to congressional action on tax and spending legislation, the other in the fall after action on budget-related measures has been completed.

The House Budget Committee has twenty-five members, selected according to a statutory formula: five each from the House Appropriations and Ways and Means committees, thirteen from other standing committees, and one each from the majority and minority leaderships. Appointments to the committee are to be made without regard to seniority, and no member may serve on the committee for more than four years during any ten-year period. Brock Adams of Washington became the House Budget Committee chairman, at the start of the Ninety-fourth Congress. The Senate Budget Committee has sixteen members, selected by regular party process, and the Senate rule limiting senators to no more than two major committees will apply to the Budget Committee when the Ninety-fifth Congress convenes in 1977. This means a much wider sharing of committee power in the Senate than would have been possible if a quota system had been adopted for Budget Committee assignments. Edmund Muskie of Maine was named the first chairman.

The new law established the Congressional Budget Office (CBO) as an informational and analytic arm of Congress. CBO is empowered to secure budget data from executive agencies and is expected to provide Congress with alternatives to the president's budget. The act opens CBO's services to all committees and members of Congress, in contrast to the Joint Study Committee's proposal to make the staff's assistance available only to the budget committees. But the act arrays CBO's duties according to four orders of priority, ranging from the budget committees to the membership at large. Yet the overall effect will be to enhance the budget competence of congressmen who do not serve on budget-related committees and to make them more independent not only of the executive branch but also of the tax and appropriating committees. By joint appointment of the speaker and president pro tempore, on recommendation of the two new chairmen, Alice M. Rivlin was named the first CBO director. She had been an HEW assistant secretary and a Brookings Institution staff member and was the author of *Systematic Thinking for Social Action*.

The budget committees are to report the first budget resolution to their respective Houses by April 15 of each year, and a full month is allowed for floor action and any necessary conference prior to the May 15 adoption date. A significant innovation is that preparation of the first budget resolution is to be guided by reports from each standing committee of the House and the Senate concerning budget matters within its jurisdiction. This novel arrangement formally recognizes that budget legislation affects all congressional committees and should not be confined to the few that have specific tax or appropriations jurisdiction.

The first resolution is to set the appropriate levels of total new budget authority and outlays, federal revenues, public debt, and budget surplus or deficit. Total new budget authority and outlays are to be allocated among the major budget functions (such as national defense, veterans' benefits, and income security), with further subdivisions for each function to be included in Budget Committee reports or, optionally, in the resolution itself. Congress is thus given an opportunity explicitly to set budget priorities in a context that forces it to assess the relative value of defense versus health, health versus revenue sharing, and so on. The process thus has enormous potential for inducing more budget conflict, for Congress no longer will have the convenience of avoiding priority fights.

The first budget resolution will function as a guideline for Congress when it takes up individual revenue, spending, and debt bills. Congress will be permitted to consider and adopt legislation not in accord with its own budget resolution, but by means of a scorekeeping procedure, it will be constantly informed of the effects of its actions on the congressional budget. Because this and subsequent budget determinations will be in the form of concurrent resolutions, they will not have the force of law, nor will they directly limit actual federal expenditures. Their sole effect will be to guide or restrain Congress in its actions on budget-related legislation.

Following adoption of the initial budget resolution, appropriation bills will proceed through Congress in much the same manner as before. The bills will be taken up individually, but it is contemplated that floor action will be completed shortly after Labor Day, or earlier if possible. The fiscal calendar is to be shifted to an October 1-September 30 cycle, thereby giving Congress three additional months within which to complete the myriad steps of its budget process.

A second budget resolution is to be adopted by September 15. It may retain or revise the levels set in the first resolution. The second resolution can set into motion a reconciliation process in which the amounts in the various tax and spending bills are brought into alignment with the congressional budget. By means of its second resolution, Congress can direct the appropriations committees to report legislation adjusting appropriations or the House Ways and Means and Senate Finance committees to report changes in the tax laws. Changes recommended by various committees pursuant to the second budget resolution are to be reported in a reconciliation bill (or resolution, in some cases) whose enactment is scheduled by September 25, only a few days before the new fiscal year is to commence.

It is at the reconciliation stage that the budget process will be most vulnerable to deep conflicts. The potential divisions within Congress are numerous: between those who seek reconciliation by adjusting tax rates and those who prefer to change spending legislation, between those who prefer one set of spending priorities and those who favor another, and between those who support one level of overall spending and those who want more spending for particular programs. All budgetary conflicts will converge at the reconciliation stage, and this new and untested procedure might not be able to bear the burdens cast upon it. Of course, reconciliation can become nothing more than the ratification of all congressional decisions made in the course of the year. Congress will have the option of mending its fences by limiting the potency of its new budget process.

With enactment of the reconciliation bill, the congressional budget process will be completed. At this point, Congress may not consider any revenue or spending legislation that would breach any of the levels specified in the second resolution. It will be out of order to vote on a supplemental appropriation if it would cause spending to rise above the levels of the second resolution or on a bill to reduce revenues below the budget totals. However, Congress may adopt a new budget resolution adjusting any of the amounts any time during the fiscal year.

An important purpose of the 1974 act is to bring backdoor spending under tighter appropriations control. New contract or borrowing authority is to be available only to the extent provided in appropriations. These forms of legislation will become standard authorizations funded through appropriation measures. Legislation providing new entitlements cannot be considered until the first budget resolution has been adopted and cannot take effect until the next fiscal year starts, thus subjecting them to the discipline of the congressional budget process. If an entitlement exceeds the allocations in the latest budget resolution, it will be referred to the Appropriations Committee (under a fifteen-day time limit) for review and possible amendment. The new procedures do not apply to existing backdoor spending nor to social security programs, most trust funds, and certain other types of expenditures.

The Fight Goes On

The budget scene will not be quieted by the new enactment. As a bundle of compromises, the Congressional Budget Act papered over many of the divisions within Congress over budget policy and budget power. The backdoor spending provisions were one such compromise, balancing the claims of the appropriations committees against the spending interests of the authorizing committees. What emerged was a mixed package, new jurisdiction for appropriations, but with major exceptions and all existing backdoors protected. The appropriations committees also wrestled with the authorizing committees regarding the timetable of the new congressional process. The 1974 law establishes a May 15 deadline for the reporting of authorizing legislation. The authorizing committees preferred no deadline at all; the appropriations committees wanted it applied to the enactment stage.

The format of the budget resolution was a compromise between those who wanted early ceilings on spending and those who preferred that the resolution serve only as a target. By providing for spending allocations by major function, the new law resolved the conflict between those who insisted that the resolution deal only with budget aggregates and those who wanted decisions made by appropriation categories.

The new process will enlarge the potential for conflict within Congress, because it both expands the range of participation and moves Congress in the direction of forced choices. The socialization of conflict will be facilitated by the placement of new budget committees in the process, the new role of authorizing committees in staking budget claims, and the spreading of budget competence to all committees and members. The congressional budget process will be much more open than the tax and appropriations procedures have been.

Making explicit matters that had been veiled will also fuel the budget wars. Priorities will have to be decided; the parts of the budget will have to be consistent with the whole; Congress will have to go on record as regards the budget surplus or deficit; tax expenditures will be publicly displayed; the costs of legislation and its impact on the congressional budget will be identified.

But Congress will not allow itself to be deadlocked by the new process. Procedural roadblocks will be brushed aside if they threaten legislative paralysis or thwart a determined majority. Congress will sooner change its budget process than permit itself to be stalled by the rigors of budgeting. The congressional budget process will prosper only if it proves workable within the legislative arena. The verdict is yet to come, but it will be favorable if Congress succeeds in managing budget conflict while giving full expression to the many interests operative in the legislative process.

White House Channels to the Hill

RALPH K. HUITT

Although it does not appear in the official text released by the White House, a line in President Ford's 1975 State of the Union message drew laughter and applause—he said he "wanted a marriage, not a honeymoon" with Congress. The analogy is apt and useful if not pushed too far. Congress and the president *are* a constitutional marriage of presumed equals.

What goes into a successful marriage? Much has been written on that question, but two elements seem to be indispensable: that both parties honestly want it to succeed and (what is not so obvious) that workable arrangements be established which make the crucial day-to-day lives flow together easily without letting every chore or responsibility become a possible confrontation. The latter is especially true if both partners are working, as Congress and the president are. Who cooks dinner after both have worked all day? Who shops, cleans the house, and balances the check book? Many unions between caring couples break down for want of arrangements to answer these questions.

This essay is an analysis of what arrangements between the president and Congress are most likely to make that partnership in government productive and reinforcing to both sides. The evidence and argument draw somewhat on the resources of the library, but more than that on the experience of the author in a particular position in the network of executive-congressional relations, namely, as assistant secretary for legislation in the Department of Health, Education and Welfare in the Johnson administration, from mid-1965 until January 20, 1969.

A participant-observer has certain advantages and suffers from some disabilities. He sees much close at hand; he is privy to secrets and confidences; his view is intense and unremitting. But the range of his view is limited; he is like the front-line officer who knows with poignant im-

Research assistance for this essay was provided by the American Political Science Association's "Study of Congress," which was financed by the Carnegie Corporation of New York. The author is, of course, solely responsible for its contents.

mediacy what occurs in his terrain but is denied a comprehension of the whole battle. President Johnson titled his account of his regime *The Vantage Point*, to say that presidents see what other people do not. He was quite right, but other people may see what presidents do not. So this is written from a vantage point. Much of it can be generalized to the whole flow of business between the president and Congress, through the intermediaries furnished by the executive departments and agencies; some of it cannot. It will rely heavily on the Johnson administration and HEW for obvious reasons, but also because Johnson was highly successful in dealing with Congress and because HEW promoted and administered a large part of the domestic legislation of the Great Society.

The principal components of the national legislative network can be briefly sketched. There is the president, hailed in the textbooks as chief legislator (and conventionally "chief" of everything else). In normal times he prepares and presents to Congress a legislative program, first in the State of the Union message and later in messages on specific subjects with draft bills to carry out his wishes. Congress usually acknowledges this leadership role by delaying action on specific measures until it receives the presidential requests, and even though the committees may give him little that he wants, they customarily take his bills as their points of departure. This may even be true when opposing parties control executive and legislature, though not necessarily so. The president also offers a budget—the heart of the matter—which allocates national resources according to his values. He is assisted in both legislative and budgetary recommendations by the Office of Management and Budget (called the Bureau of the Budget until the Nixon administration), which is the principal advisory and administrative arm of the president. He also relies heavily upon his White House staff, which has become increasingly important. The staff may be organized with a specific and known division of labor or it may be an undifferentiated amalgam. The jobs may be substantive—i.e., subject matter specialists on health, armed services, etc.—or functional, or both. The way in which the staff is organized and the extent to which its members' duties are publicly known are matters of great importance to those who have business with the upper reaches of the federal government and also to those who are *in* the federal government.

The middlemen are in the departments and agencies. Those involved may include any person in the political overlay who putatively controls the agency (for convenience, the word "agency" will be used for all administrative organizations) and also the principal civil servants. Those of most concern here are the legislative officers (whose titles may be "assistant secretary," "legislative liaison officers," etc.) who, with their staffs, attempt to push the president's legislation through Congress.

The legislative powers of Congress are exercised through a kind of feudal system, in which the powers of each house are parcelled out among barons called "committee chairmen," who share them by further parcelling them out among subcommittee chairmen. The relationships between the two layers of vassals are sensitive and important as to the questions of how much participation is allowed or forced by the ordinary members of the committees and subcommittees. The precise relationships, committee by committee, are of utmost concern to the legislative officers of the agencies, to whom a mistake in comprehension may be disastrous. So is an accurate assessment of the caliber of legislative staff and their respective relationships with their principals. They can be enormously important, but it is not enough to know titles; the staff man's knowledge of his subject and precise influence on his boss are what matter. The provision of professional staff in the late 1940s was revolutionary in its enhancement of the effectiveness of Congress. For the lobbyist of Congress, inside and outside the government, it both simplified and complicated his working life.

The Presidency

Lyndon Johnson brought to his "marriage" with Congress the best of attitudes. He had served in both houses; more than that, he was at home in them. He knew intimately their procedures and values, and he shared them. With his friends and mentors, Sam Rayburn and Richard Russell, he knew what made them work, how to move indirectly to establish situations in which what he wanted to happen did happen. In the thirty years after Roosevelt, all presidents except Eisenhower had served as members of Congress, but only Johnson had been a prime mover in legislative affairs. Ford had been a leader, but he was in the minority party.

Examples of Johnson's respect for Congress are many. He frequently told his legislative representatives, both White House and agency, not to forget that "not all the patriotism and wisdom reside in the Executive branch. They [Congress] will change our bills and often as not, they will improve them." Good as his word, he often took much-altered bills, made them law in public signing ceremonies and hailed them as "victories." And so they were—a good act on an important matter was a victory for him, Congress, and the nation.

In 1967, the president sent to Congress an air-pollution control bill. It had been developed in HEW, which would administer it, and it was considered a good bill. The relevant subcommittee in the Senate was chaired by Edmund Muskie, who knew much about the subject, as did his staff. The subcommittee wrote a good bill which, in many important respects, differed from the administration bill. The subcommittee supported its bill unanimously. Johnson heeded HEW advice that he accept the Muskie bill before it even went to the full committee. It passed the full committee and Senate unanimously. With administration support, it passed easily in the House. Vice President Humphrey, also a true Congress man, enthusiastically endorsed the action.

On another occasion, Johnson said to the agency legislative officers, "We are always asking Congress to help us. Let's offer to help them." Whereupon he directed each person to submit names of five members of Congress he knew best. The White House staff then assigned names, five to each agency legislative officer who was to ask each, "What can I do for you?" The congressional requests proved in many cases to be no more feasible than the requests made of *them*, but each got an honest try.

Johnson's staff had the necessary components of a White House competency to deal with Congress. There were subject-matter people. There was, for health and education, Douglass Cater, a highly intelligent and sensitive man who learned what was on the books, merits and demerits of proposals, and the nuances of relationships among individuals and groups interested in his policy area. Most important, he was accessible, not only to Congress and agency people, but also to interest groups, whose legitimacy he recognized. He was the crucial "way into the White House" without which all interested parties, official and private, are baffled and sometimes outraged. Nixon's decision, at the outset of his administration, to have no specialists effectively shut off access to the White House for hundreds of interest groups—as he probably intended. Ford's administration in its first year, by contrast, was an exceedingly open administration. He made himself available to many groups, and his staff was hospitable and cooperative. But the essential ingredient, staff persons designated to become expert in policy areas and to be accessible to outside interest experts, had not (as of early 1975) been supplied.

The other component was a legislative staff, divided in its work between the two houses of Congress. It was headed during the earlier part of Johnson's administration by Henry Hall Wilson, a cool, unperturbable, and knowledgeable performer, one of whose strengths was his ability to give an agency legislative officer specific tactical advice applicable to the latter's unique situation. When Wilson resigned he was replaced by Harold Barefoot Sanders, a former assistant attorney general, who supported the agency legislative officers in all their efforts and kept in touch by spending many hours on the Hill himself. Mike Manatos, who handled the Senate, had an especially close relationship with the Democratic majority leader. The other members of the staff shared the expertise and diligence of their leaders. From time to time the fabled wizard, Lawrence O'Brien, was called in, but, being a modest man who knew he had lost day-to-day touch, he usually supported the resident legislative directors rather than taking charge.

The legislative staff performed some invaluable services. First, they gave overall direction to the massive Johnson program usually totaling approximately a hundred bills a year. This they did by requiring each weekend a detailed bill-by-bill status report from each legislative officer for the legislation assigned to him. This was followed by a meeting of all legislative officers with the White House staff, at first on late Friday afternoon—a grim hour which, moreover, came before the reports had been assimilated and analyzed. The time was changed to eight-thirty on Monday morning, by which time, through the simple expedient of working all weekend, the staff could have an agenda, receive oral reports, and lead discussions on the most urgent items.

Ranking executive officers were frequently there, sometimes to give briefings on a national problem in their charge. Vice President Hubert Humphrey was a near-regular attendant. About every six weeks the president himself dropped in. His special brand of humor often convulsed the group. He told the legislative officers how to do their jobs, how to be a congressman, and how to be president of the United States. Of course, the concern of high officers and the president with their work raised the morale of the legislative officers to a very high level. The White House staff recognized this and were liberal in allowing a legislative officer occasionally to bring a member of his own staff to make a special report. When this person found himself reporting to the president, his reaction was understandable and predictable.

A second service of the White House staff was to give the agency legislative officers, as well as legislators themselves, access to the president. Bryce Harlow, counsellor to Presidents Eisenhower and Nixon, who handled congressional relations for both of them, has stressed that one essential of "this highly specialized activity is access—continuing, instant access to the power structure of the Executive Branch, particularly of course to the President, Vice President and Cabinet."[1] He tells how he woke President Eisenhower one night to get a presidential decision for Speaker Rayburn and was able to get an answer within twenty minutes. Few will question his comment that "there are never many people who can with impunity barge in on the President of the United States in the middle of the night and roust him out of bed." Certainly the notion of an agency legislative officer doing that to Lyndon Johnson is enough to give one the shakes retrospectively.

Nevertheless, as Harlow says, access to the president added cubits to the height of his agents. But no legislative officer needed the liberty to reach President Johnson directly. The White House congressional staff and Cater, the substantive man, provided access for them. If a congressman raised questions or wanted something said to the president, it could be done through channels. For example, one day a legislative officer ran into two congressmen at lunch. Their civil rights record was impeccable,

[1] *Center House Bulletin* 4 (Winter 1974), p. 7.

but they said their blue-collar constituents needed to hear the president say he wanted to help "all the American people." Two weeks later there was a paragraph on that theme in the State of the Union message. Needless to say, that gave the legislative officer that priceless asset, credibility.

But what if a president does not want a marriage with Congress? The Constitution does not say that he must. Nixon did not seem titillated by the prospect. In fact, he seemed to balk Congress by turning the relationship upside down. Historically, the principal checks Congress has had on the president come from maintaining control of the negatives—that is, the president asks for what he wants, and congressional power comes from the liberty to decide how much of it to let him have or what to give him in its place. But Nixon did not seem to want anything from Congress. To be sure, he initiated domestic programs and proclaimed priorities, but he seemed to lose interest in them quickly. In fact, Congress found itself upbraiding him for not really trying to get what he said he wanted, which many members wanted more than he did.

Trying to oppose Nixon on domestic programs was, as some congressmen put it, like "pushing on a string." There was no resistance. Instead, Nixon tried to run things without Congress. Impounding funds, deferring the spending of them, shifting money from one purpose to another—these gave him control of what really mattered, the allocation of government resources. He had effectively got control of the negatives, a role reversal that seemed for a time to bemuse Congress. In time, all this was rather well closed down by the courts and Congress, and the question of what he would do in place of this strategy was relegated to speculation by Watergate.

In the first year of his administration, Ford seemed like a suitor who could not make up his mind. His preoccupation was with the three great problems of the day—inflation-recession, energy-environment, and the world food shortage—but his position vis-à-vis Congress seemed to swing between extremes. At one moment he would call for bipartisan cooperation with Congress; at the next, he seemed to be setting Congress up as his opponent in 1976. Certainly he did not assume the traditional leadership role of pressing a domestic program on all fronts, using his chief administrators and their minions to urge his will on the Hill. In the meantime, Congress was having its own problems with an uneconomical majority of Democrats, with the freshman members employing the unlikely device of the caucus to make uncertain the customary arrangements for leadership within the House of Representatives itself. So, much more than nostalgia would be involved in a wish that the relationship could be returned to the traditional posture, with presidential initiative supported by his administration and with a responsible congressional leadership responding in the usual way.

The Middlemen

A presidential program, with its variegated subject matter and its ties to the workings of a multiplicity of agency programs, cannot be carried to Congress by the White House staff. That staff may direct, coordinate, solve problems, and give support, but like soldier ants pushing leaves, the agency legislative officers try to move their programs. Almost every agency will have a legislative officer to do that or to lead a staff in doing it. These officials vary in rank within their agencies and in the responsibilities assigned to them. Ideally, the legislative officer should be a presidential appointee, carrying a title comparable to assistant secretary. There are many reasons for this. First, to understate the case, Washington is a status-conscious city. No agency is helped when its officer is upstaged or ignored. Second, a person of such a rank is more likely to have the ear of his chief (the secretary of a department or the administrator or director of an agency) whose principal legislative adviser he is supposed to be. Third, when the principal officers in an agency are called in for counsel on policy, a person who is not of the appropriate rank may be overlooked. In Johnson's HEW, for instance, the chief frequently called his assistant secretaries together for consultation. Everyone agreed that the information officer (i.e., the public affairs officer) should be present; he had professional experience and insights that were needed. But often he was not called, at the cost of subsequent embarrassment. In 1975 the public affairs officer was an assistant secretary, as he should be.

The styles of legislative officers and the way they employ the talents of their staffs differ widely, of course. The position of assistant secretary for legislation at HEW provides a good example of contrasting styles.

The incumbent of this office throughout the Kennedy years and until mid-1965 in the Johnson administration was Wilbur Cohen, a rare combination of the experienced and wily civil servant who has a creative grasp of social legislation and the political instincts and skills of a ward leader. He had been a central participant in the development and passage of the original New Deal social security and welfare legislation. His interest remained so strong that even as under secretary of HEW, the second-ranking job in the department, he took part one year in more than sixty-five executive sessions of the Ways and Means Committee, each lasting several hours, while it "marked-up" (considered and amended, line by line) the social security bill. At the same time he carried the heavy burden of his regular job.

As a legislative operative, Cohen was almost wholly personal in his approach. He had deliberately and assiduously courted and cultivated Wilbur Mills and Lister Hill, chairmen respectively of House Ways and

Means and Senate Labor and Public Welfare committees (Hill was also chairman of the Senate appropriations subcommittee that funded health and education) until the trust and understanding between him and the chairmen were intimate and complete. He used his staff members as extensions of himself to carry out an assigned task. As one of them said later, to "get into the action, I would sit in Wilbur's outer office until he needed something. Then I was the handiest man and got the job." Cohen's method was obviously successful, but it took a Cohen to practice it. To find an identical replacement for him would have required a person with the persuasive skills of a confidence man, the skin of the rhinoceros, the stamina of a mountain goat, an almost total recall of all legislation he had passed, and total confidence that he knew what should be done next.

His replacement did not fit this description, nor did he want to try. He was a professor—with experience on the Hill, it is true, but indubitably a professor. He inherited a staff but, like most professors, he had never managed to have a staff of more than, rather late, a half-time assistant. So for several weeks he tried to do everything, while the staff languished and morale sagged. Then he realized that what the staff did would magnify his own performance. So some changes were made, and the staff pulled together. Each staff member was given responsibility for a primary subject area (e.g., education) and a secondary (e.g., welfare) so there would always be a specialist and a backup person in each subject. They were free to operate and report. Each followed his legislation across the rotunda, working with both houses. Each assumed a self-imposed responsibility. They worked when they needed to, regardless of hours, and tried to balance the time later. They did what was needed: one bill was passed, for example, because a staff person followed a congressman to the airport and secured a proxy so that a conference committee could complete its work. The success of this staff has given the author a strong bias toward this way of proceeding and the conviction that the staff is the boss's principal constituency. As it goes, so goes he.

The style is not the crucial ingredient; there are many roads to Damascus. More important are functions performed by legislative officers for their chiefs in connecting the agency to Congress. A logical one is to serve as his political adviser. An experienced chief may need little advice; a newcomer may even need to be shielded from the earthier aspects of what must be done in his name. Congressional politics often seem rough because, generally speaking, its practitioners are professionals who, like lawyers serving the court, do what is necessary to keep the system operational. They speak the same language and seldom nurse antagonisms. Their politics can seem shockingly blunt to those accustomed to the more circuitous manipulations in business, on campus, or in church.

The legislative officer should participate in the making of legislative policy. Until about 1967 he was the central figure in this process. In HEW, for instance, he issued a call to the agency heads in the department for new legislative proposals at about the same time the budget officer asked for budget requests—in the middle or late summer. In response came huge packages, each including a number of ,"dogs" that had been around for years, of the sort the commissioner preferred to let the legislative officer kill rather than do it himself. Once these items were eliminated, there could be serious discussions between the legislative and agency staffs. Ultimately a package for each agency, cleared through a "legislative committee" of the other assistant secretaries, chaired by the under secretary, was taken to the secretary for formal hearings. He refined, subtracted, and added, then *his* total package was sent to the White House in October or November. Then there ensued a period of negotiations by the department officers with the White House staff and BOB (now OMB) officials. Many changes would be made and new packages prepared, up until the time the president sent his legislative messages to the Hill, one at a time, accompanied by bills.

One serious weakness in this system was its timing. The preparation period for the next year's program came just as the legislative officer was also burdened with the heaviest responsibilities for passing the current year's legislation. Congress settles down after Labor Day, often working sixteen hours daily and even on weekends. It was not possible for the legislative officer to do both jobs properly. Moreover, it was questionable whether he and his staff were the best people in the department to control formulation of policy. President Johnson's order to every executive agency to establish the Planning-Programming-Budgeting System (PPBS) brought into each of them some bright, highly trained people whose job was to think about policy all the time. These groups logically and inevitably began to direct legislative planning and, long after the demise of PPBS, most agencies still have an office of planning and evaluation, whatever it is called. Nevertheless, it is a mistake not to include the legislative officer in the process of legislative planning. First, he is needed to suggest what the Congress will and will not take, a matter about which the planner often knows little and sometimes cares less. Second, the legislative officer's hand is greatly strengthened on the Hill if he can explain how the planning decision came about.

A variation occurred during the administration of President Johnson in his full term. Joseph Califano, a special assistant to the president, was put in charge of all legislative planning. To get ideas, Califano traveled around the country, brainstorming after dinner with university professors who were specialists in the fields he was interested in. The ideas thus collected were assigned to "task forces" of competent people to develop into policy proposals, when feasible. Their responses could be used or reassigned, in whole or in part, to other task forces. What finally emerged was what pleased Califano and the president. The advantages of this method were that it was highly flexible, it centralized control in the White House and so in the president, and it tended to eliminate much of the burdensome negotiations between agencies and the presidential establishment. Its weakness was that it sowed fear and distrust almost everywhere in the agencies. It was an element in the growth of the "imperial presidency." The agency's officers tended to feel cut out. Who was on the task forces? Often this was not disclosed; the very existence of the task forces was officially denied. Agency chiefs were not mollified to know their lieutenants were often included; they wondered *whose* policy the lieutenant was promoting.

Then the bills must be passed, if possible. First, they must be explained, beginning with the chairmen. No knowledgeable operator talks to the ranks until the leader has been briefed. With the same party controlling the White House and Congress, this can be quite an event—a veritable state visit of the secretary with his principal officers for that substantive area. The lesser committee members get staff visits, as promptly as possible, with attention paid to the minority (who on occasion will save the day) and to staff on both sides of the aisle. Much legislation is put together by consensus, which must be sustained at all cost.

Ultimately, a hearing will be scheduled on a bill. (The notice is usually short. It may be given, for example, on Thursday night for a Tuesday hearing.) The hearing is a great, flexible invention of the congressional committees. There are hearings for many and disparate purposes. The legislative officer must know what kind of hearing he must prepare for, just as a rodeo performer should know about the horse he is to ride. Perhaps an explication of some of the types will be helpful.

Passing new legislation, or revising and extending old legislation is the most frequent and important kind of hearing. What is required is expertise on the question at hand. Only the clumsy or unprepared have anything to fear. This hearing kills off tourist spectators, because experts are talking to experts in their own shorthand, but it is most reassuring to someone who wonders whether Congress is competent and responsible.

When the committee finds it really needs to learn something, it can command the best faculty in the nation. An example was the long hearing of the Joint Atomic Energy Committee on radiation fallout. The printed hearings became graduate texts in universities. The only hazard to the government official is that this company may make him look uneducated.

In an interest-group conflict the committee lets the two sides fight it out—though the majority usually is on one side or the other. Each side will tiptoe before its enemies and crow like roosters before its friends. The government agency will know which side it is on and emulate its friends in the private sector.

A committee or subcommittee with a definite commitment to some cause will search the countryside for sympathetic and impressive witnesses (i.e., those no one will attack or even question closely) to parade in a pageant. The witnesses will be coached and led through their acts. Thus television and other media coverage are obtained for whatever the cause is (e.g., abolishing rent control or feeding the hungry in Mississippi). This hearing promises nothing but grief to the government witness; if he disagrees with the subcommittee, he is heartless; if he agrees, he can almost never go to the proposed extreme.

The personal advertising hearing still happens. A chairman, often of a "task force" or select committee, will call a hearing on some cosmic subject—such as world peace or transportation for the future. There is no proposal, no focus, so any question can be asked of any witness. The subject is the first clue as to the character of the hearing. The second is that the chairman wants only blue-chip witnesses—one each day. The old tactic of getting one headline, then adjourning, may be employed. There are many counters. One is to send the chief, but surround him with technicians. At the first detailed question, embroil the chairman with the technicians. The proof that this has succeeded comes when the television lights are switched off. Another tactic, which takes self-assurance, is for the chief to go absolutely alone and refuse to answer any question that is not directed at his level. The chief looks magnificent when he succeeds.

An event may upset many people. Nothing can be done about it but a safety valve may be provided by a cathartic hearing. The relief of General MacArthur in the Far East was an example. The joint committee hearing daily reduced the dramatic importance of the witness from the general himself on the first day down to foreign policy technicians. This gradually deflated the issue, and it *appeared* that something had been done. A useful variation is one that lifts the fire from a public official. A legislative officer who can arrange an investigative hearing by a friendly committee many times can save a useful public career.

There is no need for the present purposes to review the differences in the rules and procedures of the House and Senate. It should suffice to suggest the way their differences affect the legislative officer, public or private, who has to deal with them. House action on an important bill is a nightmarish experience for the legislative officer. After the comfortable access to committee members and their careful consideration of the bill, everything may easily fly to pieces on the floor. The bill may go to the Committee of the Whole (the House itself, but with a 100 member quorum and simplified procedures yet with a verbatim record), where changes may be made. The recent rule that permits the requirement of a record vote in the committee has ended an old abuse: a change made by a small number of members off the record. When the committee "rises," calling the House officially into session again, a group may find they have a temporary majority and may rewrite the bill through amendments then and there. The legislative officer sits helpless as his work goes down the drain. He sits in the gallery, forbidden even to take notes. He has little communication with the floor leaders for the bill. He can send in a card asking one of them to meet him in the corridor, but obviously this cannot be repeated often. Staff members are no help; only the committee staffs, a few members for each side, are allowed on the floor. Moreover, there will almost certainly be no interruption. The House will dispose of the bill that day, even if they must stay until early the next morning. The legislative officer can only remember ruefully George Washington's calling the House the cup, the Senate the saucer: the tea is poured from the cup into the saucer to cool it.

The Senate can indeed cool it. One of the glories of the Senate is that it seems to have an institutional intuition for recognizing issues that need to be held up and talked over. Little that matters is handled hurriedly in the Senate. If unexpected opposition appears when a bill is called up, the majority leader usually puts it aside (a bill may be the official business of the Senate for days while other bills are discussed and passed). This provides a period for talk and negotiation off the floor, where so much Senate work is done. In fact, Lyndon Johnson as majority leader put together his majority on an important bill before he ever let it be debated on the floor. The Senate, with its small membership, can carry on bargaining; it is even possible to calculate with fair success what the vote is likely to be (almost an impossibility on a close vote in the massive House membership). Even when the bill is receiving floor consideration, communication with the floor is simple; each member may take two staff aides in with him and they are readily available to their friends. The legislative officer may lose in the Senate, but he need not fear sudden death.

The party leaders in the two houses are not very important to the legislative officer until legislation reaches the floor. The party leaders then assume responsibility for passing it (assuming the president is of their party. In the House, before the bill is allowed to reach the floor, the leadership will make every effort to get a "head count" of the likely result. Administration legislative staff, both of the agency and of the White House, will work with friendly interest groups in an effort to find out through the local constituencies of members how they will vote —and, of course, persuade them to vote "right," if possible. The bill may be held up several weeks while this effort is being made. In the Senate it is easy to guess, from voting records, where the problems are. The extent to which the majority leader will attempt to corral a majority depends on the leader's perception of his job. Johnson saw it as a major part of his job; Mansfield has not.

Conclusion

There is a fearful amount of mythology on the question of what is required for successful "lobbying" of Congress. One is the myth of the "cocktail circuit"—that the "social lobby" is important. The truth is that the true movers and shakers lack energy, time, or inclination to play that game. The only likely way to get a member to a cocktail party is to hold it in the Capitol at six o'clock, so he can drop in on his way to dinner; assure him that his constituents will be there; and promise to have a professional photographer on hand.

Another myth is that "arm-twisting" makes members vote right. Only a handful of members at most live in districts where a single interest can do that. A president might succeed with it in a limited way, but he will pay a high price. Congressmen like bullying no better than other people do, and they will exact a price when they can. As one long-time member put it, "The rule here is to forgive—and remember."

The contention that money is the most potent influence is not so easy to deal with. The climate of Watergate lingers, and the problem of campaign financing cannot be shrugged off. The administration also has the power sometimes to guide projects into congressional districts in a way to help them economically and so help the members with their constituencies. But money certainly is the most dangerous tool in the trade. Members of Congress have seen great careers shattered by an indiscretion with money, and many of them are virtually paranoid about obeying the last letter of the law. A large influence for keeping lobbying clean is the fact that most of it is done by associations, such as large labor unions, business organizations, and myriads of professional groups. They have a very high stake in preserving their reputations, which have been carefully built over many years. Certainly money per se is not a factor in the relations of the president with Congress. That is just not the nature of the game.

The most effective tool is so simple it sounds naive, and so it is hard to credit. It is knowledge, expertise, and a command of the business at hand. The member wants to do his job well and succeed as a congressman. The person who can help him to do that, who knows how to solve a problem—especially if he can offer a "little language," i.e., a well drafted provision that can go into the bill—never has trouble getting access and a thoughtful hearing. Such persons are found in both the public and private sectors; most of them go to the Hill by invitation.

The final word, which may be taken as Holy Writ by practitioners, is put with absolute accuracy by Bryce Harlow, who says that in dealing with Congress, "One's word must be his bond. I know of no major profession other than politics that uses the spoken word as lawyers use signed contracts, nor is there any other profession in which the penalty for perfidy is as swift and as absolute. In this allegedly seamy business of politics, when one violates his personal word, he becomes at once—and permanently—a pariah, while in most other pursuits he merely pays a legal or professional penalty, then proceeds as before."[2]

The initiative for continuing good relations must come from the president, but both he and the Congress must want to get along. Good will, though, is not enough. The president's purposes must be advanced by dedicated, skilled persons, trained and organized for that enterprise.

[2] Ibid.

Congress, the Media, and the President

MAX M. KAMPELMAN

Americans have been coping in recent months with problems of executive power and of corruptions of that power. Both their thoughts and consciences are troubled. Constitutional analyses examining the intent of the framers in delineating the powers of the Congress and the president are gaining fresh currency. Writers who once glorified the presidency now attack its imperial qualities. But some members of Congress who only recently worked to curtail the powers of the presidency have lately begun to concern themselves as much with the potential danger of an impotent presidency as they once did about an imperial presidency.

These deliberations take place with a sharp awareness of public opinion. The Congress and the president seek not only to respond to public wishes, but also to influence that opinion. It is via the media that the institutions of government communicate with the electorate, and there has been ample evidence to conclude that it is through the media that public attitudes are highly influenced.

The conflict between the executive and legislative branches is an aspect of the historic question of power in a democratic society. What is new is that the question and the conflict have stirred public interest and attention to an intensity stimulated by the media and the all-pervasive influence of their growing power. Indeed, the relatively unrestrained power of the media may well represent an even greater challenge to this democratic society than the other questions of power it faces.

Power itself is not anathema to a democracy. But it does require a wariness on the part of those subject to it. In the Constitutional Convention, accordingly, the framers were concerned about majority despotism and the dominance of legislatures over the executive, as well as about a return to royal power in the executive. The potential abuse of majority power through legislative dominance was to be met by two different approaches. First, the representative principle was to be a harmonizing influence to provide a majority coalition. Majority by coalition and compromise of diverse and clashing interests were to make the system function and produce a sense of the national interest.

The second way to meet the threat of legislative majority tyranny was through the creation of an elected, strong president. The separation of powers was a corollary device to discourage majority tyranny. Power divided was power less likely to be used oppressively. The framers knew that. Ambition was to be made to counteract ambition.

The present constitutional debate is part of the developing transformation of American society. The will of the people has always been a metaphysical first principle for democracy. From the outset, however, the dispute as to how to read specific meaning into that concept has been intensely debated, with varying claims for dominance being made at different times by the president and by the Congress, by the state legislatures and the national government, by interest groups, and more recently by the media.

During most of the last half of the nineteenth century, except for the period of Abraham Lincoln, the presidency was much weaker than Congress. But with Franklin Roosevelt came a strong presidency and a general disposition in the public, among opinion leaders and in academic circles, to welcome it. Congress, it was argued, failed to represent all the social values of society because important and vital interests were unsatisfactorily represented in that body. The president was, therefore, looked upon as the more likely to exercise responsible governance. The president was considered sensitive to long-range, broad considerations. He was thought to encompass the totality of interests that would be affected by public policy. Furthermore, it was argued that the public had a conception of the president as a national leader, and this created an expectation that differed quite markedly from images identified with the Congress. It was also this expectation that provided the chief executive with the means for performing, since he could organize a nationwide public to support his policies. The presidency was the best pulpit in the land. The media equipped the pulpit with loudspeakers, but the news photographers, reporters, and commentators were not content to be mere amplifiers.

Criticism of the Congress became fair game. Will Rogers, on his first visit to Italy, said: "I didn't know before I got there that Rome had senators. Now I know why it declined." It was also argued that even the civil service bureaucracy was more representative than Congress in identifying the will of the people. These bureaucrats were recruited through a process that made them representative of the national best interests, from constituencies not otherwise represented.

This philosophical propresidency tendency was strengthened by the developing technology in communication. Presidents, learning from

Franklin Roosevelt's use of radio, began to use this medium increasingly as a way of reaching people. The combination of the power of the presidency with the effectiveness of television even further magnified that power of the presidency in the competition with Congress for national support.

A pattern developed under which the president learned to ask for and then did receive ready access to the press and television media whenever he insisted that his message was of national significance. No single congressman or group of congressmen could match that initiative, access, control, direction, or command over the major media facilities. It took inordinate effort, threats, pressure, and legal action for the opposition political party to gain some acceptance of its claims that much of the communications concentration by the president was of a political nature that required equal access for a response. Even when granted, however, the impact was grossly unequal since no other political figure and no legislator could come close to matching the president's appeal for attention.

This immense propresident bias was further strengthened as members of Congress, who could once try to counter presidential influence by long periods of home visits during recess periods, now found that the complexities of government kept Congress in session almost continually.

And yet the fact that Congress was a politically representative body made it vulnerable to attacks. Of the three branches of government, the legislature has been the most accessible. Unlike the president and justices of the Supreme Court, congressmen do not walk separated from their fellowmen by the Secret Service or by black robes.

It is true that Congress also has media tools available to it. Facilities are available to mass produce congressional newsletters to the constituents, mailed postage free. Few congressmen fail to take advantage of them. There are also extensive mailings of press releases to interest groups oriented to the specific subject matter. Congressional facilities also include highly professional radio and television studios in which congressmen record talks, messages, and programs that are transmitted to their states or districts. Many congressmen have their messages broadcast either on local news programs or as special reports to the people. With intelligent and active use of the mails and air waves, congressmen can sell themselves and their programs to their publics. The benefits, however, are individual and not institutional.

With the Vietnam war and the developing passionate hostility to it becoming increasingly evident across the nation, a change began to appear in the nature and tone of the constitutional debate. This hostility became even more prevalent with the election of Richard Nixon. No previous war had been so graphically, so devastatingly, so unrelentingly reported in the seemingly endless rounds of daily newscasts, every evening on the screens in every home. Antiwar members of Congress, primarily Democrats, supported by large segments of the media and by increasing numbers of social scientists, began to talk and write about the dangers to a democratic society arising out of the unprecedented powers in foreign policy assumed by the presidency. With the unraveling of the Watergate corruption, the media and campus attacks against the powers of the president began to become even stronger. Congress was prodded and challenged, both from within and without, to assume greater responsibility and assertiveness in both domestic and international arenas.

When the Congress finally reacted and responded to the Vietnam war and Watergate, it did so with an explosive impact:

• The War Powers Act enacted by Congress in 1973 drastically and effectively curtailed the power of the president to utilize the armed forces abroad, a power traditionally unchallenged as an integral part of his power as commander in chief.

• The anti-Vietnam war amendment to the 1973 supplemental appropriation bill effectively prevented the president from undertaking realistic military response to any Communist military move in South Vietnam in violation of the Paris Peace Agreement.

• The Turkish aid ban, threatening the southern tier of NATO, has been characterized by the president as counterproductive to a Cyprus settlement. In mid-1975 it remained a point of contention between the president and the Congress.

• The tariff discrimination against OPEC designed to punish the oil producers who had participated in the embargo served also to punish Venezuela, Indonesia, and Nigeria, who had not.

• An incumbent president was driven from office.

In the face of these assertions of legislative power, President Ford and Secretary of State Kissinger have been alternately cajoling and pressuring both American public opinion and the Congress to redress the balance, a balance that they consider has been lost. But as Averell Harriman once said: "No foreign policy will stick unless the American people are behind it. And unless Congress understands it, the American people aren't going to understand it."

The present confrontation between Congress and President Ford is a complex mixture of partisanship and traditional constitutional rivalry. The confrontation appears to arise primarily out of a greater sense of confidence by Congress, Republicans and Democrats alike. What Congress considers to have been previous abuses of presidential power in Vietnam and Watergate have produced a determination to reassert an earlier constitutional balance. This feeling seems to be particularly strong with newly elected members of Congress. The achievement of bipartisanship, however, is not easy. Nor is it easily defined. Congress obviously believes that it does not mean automatic legislative support for presidential policy. It is also clear that bipartisanship in foreign policy does not exclude full debate. Nor is it necessary for that bipartisanship to include all aspects of foreign policy.

The need for accommodation and balance is becoming increasingly crucial. America's first defeat in war dramatically illustrated that need, and its domestic and international impact will become increasingly felt. Adverse developments in Asia, Portugal, the Mediterranean, and the Middle East will have inevitable and disturbing political aftereffects on American public opinion. Basic national interests are at stake. A newspaper as critical of the Vietnam war and of President Ford as the *New York Times* recently warned that "a weakened Presidency does not necessarily mean a correspondingly stronger Congress."

Congress's investigation of the CIA illustrates the crisis, the challenge, and the opportunity ahead. There are some important questions: Are there, for example, too many intelligence agencies functioning and vying for power? How does one define a line between freedom and security? How is authority to be exercised over intelligence services? How are intelligence operations to be kept nonpolitical? How is the "right to know" to be preserved while preventing irresponsible dissemination of classified information? Indeed, how can a democratic government operate without secrecy?

These serious questions require careful consideration by Congress and by the executive branch. But pursuing these inquiries through headlines and sensational "scoops" has seriously damaged the American intelligence structure.

With this background of crisis and controversy, the growing power of the media in the nation and particularly in Washington has injected a new and often decisive ingredient into government and political decision making. It is one thing to note the obvious, that the media have constitutional safeguards as the primary means of communication between the American people and their government and with the world. The media have never been just an institution to report events. But in current circumstances they have become, on an unprecedented scale, a stimulator and sometimes a creator of events, as well as active participants in events. Recognition of this reality is revealed in a statement of Ben Bradlee, the pragmatic and realistic executive editor of the *Washington Post:* "The press won in Watergate." An astute observer and student of the American political system, he understood the implications of that declaration of victory and went on to say: "I believe though that power corrupts. We are in a powerful position and I hope we don't misuse it."

It has already been noted that power in itself is not anathema to a democratic society. The power of the media, however, is a serious threat because it is relatively unrestrained. Felix Frankfurter once wrote:

"Freedom of the press . . . is not an end in itself but a means to the end of a free society. . . . A free press is vital to a democratic society because its freedom gives it power. Power in a democracy implies responsibility in its exercise. No institution in a democracy can have absolute power. Nor can the limits of power which enforce responsibility be finally determined by the limited power itself." The American press is perhaps the most powerful institution in the country next to the presidency, but restraints on its power are inadequate and becoming more so.

Walter Lippmann in 1920 gave his conception of that power when he wrote: "The news of the day as it reaches the newspaper office is an incredible medley of fact, propaganda, rumor, suspicion, clues, hopes and fears. . . . The power to determine each day what shall seem important and what shall be neglected is power unlike any that has been exercised since the Pope lost his hold on the secular mind."

More recently, Douglass Cater stated it this way: "Communications media have a vast power to shape government—both its policies and its leaders. This is not an editorial page power. It is the power to select—out of the tens of thousands of words spoken in Washington each day and the tens of dozens of events—which words and events are projected for mankind to see. Equally powerful is the media's capacity to ignore; those words and events that fail to get projected might as well not have occurred." That awesome power is even greater today. Competition is no longer a restraining force in the press as increasing numbers of cities become noncompetitive. There were in 1975 fewer than forty-five cities with two or more competing dailies and about 1,500 cities with a noncompetitive daily press. And each year more and more of these noncompetitive dailies are purchased by the big corporate chains.

Libel laws once restrained the press, but recent Supreme Court decisions have reduced their impact. In *The New York Times* v. *Sullivan*, decided in 1964, the Court held that public officials could sue and collect for libel only if the libel was uttered "with reckless disregard of whether it was false or not." This double standard against public officials and in favor of newspapers was further broadened to include "public figures" and then to private individuals who might be involved "in an event of public or general concern." Only in recent months did the Court begin to apply the brakes with respect to private individuals, when it held in a split decision, in *Elmer Gertz* v. *Robert Welch, Inc.*, that a private individual who has not accepted public office or assumed an "influential role in society" could sue for libel to protect his good name.

Ben Bagdikian, the newspaperman critic of newspapers, pointed out a further concomitant of media power when he noted that the press is protected not only by the Constitution, but very often by a government hesitancy to invoke the restraints of other laws permitted by the Constitution. Thus "the press is traditionally permitted to go farther and is reprimanded more gently than other enterprises." Nobody likes to make enemies with the town criers.

The media, in short, constitute a powerful, ever-growing institution, with huge financial resources to supplement the power they wield through control over the dissemination of news, but with fewer and fewer restraints on that power.

Relatively unbridled power is a threat to a democracy no matter how well intentioned its custodian. When good intentions are coupled with a sense of professionalism the likelihood of self-restraint can be reasonably hoped for. Regrettably, many of the ingredients of professionalism are lacking in journalism. Here, Irving Kristol's characterization of "the underdeveloped profession" comes to mind.

Professions provide procedures for qualifying and disqualifying their practitioners. Lawyers, doctors, and all other professionals must reach a level of training and learning before they are admitted. There are no formal standards for admission to journalism. There is no universally accepted code of professional ethics to guide and judge the behavior of newsmen or their editors. There is no procedure, external or internal, for suspending or otherwise condemning those who do not live up to a pattern of responsible conduct. Even stockbrokers who sell securities must first pass an examination to qualify and can be barred from selling their wares to the public in cases of fraud or failure to disclose pertinent data. But the newsman and his editor can, with impunity, sell wares that pollute the wells of information.

Recognizing this problem and the need for self-restraint, the Twentieth Century Fund, with the advice of some leading figures in American journalism, endorsed the creation of a newspaper council to receive and air complaints against the press by aggrieved persons. Even this timid but forward step, based on the widely accepted example of Great Britain's Press Council, was repudiated by the *New York Times* and the *Washington Post*, which refused to cooperate with the council. The likelihood of professional self-restraint received another setback recently when the American Society of Newspaper Editors voted by a three-to-one margin against establishing even its own internal grievance committee.

Effective democracy depends on sound public opinion, and that, in turn, depends on reliable information. James Madison said: "Knowledge will forever govern ignorance. And a people who mean to be their own governors must arm themselves with the power knowledge gives. A popular government without popular information is but a prologue to a farce, or a tragedy, or perhaps both." Distortions of content or emphasis, no matter how righteous the motivation, tend to corrupt the information flow necessary for the effective functioning of a democratic society.

A significant segment of the media, however, has become impatient with its information dissemination role. It is not easy and frequently not exciting simply to report events. Thus, there has been a tendency in recent years for imaginative, socially dedicated journalists to go beyond normal reporting in order to seek fuller expression of their talents or social views. According to the "new journalism," the responsibility of the press is "to discover truth," not merely to report facts. Words like "objectivity" are frequently dismissed as undesirable, as well as impossible of attainment. New forms of "advocacy journalism" or "personal journalism" have become popular among journalists, with the reporter encouraged to indicate his point of view in his news stories.

Added to that are the excitement and glorification that have come to surround investigative journalism, once known as "muckraking." It is the investigative reporter who receives the awards that journalists bestow upon themselves, who writes the lucrative books, and who has become the superman of the fourth estate. A social messianic role for the media has developed, which, added to the already feverish drive for the sensational story and the "scoop," leads to distortions not only in the news stories themselves, but also in the balance of news in newspapers and television programs.

It is not only critics of the press who understand or highlight these concerns. In responding to an article by Daniel P. Moynihan accusing the press of reflecting the general adversary culture of the intellectual elite, Max Frankel, the distinguished journalist of the *New York Times*, admitted the tendency of some journalists, the newer recruits, to be impatient with standards of objectivity or "with any standard that would prevent them from placing their own views before the public."

Competition, an adversary relationship between the government and the press, is not new. It is as old as the presidency itself. George Washington, for example, was generally scornful of public printers and resorted to a primitive device of playing favorites in order to get a good press. He would, for instance, hand the only copy of one of his important speeches to a single Philadelphia newspaper. Other newspapers called him "treacherous," "mischievous," "inefficient," and "pusillanimous." Indeed, George Washington himself inserted in an early draft of his farewell address an attack on the press which Hamilton struck from a later draft. John Adams proposed the establishment of a newspaper that would speak for the president. Thomas Jefferson played favorites by anointing a single newspaper, the *National Intelligencer*, as his voice. Other newspapers accused him of being an atheist, keeping a mistress, trying to seduce a friend's wife, and padding his expense account. Jefferson then retaliated by proposing that editors should divide their newspapers into sections labeled "truth," "probabilities," "possibilities," and "lies," observing that the first section would be the smallest and the last the largest.

After Jefferson began the policy of employing an official newspaper, succeeding presidents for the next half century continued in that course. It was not until Abraham Lincoln that the practice was discontinued. Andrew Jackson was the first president to adopt a systematic policy of appointing newspapermen to public office. Lincoln did not have an official government journal, but he did have the loyal and faithful support of Joseph Medill, of the *Chicago Tribune*, who at one point circulated through Congress a strong letter endorsing Lincoln for president. When Lincoln himself began to think that the push was too intense and asked Medill about the vice presidency, the publisher was adamant and said: "Now it is the Presidency or nothing." Medill, one of the founders of the Republican party, persuaded the party leaders to hold a nominating convention in Chicago in 1860 and then took over the pivotal arrangement responsibilities, distributing all of the available spectator seats to the supporters of Lincoln.

President-elect Cleveland held daily press conferences up until his inauguration in 1884, after which the conferences lapsed from daily to occasional. Under McKinley, the president's secretary met daily with press representatives. William Howard Taft, partly as a means of drawing popular attention to his program, developed the institution of the special message to Congress. During his four years in the White House, he sent twenty special messages, a potent legislative instrument, but also useful as an instrument of public relations. In 1913, Woodrow Wilson conceived the presidential press conference to "take the people of the country into his confidence," but Wilson himself soon lost confidence in his own invention and simply stopped seeing the press.

Franklin Roosevelt highlighted his problems with the press in an effort to turn them to his own advantage. Most of his troubles were with the owners and the editorial page writers, but he once tried to stand a reporter in a corner with a dunce cap on his head. On another occasion, he awarded the German Iron Cross to a newspaper correspondent. Roosevelt's ultimate weapon, however, was his radio fireside chats which reached the people directly to outweigh whatever negative impressions were communicated by the newspapers about him and his record. Harry Truman was in continuous fights with one or another newspaperman. Even President Eisenhower once stalked angrily out of a news conference when pressed on the subject of McCarthyism. John F. Kennedy would frequently telephone reporters to complain about their stories and once announced that he had canceled his subscription to the *New York Herald Tribune*. He also tried to have a newspaperman taken off an assignment. The relationships between Lyndon Johnson and the press were a source of constant discussion, deteriorating the longer the Vietnam war continued. It was under Johnson that the words "credibility gap" gained prominence. The height of hostility was, of course, reached with President Nixon's outspoken antagonism, openly reciprocated.

Much of the traditional attitude of the press toward government is in itself indigenous to democracy with its instinctive suspicion and distrust of authority in general and of concentrated political and economic power specifically. But the problem seems to be taking on a different and more intense dimension.

There are troublesome signs that a homogeneity of political, social, and economic attitudes is developing in the media. Theodore White recently wrote that increasing numbers of those who become journalists are of a "self-selected group," drawn from a social and educational elite affected by the "adversary culture."

The issue, however, is not the background and point of view of those who are in the media. It is rather an emerging view that there is a vital role for the media to perform, beyond the informational, namely, to put before the public the needs of society as journalists see them. For large numbers, this role is both a more essential and a more attractive one than the mere reporting of information. This was stated clearly and approvingly by Roger Mudd, who wrote: "What the national media, and mainly television, have done is to believe that their chief duty is to put before the nation its unfinished business: pollution, Vietnam War, discrimination, continuing violence, motor traffic, slums. The media have become the nation's critics. As critics, no political administration, regardless of how hard it tries, will satisfy them."

This view is an outgrowth of and yet far beyond the old muckraking tradition of the 1880-1914 period with its instinctive suspicions of concentrations of power and its emphasis on the mismanagement of the public's business. Now the media are assuming for themselves the establishment of the nation's political agenda—which has traditionally been the prerogative of the politician. Whereas the journalist used to think of himself as a defender of the people, increasingly now he conceives of himself as a spokesman for the people. This obviously assumes that his values are the values of the people. The assumption, however, is subject to serious challenge. Robert L. Bartley of the *Wall Street Journal*, basing his conclusions on a Daniel Yankelovich survey, has asserted the existence of a serious "gap" in values between the bulk of journalists and society as a whole.

The effect of the growing homogeneity among journalists coupled with their new political and social role reached its culmination in the reporting of the Vietnam war. There is evidence that television particularly became a potent influence in turning public opinion against the war. Edward Jay Epstein has asserted that the three television networks all began treating the war negatively after the Tet offensive. Dr. Ernest Lefever, in his analysis of all the CBS evening news programs in 1972, produced impressive data in that regard. He found that the stories on Vietnam critical of United States policy were aired 651 times that year as compared to 153 times when themes supportive of American policies were aired. Criticism outnumbered support by 81 percent to 19 percent. The most frequent theme that "U.S. involvement is wrong because the war is cruel, expensive or senseless" was aired 254 times or about 5 times a week. Statements made by those who were critical of official policies and wanted the United States either to cut back or get out were quoted 842 times in 1972, while "hawks" who wanted to see the war pursued more virogously were quoted 23 times that year—a ratio of 36 to 1.

James Reston, on April 30, 1975, drew this conclusion: "Maybe the historians will agree that the reporters and the cameras were decisive in the end. They brought the issue of the war to the people, before the Congress or the courts, and forced the withdrawal of American power from Vietnam." David Broder talked about "the breaking of the President" starting with Lyndon Johnson and then Richard Nixon. This is done, Broder asserted, by first arrogating to the press a position of moral superiority. Thus, if the press is opposed to the war, the war is labeled as immoral, indecent, and intolerable.

Not all are happy with this role. Robert Bartley, a critic of the adversary culture represented by many of his colleagues, wrote that the essence of professionalism is to set personal attitudes aside when writing stories or preparing a broadcast. He noted many instances of an absence of professionalism, with bias present in the selection of stories and in the images that the reporter carries in his head that lead him to ask the question he selects. Many reporters, he argued, often tended to think of themselves as representing the people in a disinterested way with a purity of motive that a self-serving politician cannot hope to duplicate. "Thus if the politician attacks the press, he is attacking democracy itself."

These criticisms of the media are serious and have produced a diminishing public confidence in journalism. A. H. Raskin, of the New York Times, wrote: "No week passes without someone prominent in politics, industry, labor or civic affairs complaining to me, always in virtually identical terms: 'Whenever I read a story about something in which I really know what is going on, I am astonished at how little of what is important gets into the papers—and often that little is wrong.' The most upsetting thing about these complaints is the frequency with which they come from scientists, economists and other academicians temporarily involved in government policy but without any proprietary concern for who runs the White House or city hall." His colleague James Reston warned: "The credit of the American newspapers with the American people for accuracy and judgment is not high."

At the end of his second term in office, Harry Truman wrote to a friend: "I really look with commiseration over the great body of my fellow citizens, who, reading newspapers, live and die in the belief that they have known something of what has been passing in the world in their time."

Theodore Sorensen, after returning to private life, wrote: "In the White House I felt sorry for those who had to make judgments on the basis of daily newspapers." And Arthur M. Schlesinger, Jr., told the American Historical Association that after being in on the making of history he could never take the testimony of press reports on such matters seriously again. "Their relationship to reality is often less than the shadows in Plato's cave," he declared.

Whether the media can face up to legitimate criticism is not clear. Raskin expressed doubts: "The real long-range menace to America's daily newspapers . . . lies in the unshatterable smugness of their publishers and editors . . . . None is so addicted as the press to self-righteousness, self-satisfaction and self-congratulation." Columnist George Will noted the ingenious theory contrived by the press according to which any criticisms are transformed into proof that it is doing an excellent job.

To those in journalism concerned about outside government regulation, the real lesson of history is that self-regulation is the best defense against such attacks. The need for the press to come up with initiatives of its own to help meet the serious problems created by its great power is unmistakable.

The task is not simple. A serious, professional effort, for example, might well require a self-reformation that would take on the characteristics of a self-revolution. The recruitment and training of editors and reporters would require change. News stories would have to be written less hastily; they would probably be longer and in greater depth, possibly at the risk of not being as lively. The challenge is for the press to come up with its own standards of professionalism and adapt those standards to the realities of its responsibilities.

A code of ethics is needed that will address itself to the problem of personal bias on the part of writers and editors. Legislation is needed to minimize the inequitable protections now afforded the press in libel litigation by permitting public figures to sue for declaratory judgments when they believe they are defamed even if little or no money damages flow as a legal consequence. A law somewhat like that suggested by Senator McIntyre should limit the number of newspapers a company could own and prohibit newspaper ownership of television or radio stations in the same metropolitan area. Newspapers like the *New York Times* and the *Washington Post* should accept the establishment of an independent press council to consider complaints arising out of alleged unfair press treatment. Finally, the major newspapers and television stations should establish their own independent ombudsmen who are not members of their staff, with authority to do something about valid complaints.

The American press is not monolithic, but it acts too often as it it were.

The best of its newspapers are better than any others in the world. The tragedy is that many of the "best" journals have a complacency and arrogance that is inhospitable to any kind of self-regulation. They continue congratulating themselves on their role in ridding the country of Richard Nixon; they give themselves awards for their investigative performance; and they ignore critical articles as they increase their profits, their net worth, and their power. Their failure to provide a leadership standard of responsibility is a loss to society felt far beyond the circulation areas of New York and Washington. Journalists should be capable of tackling the questions raised and supplying answers worthy of a responsible fourth estate.

The nation is going through the most serious constitutional crisis of its history since the Civil War. An informed electorate and intelligent debate are needed. Legislative and executive institutions need strengthening and revitalizing.

The current debate on defense policy, foreign commitments, and the intelligence role reflects a failure of the nation to develop a political theory adequate to its new role as a world power. In recent years the United States has been confronted with a perplexing variety of responsibilities, many of which are unfamiliar and morally uncomfortable for a country only a few decades away from innocence and isolation. Indeed, as Churchill said, the United States has had a perilously short apprenticeship for the burdens of power.

Decency and pragmatism are good but not enough. The nation also needs a working political philosophy that will help it deal effectively with the problems of power. The whole concept of power has been given a modern twist by revolutionary developments in technology and communications. Furthermore, the existence of messianic political movements backed by massive military power has added a complexity to the threat abroad.

The traditional American political philosophy based on nineteenth century liberal rationalism is no longer adequate. Problems can no longer be realistically faced by asserting slogans dealing with freedom of the individual and emphasizing the limits of government. The concept of human freedom and the need to limit power must be dealt with pragmatically within the framework of national security. James Madison and Alexander Hamilton understood the complex relationships that exist between freedom and authority, but that understanding is frequently missing from the debates of today.

The power of the media is real. Their influence will continue to be great. How constructive a role they can play in helping the institutions of government to assist the nation in its maturation as a responsible world power, committed to democratic values, is, however, regrettably far from clear. The stakes are high.

Sources of Domestic Policy Initiatives

RICHARD M. PIOUS

A policy initiative is more than a change of mind; it is also a proposal for authoritative implementing action by the government. It is a serious attempt to move the nation in new directions, rather than simply a rhetorical flourish or a tactical ploy. It is a political decision to take an innovation and gear it to action channels, such as the legislative or budgetary processes, and to apply pressure to move proposals in these channels. In short, it is an attempt to make things happen.

For the bureaucrat, a policy initiative is more than a routine decision and more than an incremental adjustment in standard operating procedures. It is a set of new programs whose adoption would have significant organizational consequences: a break in standard routines, an addition to existing repertoires, a change of jurisdiction or mission for one or more agencies, and possible changes in prospects for advancement.

At the outset it is convenient to distinguish two general types of policy iniative, first-stage and second-stage, because, whether in the executive or the legislative branch, they are associated with quite distinct types of political impulses and processes. First-stage initiation occurs after processes that include the discovery and accumulation of new factual information (through data collection, experimentation, random search, or extrapolation and prediction), novel analytical insights, and invention of new techniques for collective action. Once innovations developed through these processes are taken seriously by administrators and legislators, first-stage policy initiation has begun. Second-stage initiation occurs through feedback from existing government operations and is derived from information gathered through audits, legislative oversight, and internally or externally generated evaluations of agency performance.

This essay focuses on the sources of domestic policy initiatives and deals with two issues: first, the changes that have occurred in the capacity of the executive and legislative branches to take policy initiatives; second, the conditions under which such initiatives are primarily first-stage (emphasizing innovation) or second-stage (emphasizing efficiency, due process, and other procedural values).

The President as Initiator-in-Chief

The president's constitutional duty to "give to the Congress information of the state of the Union" and to "recommend to their consideration such measures as he shall judge necessary and expedient" finds its statutory counterpart in legislation that directs the president to develop programs for congressional consideration. He must submit a budget, an economic report, a manpower report, an environmental report, and numerous others. Even more important than these official requirements is the custom, developed since the New Deal and fully institutionalized by Truman and Eisenhower, for the president to introduce a program at the beginning of each congressional session based on the messages he must deliver and on special messages accompanying drafts of legislation.

There is nothing in the constitution, the laws, or the customs of the national government that compels the president to exercise these powers to fit his own purposes. But there are several reasons why a president might wish to become initiator-in-chief. First, he may view innovation as good partisan politics: if his electoral coalition includes blocs committed to social change, his proposals may be payoffs for his followers. Second, he may find it to his tactical advantage to define and present his own program, for that way he asserts himself both as party leader and manager of the executive branch. He may steal proposals from either party, from the departments, or from interest groups, thereby gaining the reputation of Great Lawgiver. Third, a president may wish to take the initiative in order to forestall or upstage a more comprehensive program from being developed by his opponents, especially if his proposal embodies the symbols rather than the substance of the innovation. Fourth, a president may find interest groups from both the private and public sectors (including the more than five thousand research institutes, foundations, and university centers) offering him their ideas, and he may be receptive to some of these ideas because as he demonstrates the ability to define national problems and propose solutions for them, his reputation and effectiveness as a politician in the Washington community increases. Finally, in a time of national crisis, a president may respond to demands for change in order to minimize social disorder or potential class or group conflict, or simply because people generally, and the media particularly, look to him for "leadership." His proposals for the temporary redistribution of wealth or income in this case are essentially conservative, relating primarily to his responsibilities as chief preserver of the public order—once known as "domestic tranquillity."

But no president finds all these factors maximized in his administration. Not all presidents are elected by a coalition demanding innovation in domestic programs; it is a myth that a presidential electoral coalition must be urban-centered, liberal, and committed to reconstruction of central cities and redistribution of wealth and opportunity. The reality is that party identification and group identification as factors in determining voter choice have weakened; that voting blocs seeking distributive payoffs may be smaller than a "new majority" of heterogeneous voters whose "message" to politicians involves a deep-seated mistrust of social innovation and large-scale distributions to the losers in American social and economic competition.

Not all presidents have paid attention to domestic programs. For several presidents, diplomacy and military adventures crowded out domestic concerns. Some recent presidents, faced with hostile legislative majorities and a bureaucracy for which they had no empathy, did not care much for their reputation in the Washington community and did not try to lead bureaucrats to bigger and better things. These presidents did not always prefer to accommodate officials or interest groups in their requests for the application of technological or social inventions. In short, not all presidents have cared about domestic policy initiatives or cared enough about them to exert the effort required to move them through the legislative and budgetary processes. In such cases, department secretaries and bureau chiefs were on their own, subject to obstacles if not vetos in the Executive Office of the President.

Finally, a president faced with a major systemic crisis might rely on already existing, built-in stabilizers, such as welfare, social security, unemployment insurance, food stamps, and private sector benefits. With these payout mechanisms already in place, a major recession or even a depression may not pose the immediate threat to social stability that prompted many New Deal measures. The president may suggest minor modifications in the distributions, such as a small tax rebate or tax cut, a social security bonus, or an extension of unemployment insurance. Incrementalism then replaces policy initiation.

The orthodox analysis of presidential-congressional relations, at least since the New Deal, has emphasized incentives for the president to initiate the important programs. Political scientists and historians (especially those who once worked for presidents) have argued that a primary role of the president is initiator-in-chief, that his policies are in "the public interest" since he is elected by a national constituency, and that the president, by virtue of both his electoral majority and his unique perspective, is the only man (in the only government institution) who can develop a viable, comprehensive, rational program. Some commentators, in the heyday of the New Frontier and Great Society, even argued that Congress should reform itself (i.e., get out of the president's way) by deemphasizing its legislative role and concentrating instead on oversight of administration. In effect, a new form of separation of powers was being proposed—the president would legislate, and Congress would have both a veto power and a significant input into the administrative process.

The characterization of the president as initiator-in-chief provided interesting dramatic narratives (especially in the histories of several Democratic administrations), and the proposals to end the "obstructive" role of Congress in the legislative process seemed attractive at the time, although they remind one of Theodore Roosevelt's passionate wish to be both president *and* Congress for just one minute. In any event, neither the narratives nor the proposals were grounded in an adequate understanding of the limits of the presidency as initiator of domestic programs.

Even the so-called institutionalized presidency cannot overcome the separation of powers, for the large White House Office and the several presidential agencies that preside over the bureaucratic-scientific-intellectual alliances provide the president with neither the expertise nor the political resources necessary to maintain the role of chief initiator. A closer look at the Executive Office of the President may dispel the illusion that the presidency has become institutionalized, or that these agencies are any substitute for electoral mandates and effective party and popular leadership. (At times it may make more sense to consider institutionalizing the incumbent rather than the office.)

One action channel of the presidency revolves around the Office of Management and Budget (OMB)[1]: bureaus submit proposals for legislation and budget justifications to departments, which in turn submit a budget and a departmental list of legislative proposals to the OMB. This presidential office prepares the president's budget requests for each fiscal year, and its "legislative clearance" enables the president to cull from departmental requests a "presidential program" to submit to Congress. To some extent the routinization of policy initiation has little to do with the president himself. The OMB goes into business for itself on most of the president's programs, especially requests for incremental changes. But its role in preparing major new first-stage initiatives has been undercut in recent administrations by White House staff assistants, working with task forces, presidential commissions, and the departments. To end the friction between the OMB and presidential staffers, an attempted division of functions was inaugurated in the Nixon administration;

---

[1] Until 1970 the Bureau of the Budget.

the OMB was given primary responsibility for implementation and program management studies (as well as preparation of the budget requests) but policy initiation was deemphasized. Its role in policy initiation has become second-stage, based on its management studies of the operations of various programs that it monitors.

Since 1970 the preparation of new presidential initiatives has been a responsibility vested—at least in theory—in the Domestic Council, an interdepartmental committee comprising most of the cabinet and several of the important independent line agencies with a presidential deputy in the chair. The description of the council provided in the *United States Government Organization Manual* is somewhat ingenuous: "The purpose of the Council is to formulate and coordinate domestic policy recommendations to the president. The Council assesses national needs and coordinates the establishment of national priorities; recommends integrated sets of policy choices; provides a rapid response to presidential needs for policy advice on pressing domestic issues; and maintains a continuous review of on-going programs from a policy standpoint."

No one believes that the council does any of these things to a significant degree. In the Nixon administration it was primarily a clearinghouse for departmental proposals to the president, a buffer to keep cabinet secretaries from the president, and a source of staff patronage for John Erlichman. It had plumbers but not policy analysts. At best, it reviewed particular proposals sent from the departments on an ad hoc basis.

In the Ford administration the staffing and direction of the council has been turned over to Vice President Rockefeller. It is too early to assess the significance of this development, for it may simply be a passing accommodation to keep a particular vice president busy. Certainly the council arrived in the institutionalized presidency about a decade too late to play an effective role in policy initiation. Had it been established in 1961, at the beginning of the New Frontier, such a council could conceivably have been instrumental in coordinating departmental proposals and might have performed the functions of the ad hoc task forces used by both Kennedy and Johnson. But by 1975, domestic retrenchment in all fields except energy research has decreased its importance. Recognizing fiscal realities, Rockefeller has oriented the council toward long-range planning—a function that has never been adequately developed in the presidency. Drawing on its own resources, contracts for studies awarded in the private sector, and the prior work of Rockefeller's Commission on Critical Choices, the council has begun to provide the president with a different perspective in assessing domestic priorities.

At the same time, the new role for the council provided the administration with an excuse to hold up program proposals, especially in health care, housing, and income maintenance. Planning is legitimate if there is a serious intention to follow up with detailed proposals and if there is an "institutional memory" so that a new administration might take advantage of the planning done by its predecessor. The OMB, for example, provides the president with such a "memory" in the budgetary process, because of the outlook and professionalization of its permanent staff. It is not clear that the highly politicized staff of the Domestic Council (and its lack of permanent officials) can provide an administration succeeding the present one with either a smooth transition or a set of policy initiatives. A new president is likely to clean house and create a new staff structure to go along with a new cabinet. The paradox is that the longer the planning perspective of a presidential agency, the more likely it is to be subject to the discontinuities imposed by the succession of a new administration.

Another presidential system for policy initiation relies on the nexus between the assistants of the White House Office and the experts from the departments, the national commissions, or the task forces. Presidential staffers can serve as a conduit for outside interest groups (or a buffer between them and the president), or as a "back channel" for bureaucrats, providing access to the president for officials with new proposals. While the memoirs of assistants such as Sherwood, Schlesinger, Sorensen, and Safire tend to emphasize the contributions of these assistants (especially the speechwriters), the outside observer may be pardoned for a more skeptical assessment.

The White House Office has grown from the three assistants Hoover acquired to the six accompanying creation of a formal office in 1939 to the more than five hundred used by Nixon and Ford. But most aides have been used for speechwriting, press and media relations and oversight, congressional liaison, national security affairs, internal management, and advance work. Few aides have been equipped by training or intellect to be policy analysts. Of those who dabble at being domestic guardians, most have been literary historians or journalists who qualify as "generalists" (i.e., people ignorant of the technical aspects of the issues but conversant with the president's passions, prejudices, and policies), or lawyers who have a trained incapacity to deal with many social policy areas. The economists, systems and operations analysts, engineers, statisticians, and social policy planners have rarely if ever been seen in the White House precincts in recent years.

But the staff of counsellors and generalists may play a role in policy initiation. Aides may provide the president with information from task forces, such as the forty-five arranged by Joseph Califano for Johnson or the seventeen organized by Charles Clapp and Arthur Burns for Nixon. Dinners may be arranged so that the president can converse with people who are specialists and can discuss a subject in some depth. The staff can bring innovations directly to the president, in effect "lobbying" him on behalf of certain constituencies, as many speechwriters have done.

Finally, the staff may take sides in bureaucratic struggles, and the fact that an assistant may have the last word can sometimes prove decisive —a recent example being the influence of the presidential staff on Ford's decision to sign the tax legislation of March 1975.

The newest method for developing initiatives in the institutionalized presidency is the use of the "supersecretary." In 1971 Nixon named several department secretaries (and the director of the Office of Economic Opportunity) as presidential assistants. Later the assistant for national security affairs, Henry Kissinger, was named secretary of state as well. The purpose of this innovation was fourfold. First, Congress had refused to consolidate the departments as the administration had requested, so Nixon was accomplishing by executive order (and later by the nomination of Kissinger) part of what Congress had refused him. Second, the reorganization was intended to reduce the number of secretaries who reported to the president. Third, it was intended to end friction between the cabinet secretaries and the presidential assistants, particularly when the secretaries were thwarted in trying to bring proposals to the president's attention. Fourth, it was to aid in developing comprehensive proposals, since the secretaries who were named assistants were told to coordinate the proposals of other secretaries and agencies, and since they were given White House staff assistance (and in some cases became directors of White House councils). In short, a hybridization between the secretary and the presidential senior assistant was developed: the supersecretary, who would preside over multiple sources of policy innovation, including departments, task forces, and councils, and would determine when the presidency would assume the role of policy initiator.

The disintegration of the Nixon administration destroyed this innovation, which had virtually placed the domestic presidency in commission. Only Secretary of State Kissinger continued as a presidential assistant—other secretaries retained as such were no longer aides nor directors of the various councils (the most notable casualty being the secretary of the treasury, who in 1975 presided over but did not direct the Economic Policy Board.) Once again a three-cornered competition reasserted itself, with department secretaries, presidential aides, and council or staff directors, each attempting to jostle others away from the president's door. The chaotic conditions under which innovations were debated and initiatives taken continued in the Ford Administration—euphemistically called an "open presidency."

But one should not place too much blame on the institutionalized presidency, just as one should not give it very much credit. Its condition is generally more an effect than a cause. The independent variable is not staff organization, but rather the attitude of the president toward the role of initiator-in-chief. Recent presidents have simply not grappled effectively with domestic problems. Both the Johnson and Nixon administrations ignored the central recommendations of several national advisory commissions (including the Commission on Civil Disorders, the Commission on Rural Poverty, the Commission on Campus Unrest, the Commission on the Causes and Prevention of Violence, the Commission on Marijuana and Drug Abuse, and the Commission on Obscenity and Pornography). The Nixon administration virtually abolished the science advisory structure created in the institutionalized presidency, including the position of science adviser and the Office of Science and Technology. In its first budget the Ford administration restricted initiatives to energy-related policies, continuing the trend set in the later years of the Nixon presidency.

Several factors contribute to the deemphasis on domestic policy initiatives by the presidency. In the New Frontier and Great Society years, planners assumed that the new programs would be funded from full-employment surpluses. Even after the involvement in Vietnam, many bureaucrats pinned their hopes on the so-called peace dividend that would free massive funds once the fighting ended. The illusions evaporated even as the military forces withdrew.

The appearance of massive full employment deficits (and even larger "real" deficits) forced policy initiators into a zero-sum game. In the absence of a major systemic crisis such as depression or urban violence, a president may sidestep the bitter social struggle involved in redistributive politics and concentrate on other issues. He may emphasize control of inflation rather than innovation in social services.

Second, many of the social programs of the New Frontier and Great Society, extended and at times even expanded by the Nixon administration, have high costs and uncertain benefits. A rational strategy for an administration is to maximize innovation only when costs can be controlled and when the certainty of the discovery and invention processes indicates high ultimate payoffs. As a result, the Ford administration has thus far committed itself only in the area of energy policy, conducting research and development by the new Energy Research and Development Administration.

When payout is high and payoff uncertain, understandably the president may prefer to innovate in a procedural context (emphasizing PPBS budgeting, management by objective, or other techniques), an organizational context (by promoting departmental consolidation and regionalization), or a federal context (New Federalism with its emphasis on general and special revenue sharing). While process rather than substance is stressed in times of fiscal austerity, second-stage innovation designed to cut "waste" can be emphasized. Meanwhile, presidents and their aides can exhort social and natural scientists to return to the drawing boards and provide innovations with greater certainty of payoffs. The president, in short, becomes curtailer-in-chief.

Congress as Innovator-in-Chief

Article I of the Constitution anticipates that the legislature will play the dominant role in domestic policy making. Both the many enumerated powers and the "necessary and proper" clause are affirmative grants, checked only by the president's suspensory veto. Congress may decide to act on its own, delegate its powers to the president, or wait for the president to take the initiative. Attitudinal and institutional pressures make the latter course more likely.

The local orientation of legislators induces them to concentrate on constituent services, private bills, porkbarrel measures, and district-oriented legislative oversight, at least until growing committee responsibilities impress them with the concerns of broader constituencies. For senators and representatives the expenditure of resources necessary to innovate may be greater than the anticipated return on investment; the opportunity cost, especially for senators with higher ambitions, may be too high to pay. By requiring the president to initiate the national agenda, and by relying on the innovations that arrive from the departments and agencies, the legislators avoid start-up costs and can then play a reactive role that better suits their interests.

But in no sense is Congress a rubber stamp for a presidential program. Whig precedents die hard; Congress still assumes that the legislature disposes of what the executive branch proposes. Even after the submission of a presidential program, Congress may retain the function of innovator-in-chief. First, it may reward the coalition of voters for the majority party: in the case of a split government, congressional Democrats become the major factor in the payoff to the urban-oriented and agricultural constituencies. Second, to the extent that bureaucrats and lobbyists cannot gain access at the departmental and presidential levels, they may make or support "end runs" to Congress to press their proposals. Even in an administration committed to innovation there is bound to be some bottlenecking of proposals, simply because there are thousands of program managers sending messages through the system and only a few White House aides and one president who can handle the "appeals" from proposals turned down or pigeonholed by the OMB or the Domestic Council.

But the most important factor in congressional policy initiation is the internal structure of the House and Senate, particularly the committee system. The standing committees, with fixed jurisdictions, whose leaders serve on the basis of seniority rather than at the pleasure of either presidents or party caucuses, have become autonomous vehicles for policy initiation. The expertise of their members in the House and the political ambitions of their members in the Senate provide committees with the incentive to engage in substantive policy making. Their influence over a bureau's statutory base, funding authorizations, appropriations, personnel policies, and organization provides the corresponding incentive for officials at the bureau and departmental levels to work closely with committee leaders in developing new proposals.

Except in times of crisis, the action channel for consideration of new programs by Congress passes through the committee structure. In hearings or at informal sessions, program officers and lobbyists press their claims. Often staff members become policy entrepreneurs and develop ties with officials, lobbyists, or persons engaged in discovery and invention. The committees have an institutional memory because senior staff members and senior legislators often serve for many years and therefore innovations can be kept under consideration through many sessions of Congress by holding hearings or issuing reports. The alliance between policy entrepreneurs, bureau officials, and committee leaders, often referred to as the "permanent government," leads to two familiar scenarios: either a president preempts the alliance and makes its proposals his own, or a leading senator or representative challenges the president by making administration inaction a major issue in national agenda politics. Most often the *innovation* has come from the permanent government, whether or not the *initiative* began there.

The role of the permanent government in policy innovation has been strengthened by several recent developments. First, the committee staffs have been enlarged as a result of the Legislative Reorganization Act of 1970, and to some extent they are becoming professionalized. There are more policy analysts and policy entrepreneurs (staff members who press for innovations that they favor), and some staffs play a key role in policy initiation—especially those of the Joint Committee on Internal Revenue and Taxation, the Joint Economic Committee, the new House and Senate Budget Committees, and the Joint Committee on Atomic Energy. Second, the 1970 act provided that committees could contract out for technical reports, particularly to such groups as the National Academy of Sciences (and its Committee on Science and Public Policy), the National Academy of Engineering, and the National Academy of Public Administration. Third, committees have begun using computers in policy analysis. The Banking and Currency committees used computer models for proposals to stimulate the housing industry and for suggestions to the Federal Reserve Board on monetary policy. Fourth, congressional committees have been expanding their role in second-stage policy initiation based on legislative oversight. To assist the oversight subcommittees that were created to implement the House Committee Reform Amendments of 1974 (and to implement the Intergovernmental Cooperation Act of 1968, which requires quadrennial review of intergovernmental categoric grant programs) the General Accounting Office has created the Office of Program Review and Evaluation, which can recommend changes in programs to congressional committees. The GAO has also been playing a role in the second-stage policy initiation regarding the general revenue sharing program.

The "pooled resources" of Congress have also been strengthened and put to work for the committees. The Congressional Research Service (until 1970 known as the Legislative Reference Service) has expanded its staff of policy analysts and has developed several computer models of use to committees in dealing with economic matters. The Technology Assessment Act of 1972 created a new congressional resource, the Office of Technology Assessment, to help committees deal with the scientific and technological aspects of legislation. The OTA in 1975 was working on continental shelf and oceanic development proposals, options for solar energy, urban mass transit, and food aid to foreign nations. If ever the argument could be made that Congress cannot take the initiative on issues that are technologically complex, the OTA should put the issue to rest.

Passage of the Congressional Budget and Impoundment Control Act of 1974 may have an impact on the process of policy innovation. This act created two new budget committees, each of which has a professional staff and several policy analysts, such as Nancy Teeters, formerly of the Brookings Institution and the Congressional Research Service, now staff director of the House committee. Each committee, in turn, is to be assisted by the Congressional Budget Office (CBO) which is required to submit a report analyzing the president's budget by April 1 of each year. In a general sense the CBO is to do for congress what the OMB does for the president. If the past performance of its director, Alice Rivlin, and its associate director, Robert Rieschauer, is any guide, it will probably play a large role in defining program alternatives for both the budget and the substantive committees. Utilizing computer models of the economy developed by Data Resources, Inc. (which may be supplemented by the models developed by Chase Econometrics, Inc. or Wharton Economic Forecasting Associates), the budget committees have begun to develop their own antirecession proposals in reaction to Ford's budget for the fiscal year 1976. Whether any of the initiatives proposed by the CBO or new budget committees will have an impact on the standing committees (especially appropriations) was, in mid-1975, an open question. The answer may be known only after the system operates fully on the 1977 fiscal year budget or later.

The orthodox generalization that the president is both chief initiator and chief legislator is simply wrong. Congress has taken the initiative on many pieces of major legislation, such as social security, collective bargaining arrangements, public housing, atomic energy, the space program, the environment, and manpower training. The very organization of the institutionalized presidency is often shaped by Congress.

Legislation specifies the National Security Council, the Council of Economic Advisers, the Council on Marine Resources and Technology, and the Council on Environmental Quality, whatever use the president makes of them. In only a few domestic areas, such as civil rights and antipoverty legislation, have presidents played the leading role in policy initiation. And even in these fields Congress eventually dominates the process. Voting rights were protected by an extension of legislation in 1970 over the opposition of the administration and in 1975 were being significantly modified to expand rights—again over administration opposition.

The pace of congressional policy initiation has increased during the Ford administration. Tax proposals were completely reworked by the committees, which not only changed the distributive thrust, but also introduced regulatory measures. Other recent initiatives coming from the legislature include pension reform, regulation of campaign finance, environmental and consumer protection, and antirecession measures.

The problem is not lack of congressional initiatives, but absence of coordinating mechanisms that can develop comprehensive programs. Separate energy proposals, for example, have come from the Democratic Advisory Council, the House Democratic Task Force on Energy, the Senate Democratic Task Force on Energy, the Democrats on the House Ways and Means Committee, and the unpredictable freshmen Democrats. How to provide for some coordination and some setting of priorities that take into account fiscal realities is still the crucial problem for the legislature.

As of mid-1975 there was little reason to believe that the congressional Democrats could solve the problem. There is always the possibility that the caucus, especially its Steering and Policy Committee, might develop a legislative program, since under the rules it may make "recommendations regarding party policy." Its January 13, 1975, proposals on energy and the economy were vague and resulted only in competition between committee leaders. In the Ninety-fourth Congress the committee structure rather than the caucus has continued to be the major action-channel. The Democratic caucus rules that provide for voting by secret ballot for committee chairpersons (and that resulted in the defeat of three chairpersons in 1975) might force some committee accountability to the caucus. But at best the caucus will exercise some restraint on irresponsible leaders—the scent of Cannonism still inhibits the leaders from a forceful attempt to centralize power and create a cohesive Democratic legislative party.

Conclusion

Economic as well as political conditions in the 1970s favor a larger role for Congress and a diminished role for the president in the process of domestic policy initiation. This promises to remain true because most innovation will be incremental rather than comprehensive and because much of it will be second-stage, based on legislative oversight. To the extent possible in the context of deficits, future program innovations are likely to be adopted through some redistribution of wealth, which may take several forms. First, additional spending coupled with deficit financing may lead to inflation and higher interest rates as the debt becomes monetized. Second, the money costs of new regulatory initiatives for consumer protection and environmental protection (one might also include pension reform, occupational safety, and affirmative action programs), if not offset by increased productivity, will increase prices. Third, direct redistribution through the tax or entitlement or welfare programs will also find supporters.

In each of these forms, Congress is suited to play a major role. First, it still considers expenditures separately from revenues, and it has not yet taken full responsibility for fiscal policy. It may prefer to act programmatically on new legislation rather than in terms of fiscal policy, in which case the big losers will be the House and Senate budget committees. Second, committees have been taking the initiative in legislation to regulate the production of goods and services, and have made such legislation a part of coalition payoffs in the electoral process. Third, tax and entitlement programs have traditionally been controlled by committees.

In the context of full employment deficits, both the Nixon and Ford administrations emphasized second-stage initiatives and made incremental cuts at the margins of social service programs. It is not clear how much this might change if a Democratic president assumed power in 1977 and put an end to the eight year pattern of split government.

Republicans had to face Watergate, but in 1977 Democrats might face a watershed: the party may have to develop new kinds of payoffs to its voter coalition. A Democratic president could either press forward with budget-busting redistributive initiatives and face the inflationary consequences or he might emphasize payoffs on social issues, such as a slowdown in busing, ending the federal role in birth control and abortion, a new crackdown on crime and pornography, and an increased emphasis on women's rights.

A rather gloomy long-term assessment of the prospects for meaningful innovation in domestic policy seems in order. No policies are truly "domestic" any longer, for decisions about population growth, standard of living, investment and production, and levels of pollution, affect to some degree life-chances for peoples elsewhere on the globe. If indeed mankind is approaching the earth's carrying limits, it will be necessary to take steps now to slow down exponential growth rates and develop a dynamic equilibrium for a restructured world economy. There is no indication that either the executive or legislative branch is sufficiently prepared to relate domestic goals and innovations to the necessary international initiatives.

So far the legislature has rejected proposals for a joint committee on national policy planning, for a presidential council of social advisers, and for a joint committee on the social report. There is no institution or set of institutions (with the possible exception of the Domestic Council) that might attempt to relate present policy initiatives to the problem of exponential growth on the basis of what the Club of Rome has referred to as the world *problematique*. In a sense, the absence of heightened awareness of what the present economic situation is really all about is truly an American *problematique*—one that at present seems without solution.

The Growth of Congressional Staffs

HARRISON W. FOX, JR.
SUSAN WEBB HAMMOND

Congressional staffs, both committee and personal, are an increasingly vital resource to members of Congress, who depend on their help in handling a varied work load. Constituents, lobbyists, and executive agencies and departments contribute to demands on Congress.

During the past decade, congressional staffs have increased rapidly in size. The legislative branch in 1974 employed over 30,000 persons, including 2,052 on committees, about 8,800 on personal staffs of senators and representatives, and 20,546 in supporting agencies, such as the Congressional Research Service (CRS), the General Accounting Office (GAO), the Office of Technology Assessment (OTA), and the Congressional Budget Office (CBO).[1] It should be noted that many of the functions performed (and hence, people employed) by such agencies as the GAO, the Government Printing Office, and the Library of Congress, serve many other public and private needs as well as those of Congress.

The effects of a growing congressional bureaucracy have received relatively little scrutiny, in comparison with the attention focused on the presidential staff and the consequences of the institutionalization of the presidency. And yet the resources represented by additional staff capability affect congressional operations significantly. Staff expertise may alter the content of specific legislative products, affect strategic maneuvering, or enhance the constituent-representative link. Staff resources are power. By their position in the congressional structure and their participation in the legislative process, staffs influence the larger political system.

This essay addresses some of the consequences of congressional staff increases.[2] It describes the growth of these resources and analyzes elements

---

[1] Joint Committee on Reduction of Federal Expenditures, *Monthly Report on Federal Personnel and Pay*, July 1974.

[2] Much of the data reported here is from research on Senate personal staff (Fox) and on House personal staff (Hammond) during the 92d Congress. During the second session of the 93d Congress (1974), a survey of committee professionals was conducted.

of staff activity and communication in order to delineate the role of staffs in Congress and, particularly, staff interaction with the presidency and the executive branch. The focus is on professional staffs, and no attempt is made to cover the manifold, elusive and sometimes illusive activities of unpaid helpers—interns, volunteers, and the like.

In comparison with staffs of the presidency and executive departments and agencies, the staff resources available to Congress were slow to develop in both quality and size. At the turn of the century and even by 1914, on the Senate side, there were fewer paid personal staff members than senators. Sixty years later, in 1974, each senator had, on the average, a staff of over twenty. Some senators employed more than fifty aides. In 1965, the Executive Office of the President had over 1,500 permanent staff positions. The Senate and House committees each had then just over 500 positions. In the ensuing decade the Executive Office of the President increased 30 percent to just over 2,000; Senate committee staffs increased 100 percent to over 1,000 positions and House staffs swelled to about 950. Congress cannot begin to match the numbers in the entire executive branch. Thus it is playing a catch-up game.

Historically, increases in the congressional staff occurred incrementally. Congressmen, sensitive to charges of unnecessary spending and concerned that a congressional bureaucracy is highly visible, hesitated to vote themselves staff assistance. In earlier eras, additional staffing was an exceedingly divisive issue. In the House, prolonged and often rancorous debate accompanied by extensive legislative maneuvering occurred. The flavor of these early years is evident in the 1896 debate on H. Res. 248, which provided additional personal staff allowances. Representative Wheeler (Democrat, Alabama) thundered: "Mr. Speaker, I tremble for my country. The impatient cries of 'vote,' 'vote,' from the Republican side of the chamber, which we have heard at every pause in this debate, are suggestive of the frantic appeals for 'votes,' 'votes,' 'votes' which we will hear from the Republican party next November. . . . A vote for this Resolution is a flagrant violation of your pledges to the people, and a grave violation of your duty as their representatives." The resolution nevertheless passed, 130-109, on a roll call vote.

Gradually, the issue has become less divisive, and disagreement is usually handled by negotiated bargaining in committee. Since 1971, the Committee on House Administration has had authority to approve additional personal staffing allowances, with no House vote required. Senate personal staffing formulas are determined by the Legislative Branch Subcommittee of the Senate Appropriations Committee. But bargaining and conflict continue to occur in committee and occasionally on the floor itself. In both houses, committee "investigative" staffing budgets must be approved by the full chamber after consideration by the Committee on House Administration or the Senate Rules and Administration Committee.

Committee Staffs

Prior to the 1840s, members of committees handled committee matters without paid assistance. Starting then, committees in both houses were authorized to hire, at first, part-time help. In 1856, full-time clerks for the Committee on Ways and Means and the Senate Finance Committee were approved. Thereafter, committee staffs became increasingly accepted, and the number of clerks so employed increased gradually. By 1924, 120 committee aides were employed in the House and 141 in the Senate.

Committee staffs have come of age in the last twenty-five years. The Legislative Reorganization Act of 1946 formally recognized professional committee staffs and provided each Senate and House committee with a permanent authorization of funds for professional and clerical help. The minority party was to receive a portion of the allowance, and the professional staff members were to perform only committee business. This bill, together with a provision in the First Supplemental Appropriations Act of 1947, which authorized senators to appoint administrative assistants, signalled congressional acceptance of professional staff aid in policy and legislative matters.

It also developed a core of permanent staff from which committee staffs could be built. Special purpose subcommittees were created and staffed by the Senate Rules and Administration, Post Office, Interstate and Foreign Commerce, and Government Operations committees in the late 1940s and early 1950s. Often these subcommittees were abolished within one to four years of their creation. But by the late 1950s a trend began to emerge, especially on the Senate Judiciary Committee, whereby subcommittees were functioning on a permanent basis with staffs.

By 1975, the so-called investigative committee staff chiefly used to staff subcommittees was well entrenched. The growth of staffs continued as the new Senate and House budget committees became operational and other committees continued to increase their requests for more staff. For instance, nearly a hundred additional investigative staff members were requested by Senate committees in their 1975 budgets.

A reciprocal relationship appears to exist between the rapid growth in committee staffs, especially in the last twenty years, and increased constituent demands and increasingly complex legislative agendas. In the House, committees employed 182 aides in 1947. Staffs nearly doubled, to 348, ten years later, and by 1975 had increased nearly 500 percent, to more than 900. The major increase took place in the investigative staff (from 33 to 706 since 1947), which the House, until recently, has preferred to increase rather than to permit the number of permanent staff positions on the committees to grow. In 1947 there were 222 Senate committee staff members. By 1965 this number had doubled, and in 1975 there were over one thousand, about evenly distributed between professionals and clerks, as shown in table 1.

TABLE 1

House and Senate Standing Committee
and Subcommittee Staff (selected years)

| | Number Employed | |
Year	House	Senate
1947	182	222
1957	348	371
1962	466	472
1965	506	448
1972	727	814
1975	952	1,120

Source: Reports of the Secretary of the Senate and Select Committee on Committees, U.S. House of Representatives, 1974.
Note: The number employed includes professional and clerical employees.

Personal Office Staffs

After 1946 the increases in authorizations for personal staffs also accelerated. But it was not until 1970, in the Legislative Reorganization Act of that year (P.L. 91-510), that the professionalization of House personal aides got specific statutory recognition. Between 1893, when clerks were first approved for members other than committee chairmen in the House, and 1946, personal staffs increased from one or two to a maximum of five for each representative. Since 1946, additional numbers have been approved fairly regularly: to eight by 1955, to ten by 1965, and to eighteen in March 1975. Table 2 shows the growth in totals to the 1975 level above 6,000.

TABLE 2

Personal Staff Employees of Members of Congress,
Selected Years

Year	Senate	House
1891	39	—
1914	72	No limit on number of staff; staff allowance of $1500 a year per representative
1930	280	870
1935	424	870
1947	590	1,449
1957	1,115	2,441
1967	1,749	4,055
1972	2,426	5,280
1975	2,600	6,114

Sources: Reports of the Secretary of the Senate; *Congressional Record*; Hearings Subcommittee on Legislative Appropriations, U.S. House of Representatives, FY 1949–76.
Notes: Figures for 1891-1947 are based on authorized positions. Figures quoted for the House are based on clerk-hire payroll for a selected month during the year. Months vary.

Senate personal staffs were first authorized in 1885, eight years earlier than in the House. The total number of personal aides on that side increased from thirty-nine in 1891 to 590 in 1946 and to over 2,000 in 1975. Of that number, about one-fourth are professionals.

Other Staff Groups

Although two of the specialized congressional staff groups that offer support services have been in existence for many years, their expansion, as well as the addition of other support groups, has been a relatively recent development. The Legislative Reference Service, now the Congressional Research Service (CRS), in the Library of Congress was formally established in 1914, adapting the state model pioneered in Wisconsin. Activities were expanded somewhat in 1946, and additional duties and a major increase in professional employees were mandated by the 1970 Legislative Reorganization Act. (See table 3.) The CRS serves as a source of expertise for individual congressmen and for committees. The General Accounting Office, established in 1921, has since that time expanded its work to include analyses of executive branch expenditures and program management. Personnel of the GAO are working more closely each year with congressmen and personal and committee staffs.

TABLE 3

Total Employees, Congressional Research Service
(Legislative Reference Service)

Year	Number
1947	131
1952	151
1956	158
1960	180
1965	219
1969	306
1972	572
1975	703

Source: Legislative Branch Appropriations Hearings, U.S. House of Representatives, FY 1970–76.

The Office of Technology Assessment (ATO) was created in 1972 to provide technical evaluation of pending legislation, just as President Nixon was phasing out its counterpart in the White House staff. Establishment of OTA climaxed persistent efforts of former Congressman Emilio Daddario (Democrat, Connecticut) who became its first director. In 1975 it had a staff of twenty-six; its place in the cluster of overlapping staff jurisdictions had yet to be firmly secured.

The Congressional Budget Office (CBO), authorized by the Congressional Budget and Impoundment Control Act of 1974, is the most recently created support group. A director was appointed in March 1975, and by May its staff of experts already numbered about seventy-five. The CBO by then was working closely with the staff of the two budget committees. The arrangements and working relationships being established appear to offer budgetary skills which previously had been only perfunctorily available to Congress. Staffs of all three share, in many instances, a common professional background, facilitating coordination.

Staffs have grown for a number of reasons. Increased volume and complexity of legislation and federal programs, greater awareness of congressional activity on the part of constituents, and a growing acceptance of technical advisers on Capitol Hill are major reasons. In addition, the recent executive-legislative confrontation over presidential prerogatives and power has undoubtedly contributed to renewed efforts to "balance" staff and resources.

Certain trends are evident, both in committee and personal staffing. Most congressmen appreciate the need for staff assistance, although they may disagree about staff activity and numbers. Not all of them use their full allowance for personal office staff, but few dispute the right of a colleague to hire up to the maximum allowance. Most no longer begrudge reasonable increases in those allowances, which in May 1975 were raised to nearly a quarter of a million dollars for each House member. The use of staff assistance varies; some members prefer to use committee staffs for legislative work and personal staffs for constituent-related matters.

Increasing professionalization is evident, in training, previous employment, and tasks performed. Although Congress continues to be a milieu that encourages generalists, specialization is nevertheless increasing. For example, there were in 1975 more press secretaries and research assistants than ever before on House personal staffs. A number of offices employed more than one legislative assistant, making possible area or functional division of the work load, as has been the practice in the Senate for some years. Within the relatively small House staffs (up to eighteen employees, divided between Washington and district offices), tasks necessarily continued to be somewhat interchangeable. Nevertheless, a rough division of function has come to prevail at the professional level. On committees, too, the trends are similar. For example, an increasing number of subcommittee chairmen have been hiring trained professionals. Overall, congressmen seem to have been learning to use staffing resources more effectively.

Congressional Staff Activity

What do staff people do in their working hours? Two major types of staff jobs, committee and personal, cover a wide range of activities. Major personal staff tasks are handling constituent problems: casework and projects, requests for information, correspondence, and visiting with constituents and special interest groups. In addition, press and legislative work are important activities. Within the personal offices, variety marks the styles and degrees of emphasis. Senate offices with larger staffs tend to be more specialized than House offices. A Senate office may receive 14,000 or more letters in a week. Thus the staff takes care of a great number of things that a senator receives credit for even though he never knows about them. In both House and Senate personal offices, six major functions need to be performed: administration, legislative, research, press relations, correspondence, and oversight.

Administrative work is generally handled by a congressman's administrative assistant (AA) and in some Senate offices by an office manager. A professional staff member who handles constituent problems often deals with both constituents and lobbyists, supervises office personnel, and reacts to political mail.

The legislative and research functions of the office are typically handled by one or more legislative assistants (LA) and in an increasing number of offices on both sides of the Capitol, a researcher. Most House offices and all Senate offices have LAs. They may work with the member in committee, write floor remarks, perform legislative research, draft bills, read and analyze other bills, and write articles. In the Senate, even the personal staff of committee chairmen and ranking minority members do a significant amount of committee work. Unless a member controls committee staff appointments, he often feels he must rely on his own personal staff for major assistance in committee work.

Press aides and assistants advertise their member's work through any available media. Secretaries, clerks, AAs, LAs—everyone, including even the member himself—answer the mail. They provide an informational service to the constituent and produce the letter or telegram that treats a particular problem.

Finally, the personal staff aide's activities are guided by his congressman's ideology and interests, his personality, the quality and quantity of his relationships with other congressmen, the congressional environment, the home state and the realization that members are human and have families.

Committee staff people are most actively involved in drafting bills, investigating, providing information, and seeing lobbyists—activities that lead to the making of policy and the performance of oversight. In the course of such duties they are in contact with the bureaucracy on the average nearly once a day. Contact may be made to discuss future legislation, the implementation of a public law, information about a particular program or project, or any number of topics associated with program authorization, appropriation, budgeting, or oversight. Table 4 shows how

TABLE 4

Professional Committee and Personal Staff
Activities (selected)

Question: Please note how often you engage in the activities below.:	Response		
Activities	Mean		
	Senate Standing Committees n=126	House Standing Committees n=130	Senate Personal n=188
With congressman in committee: hearings	5.60	4.97	–
Writing floor remarks, speeches, and opening statements	5.30	5.38	5.97
On legislative research, bill drafting, and reading and analyzing bills	3.73	4.58	5.24
With lobbyists and special interests groups	4.57	5.25	4.70
Investigation and oversight	4.14	4.78	5.35
On correspondence other than described	4.64	4.78	3.74
On requests for information	3.69	3.47	4.56
Supervising clerical staff	4.56	4.94	–
Working with another committee	5.66	6.19	–

Source: Authors' surveys; see footnote 2.
Note: Mean calculated on basis of the following values: once each hour, 1; more than once a day, 2; once a day, 3; more than a week, 4; once a week, 5; more than once a month, 6; once a month, 7; more than once a year, 8; once a year, 9; less than once a year, 10; and not at all, 11.

often professional committee and personal staff engage in selected activities.

Since the 1930s executive agencies more and more often submit drafts of legislation to Congress for consideration and passage; some members were wont to characterize this procedure as a usurpation of legislative initiative by the executive. For its part, Congress has been delving into the administrative realm of the executive through the use of the congressional veto and by spelling out specific administrative procedures to be followed in administering a program.[3] This mixing and interchange take place mostly at the staff level.

Committee aides report that they work with congressmen in hearings, on the average, about once a week, and in markup, conference, and execu-

[3] There are two types of congressional veto. The legislative veto inserts a provision in a statute that requires an agency to submit contemplated actions to Congress for a stipulated period of time or for disapproval or approval. The committee veto is similar, except that the agency must report to a specified committee.

tive sessions about once a month. They work on legislation more frequently, "at least once a day," and write remarks approximately once a week. A prime factor leading to legislative accomplishment is the ability of a staff member to communicate with his fellow staff members and congressmen. The intensity and quality of staff activity makes little difference if an idea, amendment, or bill cannot be brought to the attention of the people working in Congress.

Communications

Communications are critical to congressional operations. Staff assistants, because of the nature of their tasks and their positions in the congressional structure, are significant elements in establishing and maintaining communications channels. They have a potential impact on the policy process at various points. Case studies describe the staff roles in specific instances.[4] The authors' own research yields data on communications patterns within Congress and also between Congress and outside groups—the executive branch, interest groups, and academic advisers, for example.

Communications channels within Congress are often haphazard. Shared characteristics, such as party, region, state, and attitude, provide a framework for communication. Congressional "class" (Congress of election) can also be a factor. Both the Ninety-fourth Congress freshmen in the House, and the "freshman" group in the Senate are illustrations. Formal channels of communication exist, based on chamber structure. But the actual use and maintenance of these channels is more usually dependent on personality and predilection of the congressional actors.

In addition, the structural dispersion of power in Congress has created pockets of interest and responsibility. Various mechanisms for coordination must be used. These include party leadership, state delegations, and regional caucuses in the House. But a great deal of overlap and duplication of effort persists, for want of effective communication. There is, for example, little coordination between House or Senate offices. No mechanism for exchange of information on office organization, division of the work load, or hours is presently operative on either side of the Capitol.

The structure of the Congress affects communication generally. Members of personal staffs call committee staffs for information on bills before the committee; virtually all staff aides deal with their opposite numbers in the bureaucracy for data and information on matters of concern to the congressman or the committee. Channels of information are developed primarily through informal contacts, facilitated in some instances by

---

⁴ For example, Stephen Bailey's *Congress Makes a Law* (New York: Columbia University Press, 1950), a study of the passage of the Employment Act of 1946, and *To Enact A Law* by Robert L. Peabody, Jeffrey M. Berry, William G. Frasure, and Jerry Goldman (New York: Praeger Publishers, 1972), a study of the Political Broadcast Act of 1970.

existing groups such as staff aides of the Democratic Study Group (DSG) members or AAs of a state delegation. But exchange of information that extends to strategy, content, and mutual accommodation, appears to occur only after an investment of trust on both sides and after some experience. Freshmen congressmen and their staffs spend a good deal of the first session building up communications networks and a backlog of information. After several months in his first session, one midwestern farm congressman had, with his staff, built up channels of information with other congressmen from his state delegation, with his state senators, and with other congressmen, on the basis of shared interests, structural groupings based both on region (Midwest) and on ideology (DSG). His interest, centered on agricultural issues, led him and his staff to cross party lines and to form bipartisan communications nets. He relied heavily on staff contacts for establishing and maintaining information sources. His staff, hired to balance district and Washington experience, had built up extensive contacts among Senate staff aides and also within the bureaucracy, private research, and interest groups in Washington.

House staff aides develop information sources within the executive branch in much the same way. In the case of personal staff, constituent requests, representative's interest, or committee assignment may bring about an initial contact, which may be made through either the formal channels or informally, based on previous social or professional contacts. Over a period of time, congressional staffers build up ongoing relationships with executive branch personnel, ferret out their own sources of expertise, and learn whom to rely on and how far to trust data.

The impact of committee assignment on interaction with the executive branch can be illustrated by the case of a congressman who moved from a legislative committee to the Appropriations Committee during a congressional session. Immediately, high level personnel from the agency scrutinized by his appropriations subcommittee called on him and his top level staff. Subsequent travel on official business and numerous exchanges on departmental expenditures ensued. Although an adversary relationship continued to exist in spite of common party membership, there was extensive and regular interchange of information.

Communications in the Senate are similar. Three patterns of communication are evident among personal staff aides. Legislative assistants are in contact with other LAs and with committee staffs in both the House and Senate. These aides also account for some of the interaction with presidential staff and executive branch personnel at the personal staff level.

Administrative aides most frequently communicate with staffs in other Senate and House offices, with the bureaucracy, and with presidential aides. Many of these Senate aides handle federal projects and similar constituent-related political matters. Press aides are in frequent contact with both journalists and their senator.

Senate aides report numerous contacts with the bureaucracy. Some 21.8 percent report contact at least every hour, 68.1 percent are in touch once a day or more, and a full 90 percent communicate with the bureaucracy at least once a week or oftener. Few contact the staff in the Executive Office of the President as frequently: only 1.1 percent report communication as often as every hour. However, 17.6 percent are in touch daily, and 41.5 percent communicate at least once a month. (See table 5.) This White House pressure tends to show up when there is an "important" vote pending and during committee consideration of major legislative issues.

TABLE 5

Communication Patterns: Professional Staffs of
Committees and Senators

	Mean		
Type of Contact	Senate Personal n=188	Senate Committee n=126	House Committee n=130
Bureaucracy	3.22	3.20	3.30
Staff in Executive Office of President	6.31	7.45	7.70

Source: Authors' surveys.
Note: Mean calculated on basis of the following values: once each hour, 1; more than once a day, 2; once a day, 3; more than a week, 4; once a week, 5; more than once a month, 6; once a month, 7; more than once a year, 8; once a year, 9; less than once a year, 10; and not at all, 11.

A Senate staff member compared House and Senate communication patterns by noting: "Staff on the Senate side are more pompous than those on the House side. You have a system of layers here—the Senators only talk to Senators, the administrative assistants to administrative assistants, the legislative assistants to legislative assistants, etc. On the House side, you find out what was going on in forty-five minutes by going from group to group in the cafeteria. Over here, I go down to the cafeteria and eat alone."

Varying communication patterns exist within the houses of Congress. One senator's AA, formerly an AA on the House side, described the difference. "If you wanted to find out about some piece of legislation on the House side there was always a Congressman who knew all about it. You could get him aside and he would go down the list of political as well as practical matters. Here in the Senate the Senators are not experts. You have to go to the staff. First, I call the office and find out as much as possible. Then they usually refer me to a committe staff person. Committee staff many times know the practical but not the political issues. You have to know both to make a decision on the bill."

Preliminary data on committee staff communication patterns are available from the survey conducted during 1974. On the average, committee staffs work with executive branch personnel at least once a day, and often, more frequently. This is about as frequently as with the Congressional Research Service.

Committee staffs on the average contact the presidential staff less frequently, about once a month; 28.6 percent of House professionals talk with the presidential staff once a week or more; only 8 percent are in contact once a day or more, and the average frequency of contact is once a month. The pattern for the Senate is quite similar: 24.5 percent report contact once a week or more, 8.8 percent once a day or more, and the average frequency again is about once a month.

Policy Making and Oversight

As demands on congressmen have become more intense and frequent, congressional staff members have had to assume a greater role in policy making and oversight. Often they are called on to develop substantive legislation. For instance, the Congressional Budget and Impoundment Control Act of 1974, surely one of the most important bills enacted by Congress in the last twenty-five years, was largely formulated by staff in a long series of "markup" sessions. Staff aides from the Senate Government Operations Committee began consideration of this bill. It was finally redrafted by a conference of a few select staff members from the major committees and joint committees that were concerned with the bill. Senators, indeed, are functioning more and more like directors or trustees of a large organization, giving direction to policy but not working out the details.

Congressional oversight of the executive is an indicator of the complexity of the congressional-executive relationship. Congress has rarely performed oversight in a consistent and comprehensive manner, for a number of reasons. First, even though the president has a constitutional duty to "take care that the laws be faithfully executed," the concept of oversight has not been very well defined by Congress or for that matter by students of government. Second, inadequate funding is often a major problem for a committee trying to carry on an investigation. Third, closely connected to the last reason is the lack of staff time and resources. Fourth, the political payoff of oversight is often perceived as being very limited. Only the most sensational investigation is "really worth the time and effort that members and staff have to invest in oversight."

Professional congressional staff assistants feel that they give a fair amount of attention to investigation and oversight—on the average, committee staffs are actively involved in oversight more than once a week. Personal staff professionals have a somewhat less active role in oversight.

For instance, Senate staff members engage in it slightly more than once a month. Primarily through casework and federal projects assistance, personal staffs may become involved in oversight activities. An increasing number of congressmen are organizing their offices and training their staff to be aware of oversight implications of constituent complaints. One office, for instance, has established a filing and processing system for casework that enables routinized aspects of replies to be handled quickly. The staff member in charge of casework then devotes more time to the policy implications of complaints.

In short, staff professionals can be a significant force in congressional policy making. They participate in identifying issues, determining priorities, and shaping the way an issue is addressed. They perform research, analysis, and evaluation. One aide described efforts to secure speaking invitations for his boss before groups with concerns that the aide felt important. "It's really at the speech stage where I have the greatest impact. After that, when an issue is into the legislative process, it's almost too late."

For both personal and committee professionals, office organization and the interest of the principals are major determinants of the extent of staff participation, particularly at the stages when issues are developed and when priorities are set. In some offices the staff operates within clearly defined and quite narrow limits, primarily giving technical assistance. In others, the staff is encouraged to act as policy "entrepreneurs," working on issue identification and development as part of wide-ranging responsibilities.

Staff, whether committee or personal, are hired for judgment, as well as loyalty and expertise. Many congressmen ask for and expect expressions of opinion. One aide, describing his activities, reported of his boss, "He wants our opinion and judgment." And a congressman, agreeing, said, "The staff must bring pros and cons, but they also must be able to say 'wait.'"

The growth of staffs at either end of Pennsylvania Avenue proceeds rapidly. Added staff are extra resources. Although they bring greater analytical capability to the decision-making process, there is also more potential for staff impact on policy. As in most organizations, the questions of staff role in policy making and control are central issues for debate. In the future, the productive utilization of staff resources will be a vital component of congressional action.

Congress, Shared Administration, and Executive Privilege

ROBERT G. DIXON, JR.

A unique facet of American government, to which every generation must adjust anew, is the separation of powers. The United States is the only major power that is neither a parliamentary democracy nor an executive "force state" under a tight ruling cadre. At the same time it may be the political function of Congress never to accept fully the principle of interbranch independence, at least in respect to the executive.

In 1974 the first forced presidential resignation culminated an especially agitated period of congressional-executive relations. The battlegrounds included impoundment of funds, war powers, the Agnew agony, expansion of Senate confirmation authority in an attempt to oust Budget Director Roy Ash retroactively, veto power, independence for the Office of Special Prosecutor, dismantling of the Office of Economic Opportunity, and the scope of authority in respect to executive agreements and executive orders. Finally, there was the explosive convergence of the impeachment proceedings and the special prosecutor's victory in the executive privilege ruling in *United States* v. *Nixon*.

Underlying these passing events are enduring problems of separation of powers. The history of legislative-executive relationships has been marked by a steady pressure from Congress to adopt measures and procedures conceptually closer to a regime of shared powers than to the separation the framers envisaged. The executive has lately responded with theories of absolute discretion. Executive privilege is the quintessential example, because the key to most congressional power is the inquiry process. Before reaching that key issue, however, perspective will be gained by reviewing briefly some recent examples of the congressional thrust.

The Thrust for Shared Administration

For many lesser officials, the Senate's "advice and consent" function is a simple litany; not so for the major officials. Pledges of future cooperation, especially in regard to responding to congressional inquiries, are now routinely extracted, though legally unenforceable. Some "oversight" inquiry can be attempted, as for example in the confirmation of FBI Director Clarence Kelley. The mere requirement of confirmation induces the White House to screen and eliminate controversial figures. It may even dictate the selection. Franklin Roosevelt, unsuccessful in his Supreme Court reorganization plan in 1937, went to the Senate, to Hugo Black of Alabama, for a surely confirmable candidate to fill his first vacancy on the court. Similarly, it was no accident after the ouster of Elliot Richardson as attorney general that the White House, needing to quiet controversy and get a prompt replacement, turned to the Senate itself and selected William Saxbe. Another essay in this volume deals with the congressional effort, thwarted by a veto, to manipulate the confirmation power retroactively into the removal of Roy Ash, director of the Office of Management and Budget, and with other recent issues over the extension of the confirmation requirement.

Once having enacted legislation, it is the constitutionally appointed task of Congress to sit on the sidelines and watch how the executive administers the program. The oversight function, critical though it may be, exhausts itself in factual inquiry, evaluation, determination of levels of funding, and enactment of modifying legislation as needed. All of these are important and keep bureaucrats attentive. Shared administration is something else, not part of the original constitutional order. As James Madison put it, as a member of the House of Representatives in the First Congress: "If there is a principle in our Constitution, indeed in any free Constitution, more sacred than another, it is just that it separates the legislative, Executive, and judicial powers."[1]

Congress, nevertheless, perennially seeks to move off the sidelines, seat itself in the chair of the bureaucrat, and participate directly in the administration of the law as well as its enactment. One modern device is to insert "coming into agreement" provisions in legislation, requiring that the agency's proposed implementation of the law be submitted to committees, subcommittees, or their chairmen for approval before being put into effect. This is also called "committee veto." It has consistently been viewed by presidents and attorneys general as unconstitutional and unenforceable, although there is no authoritative adjudication. Depending on the president's political strength at the moment, legislation containing such provisions may be vetoed or allowed to go into effect with

[1] *1 Annals of Congress* 581 (1834).

a presidential statement at the signing, asserting that the provision is unconstitutional and hence will not be recognized.

Alternatively, legislation may contain provisions that either would permit one House to disapprove presidential or executive agency action (called "one-house veto") or that would permit Congress by concurrent resolution to do so (the "concurrent resolution veto"). The Department of Justice views these devices, too, as unconstitutional inroads on the president's duty to execute the laws, at least when the president does not accept them.

A recent American Bar Association Committee report identifies thirty-nine examples in the Department of Health, Education and Welfare alone of congressional inroads on normal executive prerogatives in administering programs authorized by statute. For example, the regulations pending in 1975 on sex equality in public education, including sports, were subject to a provision that they could not go into effect until Congress had been given an opportunity to block them by concurrent resolution. Other provisions authorize Congress merely by committee action to block routine administrative decisions, such as the content of experimental education programs. Congressional vetoes also may affect certification for foreign oil shipments from the Alaska pipeline, and one bill pending in 1975 would require submission of the National Science Foundation's proposed grants.

These provisions for a congressional check on the president's administrative authority might be argued to be unobjectionable because of their superficial resemblance to the congressional veto provisions in the reorganization acts dating back to 1939. All presidents have welcomed reorganization act authority because it has permitted them to prepare plans for reorganization of parts of the executive branch. The acts have been in effect successively for limited time periods, the latest of which expired in 1973. The Congress was in no mood for a renewal in 1974. When a reorganization statute is operative Congress is authorized to disapprove any plan the president submits, in earlier years by concurrent resolution, but since 1949 by resolution of either House.

Under reorganization act authority, the president participates in a course of action properly characterized not as an *executive* function under Article II but as "reverse legislation." The president initiates the legislation and Congress exercises a veto power. Thus his constitutional position in respect to legislation is adequately protected; the legislative process simply begins, rather than ends, with him. By contrast, attempts at shared administration of the law through congressional veto devices operate in derogation of the president's express constitutional authority to take care that the laws be faithfully executed and in support of no authorized congressional power.

Likewise different from shared administration, but perhaps equally questionable constitutionally as inroads on the president's authorized legislative role, are attempts by Congress to provide that powers granted under a statute to the executive may be terminated by the nonstatutory device of concurrent resolution. The War Powers Act of 1973, for example —the subject of another essay in this volume—not only provides for a sixty-day cutoff on the president's emergency use of troops abroad (which itself raises constitutional questions because of the president's special authority in diplomatic and military matters), but also provides that Congress by concurrent resolution can direct termination of the action at any time short of sixty days.

Is such a concurrent resolution an act of legislation, or is it simply a limitation from the outset on the scope of authority conferred? Viewed as legislation, the device may be constitutionally flawed as an attempt to exclude the president from his role in the legislative process as authorized in Article I, Section 7, including his veto power. If the president is to participate in the creation of a statutory power—and the Constitution mandates that—should he not participate also in the discretionary decision to be made in the light of a later situation, as to when, how, and whether to terminate it? The Constitution authorizes no one-way street for the legislative process.

If the various congressional veto devices for shared administration, or for terminating earlier granted authority merely by concurrent resolution, were regarded as constitutional, a substantial transfer of executive authority to the legislative branch could occur. Under the committee veto and one-house veto devices, it would also be patchwork and a parochial shift, diffusing power irresponsibly. No single committee speaks for the entire House; neither House speaks for the entire Congress.

Governmental Confidentiality in the Public Interest

Among the most difficult questions that can arise in a democracy is determining the point when a public or legislative "right to know" is properly overborne by the principle of executive confidentiality. The question is, indeed, broader than the separation of powers. The Supreme Court in *United States* v. *Nixon* in 1974 spoke of the need "common to all governments" for "confidentiality of high level communications."[2] The need, however, is governmental—in the public interest, *not personal* to current wielders of governmental authority. The affront to this principle was the real tragedy of Nixon and his lieutenants. From the grand antithesis—the democratic citizen's need to know in order to evaluate, judge, and decide, while the government preserves certain confidentialities

[2] 418 U.S. 683, at 705, 706 (1974).

in order to be a safe, effective government—each generation must find the balance appropriate to it. The awkward truth is that no clear line marks off the "right to know" from the necessities of confidentiality. A similar difficulty arises under the First Amendment. Speech can be curbed, said Justice Holmes, when it gives rise to a clear and present danger of producing a socially repressible evil. His example was crying "fire!" in a public theater. In respect to governmental confidentiality, a parallel example of clear authority to repress would be troopship sailing dates. Both examples are extreme, unchallengeable, and singularly unhelpful in determining the reach of free speech, or the reach of proper governmental confidentiality. In respect to freedom of speech, as Professor Paul Freund pointed out recently in his Jefferson Lecture for the National Endowment for the Humanities, the cry of "fire!" is a trigger to action, reflex action, not a communication of an idea. It does not implicate the *real* interests that the First Amendment was designed to promote. Likewise, advance knowledge of troopship sailing dates does not relate to the *basic* function of evaluating government, which is the raison d'être for the "right to know."

Although all governmental confidentiality issues are in a sense interrelated, three areas of primary concern to Congress in the past two years may be distinguished: the classified document system operating under executive order; the breadth of the national security exemption from the duty of public disclosure under the recently modified Freedom of Information Act; and formal invocation of executive privilege by the president. While conceding a large and necessary executive role, Congress has been pressing to find constitutional and statutory grounds for sharing power in these fields, if not dominating the final decision on confidentiality.

The Ford administration has sought to avoid confrontation by voluntarily furnishing Congress more information than ever before available on sacrosanct agencies, such as the CIA and the FBI, including materials withheld from the public that bore on allegations regarding CIA complicity in assasination plots. By late spring 1975 there were nevertheless indications that events might force the president's hand. On May Day 1975, President Ford declined to disclose the exchange of letters and documents between President Nixon and Vietnam officials concerning assurances of United States support if the North Vietnamese dishonored the Paris Peace Accords. In the Senate, the Church committee investigating the CIA has regularly intimated to the press that it may not get all it wants. In the courts, under the amended Freedom of Information Act, which permits court scrutiny of the bona fides of a classification, suits were filed in 1975 demanding details of the work of the National Security Council and the Central Intelligence Agency.

Classified Information. The present system for classifying information for national security purposes rests on an executive order issued by President Nixon in 1972. It authorizes the categories of "top secret," "secret," and "confidential" and seeks to define each, but subjectivity is substantial and not wholly avoidable. The "top secret" classification is used, for example, when disclosure would cause "exceptionally grave damage" to the United States, such as revelation of sensitive intelligence operations.[3] The most innovative aspects of the order were the twin principles of limited intake and automatic "flush." The number of persons authorized to classify decreased in two years from 59,000 to 17,000. A provision for mandatory downgrading and declassification at the expiration of specified time periods will produce much automatic declassification.

The foundation for the classification system is the president's power under Article II of the Constitution to conduct foreign relations and to maintain the national defense as commander in chief of the armed forces. In the celebrated suit in 1971 to enjoin publication of the Pentagon Papers, *The New York Times* v. *United States,* which the government lost 6-3 on the issue of prior restraint, three of the majority justices nevertheless noted the legality of the executive classified documents system.

Hearings before a Senate Government Operations Subcommittee in May 1974 focused on various bills that would have drastically shifted the loci of power over the classified documents system. One bill would have given to a joint committee on government secrecy the power to override an executive classification decision and release the document. Another would have created a classification review commission and restricted the president's power to control it.

The prime difficulty that Congress faces in respect to the classified information system is that here administration is everything; the feasible role for legislation is limited almost exclusively to the provision of criminal sanctions, which Congress has accomplished. In other areas—commerce, welfare, and regulated industry—Congress can discharge its legislative role by making policy with some degree of precision. Particular applications of the policy by the administrative agencies can be reviewed judicially. A classification standard, however, can do little more than set this rule: documents should not be disclosed if disclosure would have a significantly adverse effect on United States interrelated foreign policy and military security interests. What is significant? What is adverse? These are ineluctably matters of judgment that do not lend themselves to further clarification by legislation.

Considerations of practicality may be the most persuasive of all. The Congress operates *in futuro;* the executive operates day by day. Even if there had been in operation in World War II a statutory system with

[3] Executive Order 11652, 37 Federal Register 5209, March 10, 1972.

specified standards for classification, the executive could not have honored any standards that would have barred classification of information concerning the Manhattan Project, the defection of a foreign counterspy, or the extent of a military reversal in a given area. If only the executive can be entrusted with classification decisions in wartime, who is going to define "peacetime"?

The unconstitutionality of those aspects of the 1974 bill that would remove from the president the final decision on the release of national security information is strongly suggested by a substantially unbroken line of judicial precedent. In the Pentagon Papers case in 1971, Justice Stewart, in an opinion joined by Justice White, articulated a basis in this field not only of constitutional power but of exclusive constitutional power in the executive as follows:

> I think there can be but one answer. . . . The responsibility must be where the power is. If the Constitution gives the Executive a large degree of *unshared power* in the conduct of foreign affairs and the maintenance of our national defense, then under the Constitution the Executive must have the largely *unshared duty* to determine and preserve the degree of internal security necessary to exercise that power successfully. . . . It is clear to me that it is the *constitutional duty of the Executive*—as a matter of *sovereign prerogative* and not as a matter of law as the courts know law—through the promulgation and enforcement of executive regulations *to protect the confidentiality necessary* to carry out its responsibilities in the fields of international relations and national defense.[4]

This is strong language, supporting not only the Article II basis for the classified document system, but the principle of confidentiality for candid exchange of opinions. Justice Marshall, likewise concurring with the refusal to enjoin publication of the purloined Pentagon Papers, nevertheless spoke of the president's constitutional authority to protect national security by "disciplining employees" and preventing "leaks."

The striking comments of Justice Stewart, quoted above, do not stand alone. Despite its commitment to the rule of law, the judiciary has on other occasions spoken of the impropriety of subjecting to conventional review the particular decisions made by the executive in respect to foreign relations and national security. The Supreme Court finds itself possessed of "neither aptitude, facilities nor responsibility" for such work, for the decisions are "delicate, complex, and involve large elements of prophecy." Nor, the Court added, "can courts sit *in camera* in order to be taken into executive confidences."[5] In regard to particular classified document decisions, in contrast to judgments concerning appropriations and policy statements, these considerations of delicacy and facilities may effectively

---

[4] 403 U.S. 713, at 728–30 (1971).
[5] C & S Airlines v. Waterman Corp. 333 U.S. 103, at 111 (1948).

disable Congress, too, wholly apart from legal arguments based on separation of powers.

The FOI national security exemption. These judicial comments may not augur well for complete success by Morton Halperin and others in current suits, under the amended Freedom of Information Act, for CIA and National Security Council information. The act creates a duty to disclose identifiable government records to anyone on request, subject to nine exemptions. The first exemption protects matters "required by Executive order to be kept secret in the interest of national defense or foreign policy."

This exemption was modified in November 1974 to authorize *in camera* court review of requested records, and the agency now has the burden of showing that the document in question is "in fact properly classified."[6] In his unsuccessful veto message, President Ford hypothesized that disclosure would be mandated if a district judge had before him an apparently reasonable contention by a plaintiff for disclosure, and the determination by the secretary of defense against disclosure seemed merely equally reasonable. Winning by shifting the burden of proof, when proof either way is difficult, is one of the oldest tricks known to law.

In respect to some classified documents, it may be difficult to settle the propriety of the classification without looking at a mass of interrelated secret material. The price of vigorous judicial action in this direction, even if the president were willing to permit it, would be to make the courts the partners of the executive in respect to foreign relations and military affairs. This would raise new questions of separation of powers. However, in commenting on the state-secret doctrine years ago, the Supreme Court said the surrounding context may indicate that secrecy is needed and "the court should not jeopardize the security which the privilege is meant to protect by insisting upon an examination of the evidence, even by the judge alone, in chambers."[7]

The president might have hypothesized a more difficult future case. Suppose that in response to a Freedom of Information request the judge demands *in camera* disclosure of codes that the State Department deems to be too sensitive to talk about at all outside the department. Is this an appropriate case for invoking executive privilege, even in the face of a court order? This is perhaps the "unfair" example that will never occur. Yet in the Civil War, President Lincoln did direct the military to ignore a habeas corpus order issued by Chief Justice Taney, in his capacity as circuit judge, on behalf of a prisoner in Fort McHenry in Baltimore.

In the long run, however, the ability of the executive to maintain

---

[6] P.L. 93–502, November 21, 1974, 5 U.S.C. § 552 (b) (1) as amended.

[7] United States v. Reynolds, 345 U.S. 1, at 10 (1953); quoted with approval in United States v. Nixon, 418 U.S. 683, 711 (1974).

needed confidences, to ward off questioning courts or a frustrated Congress striking out to fragment executive powers, will depend less on constitutional doctrines than on political power. The constitutional theory of plenary executive power in respect to certain kinds of government information, whether called state-secrets doctrine or executive privilege, palls when its political base in popular trust erodes, as the readiness to expose the CIA has shown. Confidentiality and credibility have a symbiotic relationship. In order to withhold, much must be disclosed.

Justice Stewart put it well in his Pentagon Papers opinion, already cited, when he spoke of the principle of "maximum possible disclosure" that must accompany the largely unshared power of the executive in respect to national security information: "I should suppose that moral, political, and practical considerations would dictate . . . avoiding secrecy for its own sake. For when everything is classified, then nothing is classified . . . . I should suppose, in short, that the hallmark of a truly effective internal security system would be the maximum possible disclosure, recognizing that secrecy can best be preserved only when credibility is truly maintained." This principle will be heavily tested in the forthcoming wave of suits for national security documents under the amended Freedom of Information Act.

Executive privilege. Executive privilege is a provocative, evocative, misleading term. The contention that it was a mere myth, which gained some currency at the height of Watergate, was devastatingly destroyed by the Supreme Court, 8-0, in July 1974. But the term signifies too much if taken to imply a power to close down the executive branch and bar all unapproved communications with outsiders, as the Official Secrets Act in Britain does. And it signifies too little if taken to refer to a narrow concept of communications personally with the president.

Executive privilege is a particular aspect of the government information policy already discussed and of the general principles of confidentiality common to all government, indeed common to all three branches of the separation of powers system, and to organizations generally. Few utterances are more confidential than Supreme Court conferences behind the velvet curtain. Congress has not only exempted itself from the Freedom of Information Act in respect to citizen inquiries, but it has also provided that no court subpoena is to be honored without a vote of the house concerned; thus disclosure, if made, is voluntary, and independence is preserved. Accordingly, the Senate in May 1975, by voice vote and with scarcely a pause for debate, directed the comptroller general to reject a subpoena from the Florida federal district court trying former Senator Edward J. Gurney on bribery and perjury charges. The subpoena demanded Gurney's financial disclosure statement, filed and sealed and kept in the comptroller general's custody under a Senate rule requiring a majority vote of its Committee on Standards of Conduct to permit

134 | ROBERT G. DIXON, JR.

access. Committee Chairman Howard W. Cannon said: "The surrender of a disclosure statement made in reliance on a Senate rule which protects its confidentiality would jeopardize the whole system of Senatorial disclosure."[8]

Prior to Watergate, the occasions for formal invocation of privilege by the executive against requests from Congress or the courts were surprisingly infrequent—twice each by Presidents Kennedy and Johnson, four times by Nixon prior to 1973. Invocation in the context of litigation was especially rare, perhaps because the same purpose could usually be achieved by using the state-secrets doctrine recognized in virtually all legal systems.

It is conventional to trace executive privilege back to the administration of President Washington when the issue arose on three occasions. The ill-fated expedition of Major General St. Clair into the Northwest Territory gave rise to a congressional investigation in 1792 and a request for certain executive papers. Washington's cabinet unanimously agreed on the principle that it was for the executive to decide whether disclosure could be made without injuring the public good. Disclosure was made in this instance, but on two subsequent occasions President Washington refused to honor congressional requests for papers touching on foreign relations and treaty negotiations.

Judicial involvement came early, too, but was blunted, and did not reappear until recently. Chief Justice Marshall, while sitting as circuit justice in the *Aaron Burr* cases in 1807, twice directed subpoenas *duces tecum* to President Jefferson, holding that the president was subject to such power. The president submitted some documents which in his judgment, or that of the prosecutor, could be divulged without injury, but declined to appear personally. Marshall took no further action but did observe in an opinion that the court would never "proceed against the President as against an ordinary individual."[9] Thereafter, and until 1973, the doctrine prevailed that the president is personally immune from judicial process (hence any question of executive privilege cannot be reached in a suit directly against him) but that his subordinates are not immune.

Traditionally, Congress has used the word "request" when seeking information from the president, thus negating the idea of a mandatory duty. The requests were frequently softened by the clause "if not incompatible with the public interest."[10] An 1879 report of the House Judiciary Committee concluded that neither the president nor Congress has compulsory power over the records of the other.

Senator Stennis took an analogous approach in a 1962 ruling, arising

[8] *New York Times*, May 24, 1975.
[9] United States v. Burr, 25 Fed Cas. 187, 192, No. 14, 694 (C.C.D. Va. 1807).
[10] See United States v. Curtiss-Wright Corp., 299 U.S. 304 at 321 (1936).

out of President Kennedy's refusal to disclose the name of the individual who had reviewed certain "cold war" speeches. He said he knew of "no case where the Court has ever made the Senate or the House surrender records from its files, or where the Executive has made the legislative branch surrender records from its files—and I do not think either one of them could."[11]

Although executive privilege invoked in the "public interest" is not precisely definable, recent cases of denial of information fall into the four broad categories that have been mentioned traditionally as bases for the privilege. They are foreign policy, military matters, investigative files related to law enforcement, and intragovernmental discussions of an advisory nature. The first two require no further explanation and overlap with the traditional state-secrets doctrine in the law of evidence applied by the courts, and with the national security exemption in the Freedom of Information Act.

Protection of law enforcement files involves considerations both of protection of privacy against damaging release of raw, unevaluated and univerified data, and protection of the law enforcement process itself against damaging disclosure and disruption of sources and methods. The theory of this category of executive privilege was first rationalized by President Jefferson as early as 1807, arising out of congressional inquiry into the aborted conspiracy of Aaron Burr to establish a separate government out of Spanish Mexico and Louisiana Territory.

Significantly, however, there have been intimations in communications to Congress made by or on behalf of Presidents Jackson, Polk, and Franklin Roosevelt that this "law enforcement" heading of executive privilege may not apply with full force, or at all, when official wrongdoing is involved and the information is sought by Congress in connection with an impeachment proceeding. The difficult case would be posed, of course, if the data sought simultaneously jeopardized ongoing foreign policy or military affairs interests, whether or not the president was personally implicated.

The fourth heading, advisory discussions internal to the executive branch, is illustrated by the Stennis ruling. The purpose is to promote candor and full discussion by assurance of confidentiality.

The era of Watergate began therefore with the following developed state of executive privilege. Most invocations of privilege had concerned congressional inquiries, but Congress had never sought to push the matter to a final confrontation, particularly because on a confidential basis much was shared with chairmen of key congressional committees. On the judicial side, the record—when the state-secrets doctrine is separated

[11] Hearings on Military Cold War Education and Speech Review Policies Before the Special Preparedness Subcommittee of the Senate Committee on Armed Services, 87th Cong., 2d sess. 512 (1962).

out—is virtually barren except for the Aaron Burr trial, which was a standoff between President Jefferson and Chief Justice Marshall. Finally, the theory of total immunity of the president personally from judicial process had never been successfully denied.

The disclosure by Alexander Butterfield, at an early stage of the Senate Watergate Hearings in 1973, of the existence of secret tapes of presidential conversations, coupled with multiple charges of wrongdoing in relation to the Watergate coverup and campaign finance contributions, triggered a sequence of cases that remade the constitutional law of executive privilege. In parallel actions, access to the tapes was sought by Special Prosecutor Archibald Cox and by Senator Ervin's Select Committee on Presidential Campaign Activities.

In the suit by Cox, the Court of Appeals for the District of Columbia rejected the president's total immunity argument. That argument had been based on the theory that the impeachment clause provided the only constitutional means to proceed directly against a president and also on the president's unique status as head of the nation and its highest elected official. In this ruling of October 12, 1973, the court also confirmed that a doctrine of executive privilege did exist regarding certain kinds of information. But it ruled that the privilege was subject to verification by *in camera* court inspection of documents, at least when the special prosecutor had made a "uniquely powerful showing" of the need for tapes in connection with a grand jury investigation of criminality.[12] The court added that actual submission of documents for court inspection might not be required if the president made a plausible showing that the material related to national defense or foreign relations.

The ruling in favor of Special Prosecutor Cox was followed by the president's unsuccessful attempt to have Cox compromise the matter, resulting in the "Saturday Night Massacre" of October 20, 1973. Attorney General Richardson and Deputy Attorney General Ruckelshaus resigned, and Cox was fired.

The outcome of the separate suit by the Ervin committee was quite different and may have a greater impact on future congressional-presidential relations. It was the first attempt in history by Congress to sue the president on an issue of executive privilege, and Senator Ervin and his colleagues lost. The same Court of Appeals that had ruled in Cox's favor with respect to the grand jury's request for the tapes found no equivalent need to pull chestnuts from the fire for the Senate committee. The predicate for the ruling was that presidential conversations of the sort at issue are "presumptively privileged," even when the president makes only a "generalized claim of confidentiality" and invokes neither foreign policy nor military matters. To overcome such a claim there

---

[12] Nixon v. Sirica, 487 F. 2d 700, 717 (D.C. Cir. 1973).

must be a particularized showing that the information is "demonstrably critical" to the committee's functions. The court probed the nature of these functions, and its opinion could be paraphrased as follows:

The matter involves criminality and is already under scrutiny by the grand jury, pursuing a law enforcement function not shared by the Select Committee. To be sure, the Select Committee may have a function of "oversight" over the executive branch, but in this instance the Select Committee has been upstaged by the House Judiciary Committee, which possesses the ultimate constitutional power of impeachment and is proceeding to exercise it. The Select Committee may also have a "legislative function," but that function does not depend on limitless fact-finding because law-making depends more or "predicted consequences" and "political acceptability" than on objective truth. Indeed, Congress frequently legislates on the basis of "conflicting information."[13]

From the standpoint of the actual manner of congressional operation, this description of the legislative function is difficult to fault. But it is certainly niggardly from the standpoint of laying the foundation for a showing of the compelling need to overcome a plea of executive privilege in any instance short of impeachment.

Significantly, the House Judiciary Committee never sought court subpoenas in support of its quest for additional presidential tapes for one very good reason: possible loss to the judiciary of control over impeachment. The court could choose to dismiss the request on the ground that impeachment is a political question that the Constitution commits to Congress. But if the court took the case it would have to review the concept of what is an impeachable offense in order to ascertain the relevance of the subpoena to a permissible end. The court's view of the concept of a "high" crime and "misdemeanor" could differ markedly from the congressional view. Such an adverse judicial ruling would not terminate an impeachment proceeding, but it could cripple it politically beyond hope of revival. Beyond this, the House had its own remedy: it could make presidential defiance a ground in itself for impeachment.

After the initial ruling by the Court of Appeals for the District of Columbia against President Nixon on secrecy of the tapes sought for grand jury use in October 1973, events moved with the inevitable escalation of a Greek tragedy to the similar ruling by the Supreme Court on July 24, 1974. The suit was new—for additional tapes—but the cast was the same: the special prosecutor versus the president, with Leon Jaworski substituted for Archibald Cox. The president did obey the order to submit additional tapes for grand jury purposes. And it became clear at last why Cox was fired when he refused to moderate his demands. The tapes

[13] Senate Select Committee on Presidential Campaign Activities v. Nixon, 498 F. 2d 725 (D.C. Cir. 1974). The various quoted terms are at 730–32.

did contain the "smoking gun," showing presidential knowledge of the Watergate coverup plan within a few days after the break-in. In many of its key constitutional aspects the Supreme Court ruling on executive privilege in *United States* v. *Nixon* was a replay of the Court of Appeals's ruling ten months earlier. The president was suable personally—the first such Supreme Court ruling in history. The privilege did have a basis in the Constitution. In the face of a showing of grand jury need it was not an absolute, and the materials sought had to be delivered to the district court for *in camera* examination.

But the holding was tailored narrowly to the facts of the case and carefully qualified. It could be said that the *president* lost the case, but the *presidency* won. For few presidents will ever again be in the position of Richard Nixon, trapped in a situation of implied criminality based largely on evidence the president himself had created.

The real test of the *Nixon* ruling is what it means in respect to congressional demands for executive information. The Supreme Court nominally excluded any ruling on the conflict between a "President's generalized interest in confidentiality" and congressional demands for information.[14] Three questions can be posed in tentative conclusionary fashion. First, is it not unlikely that congressional interests themselves would normally be more than "generalized" interests, especially in view of the characterization of the legislative function made by the Court of Appeals in the tapes case brought by the Ervin committee? Second, if it is likely that most congressional interests would be "generalized" interests, is it not *un*likely that the Court would elevate such a request over generalized executive assertion of confidentiality, in view of the Court's exceptionally strong separation of powers statements? Third, whether or not military and foreign relations matters present a case for absolute privilege, as intimated by the Court, does not the opinion suggest that confidentiality for such matters would prevail over any congressional request for such information? Impeachment may be an exception; yet would the fact of impeachment change at all the degree of confidentiality to which a truly sensitive military document was entitled?

If Congress had procedures for holding in confidence material received under a partial waiver of executive privilege, as some oversight committees do, the problem would be eased considerably. Such understandings tend to be disfavored by some in Congress because they preclude

---

[14] United States v. Nixon, 418 U.S. 683, 712n. The essence of the Court's limited holding is captured in the cited footnote as follows: "We are not here concerned with the balance between the President's generalized interest in confidentiality and the need for relevant evidence in civil litigation, nor with that between the confidentiality interest and congressional demands for information, nor with the President's interest in preserving state secrets. We address only the conflict between the President's assertion of a generalized privilege of confidentiality and the constitutional need for relevant evidence in criminal trials."

political use of the information obtained, but the possibility of confidential submissions should be further explored. It may be useful to revert to the Freedom of Information Act's exemptions at this point, even though they do not now apply against an official congressional request. Why not make them qualifiedly applicable to Congress? If a matter falls within an FOI exemption and is therefore deemed by both Congress and the executive to be a matter that should not be disclosed to the public generally, should not a congressional request for the very same material be subject to a valid plea of executive privilege, unless Congress is willing to provide the same security for the material as the executive branch provides? In addition to national security, the major exemptions protect privacy interests, intraagency advisory memorandums, law enforcement records, and private material furnished to the government in confidence, such as trade secrets.

Conclusion

Two enduring institutional problems in American democracy, both aggravated by Watergate, both stemming in large part from the separation of powers, are shared administration and executive privilege, broadly defined to include all aspects of governmental confidentiality. It is difficult to draw the line in congressional-presidential relations between the proper concept of oversight and the improper concept of shared administration. It is equally difficult to draw the line between the claims of the executive to safeguard certain information in the public interest and the "right to know" of both Congress and the public in the interest of accountability.

To speak of the "presidency, imperial or imperiled?" is to speak largely of these two things. Congress has an instinctive thrust toward control of the executive. It seeks ever-greater authority over executive personnel and pursues a variety of other devices toward shared administration, of which the various forms of "congressional veto" of administrative action are the most assertive and least understood. Additional devices, which have not been explored here, include recent attempts to limit the pocket veto, to create independent agencies, such as the new Federal Elections Commission, to perform executive functions, and the aborted plan of Senator Ervin in 1974 to remove the Department of Justice from the executive branch. Many of these congressional forces are enduring. They are not readily amenable to judicial check in the form of litigation over separation of powers, or to political check when the presidential faction in Congress is divided and small. Indeed, it could be said that the balance in the separation of powers system between the executive and the Congress largely exists at the sufferance of the latter, its disinclination to exercise fully the power it constitutionally possesses.

In respect to the presidency, it is important to distinguish between *power* and *abuse of power*. The presidents beloved by historians have been strong, vigorous presidents who acted to solve problems first and worried about authority later.

The courts, it seems, can save the nation from an imperial president. An enduring problem is to avoid a reactive, institutional overkill by an imperial Congress, which could leave the presidency imperiled in function under the delusive idea that power fragmented is power purified.

Senate Confirmation of Executive Appointments: The Nixon Era

RONALD C. MOE

The constitutional power of the Senate to advise and consent to appointments not otherwise specified by law—which had attracted only sporadic, though occasionally spectacular attention in recent years—emerged as a major instrument in the developing confrontation between Congress and the president in the Nixon era. Struggles over actual nominations drew headlines but were only a part of the congressional campaign to redress the balance between the two branches. Less noticed but equally important were efforts of the Senate to attach the requirement of confirmation to currently exempt offices and otherwise to impose constraints on the tenure of executive officials. Moves of the latter sort, needing a statutory basis, required the concurrence of the House, thus adding a bicameral dimension to the senatorial-presidential engagements.

The purpose of this essay is to review and analyze events along this general front, chiefly in the Ninety-third Congress (1973-74), for the light they shed on perennial issues in the exercise of this power of the Senate and particularly to mark out more sharply the objects of senatorial concern and to distinguish the tactics and circumstances that augur well for success in attaining them from those that, on the record, have proved less promising.

To accommodate space limits here, two topics appropriate to a more comprehensive treatment of the appointing power have been excluded —the contests over Nixon's nominations to vacancies on the Supreme Court and the Senate's share in the novel proceedings, introduced by the Twenty-fifth Amendment, for congressional confirmation of the appointments, first of Gerald Ford and more recently of Nelson Rockefeller to the vice presidency. These events held widespread and prolonged public attention, and stirred emotions sufficiently to remain fresh in mind.

The justices and vice president have constitutional terms and duties, however, that set them apart from statutory officials.

Until 1868 the entire Senate deliberated on nominations. Then the rule was changed to require committee reference unless otherwise ordered. In modern practice, nominations are routinely referred by the Senate's executive clerk, upon receipt from the president, to the appropriate standing committees. The committee normally notifies the senators of the state in which the office is located, if that is outside the District of Columbia, or of the state of the nominee's residence if the office is at the seat of the government. Receiving no response within seven days in session, the committee will generally suppose no objection is raised from that quarter. The committee may hold hearings or may dispense with them. The committee may act promptly—in some circumstances even in unseemly haste—or only after a delay, sometimes prolonged, or it may not act at all. Failure to act by the end of a session, or if Congress takes an intrasession recess of more than thirty days, means that the president must resubmit the name. Under these conditions the president may make a recess appointment.

Anticipated events have a way of casting shadows ahead, and so it is with the prospects of confirmation. It is not unusual, for instance, to find the White House making discreet inquiries of key senators regarding the acceptability of prospective nominees. When the president wishes to be sure that his nominee will be confirmed, he may take the precaution of naming a member of Congress in good standing, who will almost automatically be regarded as eligible for any office tendered that he or she is willing to accept. So President Franklin Roosevelt chose Senator Hugo Black for his first vacancy on the Supreme Court in 1937, and so President Nixon chose Representative Gerald Ford to be vice president in 1973.

If the president becomes aware that his selection faces rejection at the hands of the committee, the name will usually be withdrawn, either at the instigation of the nominee or under instructions from the president, thereby sparing both the president and the Senate embarrassment. While a committee may not want to reject outright a presidential nominee, it may take the hearings as an opportunity to exact pledges from the nominee before moving to confirm. So it was when the Armed Services Committee in 1953 required President Eisenhower's choice for secretary of defense, Charles Wilson, then president of General Motors, to divest himself of stock in the corporation. So the Judiciary Committee required the Watergate special prosecutor, Leon Jaworski, to promise to return to the committee if he encountered recalcitrance on the president's part in securing evidence for the Watergate trials. And so the Environmental Protection Agency administrator, say, or the secretary of transportation might be pressed for policy commitments in the administration of their agencies. As a result of a resolution passed by the Senate Democratic Caucus on January 11, 1973, all nominees are now required to agree, preliminary to confirmation, to appear before congressional committees when requested.

Nothing in the Constitution requires that senators be limited to questions of probity and competence in giving their advice and consent to nominees. While the degree of deference accorded the president in making his selections differs according to the category of office, the presumption has largely been in favor of permitting wide latitude of choice. There have been, however, numerous instances when nominees have either been rejected or subjected to sizeable negative votes because of opposition to policies with which these individuals had been associated. The nomination of Charles E. Bohlen to be ambassador to the Soviet Union in 1953, for instance, encountered considerable opposition because of previous policy statements he had made. Lewis Strauss was rejected as secretary of commerce in 1959 partly because of policies he pursued as chairman of the Atomic Energy Commission. And, more recently, the Senate Foreign Relations Committee in 1973 took what was believed to be an unprecedented step in refusing to approve a nomination to a post in the Department of State. The committee rejected G. McMurtrie Godley as assistant secretary for Far Eastern affairs for policy reasons, not on the question of competence. According to some press reports, his rejection was based on the fact that he was ambassador to Laos when the unacknowledged bombing campaign was being waged.

The Senate as an institution and senators individually and in committee have several related but distinguishable interests to be served in the exercise of their power to give or withhold consent. Some of these interests are manifest, others latent. As an institution the Senate shares responsibility for determining the probity, competence, and qualifications of appointees—a concern that rests more lightly on some shoulders than on others. Certainly the length and scope of the hearings surrounding the nominations of Richard Kleindienst and L. Patrick Gray to be attorney general and director of the Federal Bureau of Investigation suggest that rarely, if ever, have so many nominees been subjected to so much questioning as during the Nixon era.

For the good of their institution in future contests with the executive, senators perceive that they also have a collective interest in extending the scope and strengthening the effectiveness of their power to confirm. The House may go along with particular moves in that direction, out of comity or in a trade-off; but it has no instinctive institutional enthusiasm for enhancing the influence of the Senate.

Confirmation may be considered in two additional perspectives. First, as a helpful adjunct in the exercise of senatorial oversight of executive agencies, an official who has been through the ordeal of confirmation is presumably more sensitive to legislative desires and ways and less likely to attempt to invoke executive privilege when next called upon to testify. Second, senators individually and in pertinent committees tend to have a proprietary interest in the control of appointments either as patronage for themselves or as bargaining counters—even hostages— in dealings with colleagues, executive officials, White House aides, and others.

The political usefulness of confirmation proceedings to senators is limited, however, by the sheer time constraints imposed. Is it really worth spending much time quizzing a future ambassador to Upper Volta? Even patronage can become politically counterproductive to senators when they find that a nominee they have sponsored is touched with scandal or when the jealousies generated by making a senatorial choice outweigh any benefits of gratitude and loyalty that may have accrued.

Congressional Reassertion: The Executive Office

As often has happened historically, just when an institution appears to be at its zenith, it stumbles and falls, not slowly but precipitously. So it was with the American presidency soon after Richard Nixon's accession; 1970 may be arbitrarily but conveniently taken as a turning point. For a half-century before, from the passage of the Budget and Accounting Act of 1921, a combination of factors had tended to diminish the relative importance of senatorial confirmation in the general scheme of things. That act set a precedent in exempting the director of the Bureau of the Budget from the traditional requirement; he was to be unmistakably the president's man, as the budget was also to be the president's. Prevailing doctrine, down through the reports of the two Hoover Commissions and Richard Neustadt's book titled *Presidential Power* emphasized strengthening the institutional base of the presidency, expanding the coverage of the civil service—while making room also for political executives, sharply distinguished as such, and providing a continuing authority and a workable procedure for incremental reorganizations of the executive branch. Democratic control of both the White House and Congress during the 1960s also operated to erode senatorial participation in the appointing process.

Early in 1970 the president, by Reorganization Plan No. 2 of that year, boldly proposed to expand the mission of the Bureau of the Budget and to change its name accordingly to the Office of Management and Budget (OMB). He was sustained by a bipartisan margin in the House over an adverse committee report aimed at another feature of the plan, a cabinet-level Domestic Council to be presided over by a confidential assistant to the president who not only was exempt from confirmation but could plead executive privilege regarding council deliberations. This proved to be one of the last major institutional changes, enhancing his powers and affecting his Executive Office, that Nixon was able to accomplish. His highly touted reorganization proposal for rationalizing the executive branch in 1971 was disregarded by Congress, save for House committee hearings on one (and only one) of the projected four new departments.

At the commencement of the Ninety-third Congress, there were fifteen component units, not including the White House Office, within the Executive Office of the President. Five of these units were headed by persons not subject to Senate confirmation: the director and deputy director of the Office of Management and Budget, the executive secretary of the National Security Council, the executive director of the Domestic Council, the executive director of the Council on International Economic Policy, and the executive director and two deputy directors of the Office of Consumer Affairs. The latter office was transferred to the Department of Health, Education and Welfare by executive order on January 25, 1973, thereby leaving four such exempted offices.

Several bills were introduced in the Ninety-third Congress to "blanket in" the remaining heads of components in the Executive Office under the requirement of Senate confirmation. Two of the bills were to become law.

The first bill, S. 37, amended the Budget and Accounting Act of 1921 to require Senate confirmation of the director and deputy director of the Office of Management and Budget. It was passed and signed into law on March 2, 1974, after a similar bill, S. 518, had been vetoed by the president on May 18, 1973, and Congress had failed to override the veto.

The bill destined to be vetoed, S. 518, provided for the abolition of the two offices mentioned above and for their immediate reestablishment. The new offices would then be subject to senatorial confirmation. The president vetoed the bill on two grounds: that the positions in question "cannot reasonably be equated with cabinet and subcabinet posts for which confirmation is appropriate" and that this bill was an unconstitutional attempt to remove incumbents (including Roy Ash) who lawfully held these offices. The override vote in the Senate succeeded on May 22, 1973, by a vote of 66-22. In the House, however, the override attempt failed on May 23, 1973, by a vote of 236-178. The bill ultimately to be signed by the president, S. 37, provided only for the prospective confirmation of the future directors and deputy directors of the Office of Management and Budget.

The second bill related to Senate confirmation of officers in the Executive Office that became law in the Ninety-third Congress was an amendment to the International Economic Policy Act of 1972. It required that any executive director of the Council on International Economic Policy thereafter appointed would have to undergo Senate confirmation.

The Commission on Government Procurement, which Congress established in 1969, issued a report in 1972 recommending, among other things, that an office be established to develop and evaluate procurement policy. Congress passed and the president signed a bill that provided for the Office of Federal Procurement Policy within the Office of Management and Budget, headed by an administrator appointed by the president with the advice and consent of the Senate. The administrator is the only official below the level of the director and deputy director of the Office of Management and Budget who is subject to Senate confirmation.

There was considerable shuffling of offices in the Executive Office during the Ninety-third Congress. Reorganization Plan No. 1 of 1973 provided for the abolition of three units, all of which had directors subject to confirmation; the National Aeronautical and Space Council, the Office of Science and Technology, and the Office of Emergency Planning. On the other hand, three new offices were added. The first was the Federal Property Council, whose chairman does not require confirmation although the individual holding the position may have undergone confirmation for another position. Throughout the Ninety-third Congress the chairwoman was Anne Armstrong, counsellor to the president, the latter position not subject to confirmation. The second unit, the Council on Wage and Price Stability, was considered temporary, and therefore the chairman was not made subject to confirmation. The third unit created was the Energy Resources Council, with the secretary of interior designated as chairman.

In summary, at the outset of the Ninety-third Congress, Senate confirmation was not required of five of the fifteen units within the Executive Office. In the course of the Ninety-third Congress, two of these five exempt positions were included by statute under the requirement of confirmation. One of the five positions was transferred to a line department. Three units in the Executive Office were abolished by reorganization plan, all with chief executive officers requiring confirmation. And, finally, three new offices were established, two with chief executive officers not requiring confirmation.

The net result was, at the close of the Ninety-third Congress, fourteen component units in the Executive Office of the President, not including the White House Office, of which four had chief executive officers selected by the president but not subject to Senate confirmation.

Other Executive Agencies

Bills were introduced in the Ninety-third Congress altering the conditions and tenure for officers in the executive branch. The Senate, as might be expected, was more receptive to these proposals than the House.

The Justice Department was the object of considerable interest largely because of Watergate. Senator Ervin introduced two bills: one to establish a justice department independent of the executive branch (S. 2803) and another to establish an independent office of special prosecutor (S. 3652). Hearings were held on the former bill and were expanded to include the more general topic of depoliticizing the Justice Department. No further action was forthcoming.

The Federal Bureau of Investigation also attracted attention. Title VI of the Omnibus Crime Control and Safe Streets Act of 1968 required that the president nominate the director of the Federal Bureau of Investigation and that the Senate confirm this nomination. No term of office was stipulated. Prior to this law, the director had been appointed by the attorney general without Senate confirmation. Legislation (S. 2106) was introduced by Senator Robert Byrd in the Ninety-third Congress to amend title VI of this act to provide for a single, ten-year term of service. This bill passed the Senate on October 7, 1974, by a vote of 70-0. The House, however, took no action.

Senator Byrd also introduced legislation of more general applicability, namely, a bill that would *limit* to four years (concurrent with the president's term) the term for heads of executive departments (S. 755). The objective was to require cabinet officers who were retained by a president serving his second term to come before the Senate for confirmation prior to reappointment. The commission of office, therefore, would cease at the expiration of the term of the president who appointed the individual or upon the death of the president. While the bill did not inject the Congress into the process whereby the president makes a decision as to whom he will nominate to be department head in the first instance, it would require that a complete break be made between administrations, whether or not the incumbent president succeeds himself.

A third bill (S. 1828) introduced by Senator Byrd sought to have the director of the newly established Mining Enforcement and Safety Administration brought under the requirement of Senate confirmation. The original bill was amended in committee and later on the floor, and when finally passed by the Senate on July 25, 1973, the offices to be made subject for the first time to Senate confirmation included: director, National Park Service; director, Bureau of Outdoor Recreation; commissioner of reclamation; and governor of American (Eastern) Samoa. The vote in the Senate was 91-2. The House did not take any action.

Temporary Appointments

Historically, many controversies have surrounded the constitutionally permissible "recess appointments" of presidents. While the rules governing such appointments are at least reasonably explicit and have been subjected to judicial interpretation, presidents have proven to be rather inventive in circumventing these rules. The problem of temporary appointments does not end, however, with "recess appointments." There is also a problem of determining the legal status of ad interim, or temporary, appointments made by the president while the Senate is in session and capable of conducting advice and consent proceedings.

While the right of the president to fill vacancies with temporary or acting officials has never been seriously challenged, Congress has placed several statutory restrictions on this power. The most notable congressional effort to restrict presidential discretion was the Vacancies Act of 1868. This law, as later amended, limits the power of the president to appoint ad interim officers to thirty days.

Although in a number of instances recently the president has appointed an individual to "acting" status for more than thirty days without submitting his name for confirmation, the first major challenge to this practice occurred when several members of the Senate brought suit in 1973 to prevent the "dismantling" of the Office of Economic Opportunity by "Acting Director" Howard Phillips. A federal court of appeals held that the naming of an "acting director" for a period extending beyond thirty days was unconstitutional, except when there was legislation giving the president a power to make appointments without Senate confirmation or when such an appointment occurred during a Senate recess.

Legislative Branch Agencies

Four legislative agencies have chiefs appointed by the president subject to Senate confirmation: the librarian of Congress, the architect of the Capitol, the comptroller general, and the public printer. While each of these positions has a distinctive legislative history and while there remains, in each instance, more than a modicum of ambiguity and confusion regarding the status of the institution, a major common question concerns all four. Are the persons who hold these positions "officers of the legislature" or "officers of the United States"?

The principal issue is whether it is constitutional to establish an office in the legislative branch that is not an office of either house. A subsidiary question is, If one can establish an office of the legislative branch, can the office be given a tenure beyond the length of a particular Congress? This question has not been subjected to judicial interpretation. The most extensive discussion of these questions arose in connection with the passage of the Budget and Accounting Act of 1921 which provided, among other things, for the establishment of the General Accounting Office headed by a comptroller general. The majority view in Congress appeared to be that the person who holds this position ought to be an officer of the United States, thus eliminating doubt as to the validity of providing a fifteen-year term of office. If the comptroller general was to be an officer of the United States, he had to be appointed by the president.

Legislation was introduced (H.R. 63) in the Ninety-third Congress to provide for alternating Senate and House appointment to these offices. It is worth noting, perhaps, that none of the agencies in question is on record as being opposed to the present method of selecting its chief administrative officers.

Rubber Stamp or Search-and-Destroy?

Experience suggests that the type of review conducted by the Senate is related to the type of office for which the nominee is being considered. The customs of the Senate in reviewing a cabinet nominee, for instance, are considerably different from those that apply to the selection of judges.

It appears to be a well-established practice that the Senate will allow the president wide latitude in the selection of members of his cabinet. The consensus has been that if he is not given a free hand in the choice of his cabinet, he cannot be held responsible for the administration of the executive branch. Only eight cabinet nominations have been rejected on the floor of the Senate in the nation's history. The first occurred when Andrew Jackson submitted the name of Roger B. Taney to be secretary of the treasury in 1834. Four more occurred in 1843 and 1844 when John Tyler had broken with the Whigs and had become a president without a party following in Congress. Since the Civil War there have been three rejections, the most recent that of Lewis Strauss to be secretary of commerce in 1959.

The heads of independent agencies and the members of commissions tend to be given closer scrutiny by the Senate, but the degree of scrutiny varies greatly from one agency to the next. Some independent agencies, such as the General Services Administration, are considered close to the president, and he is accorded considerable discretion in appointments. Other independent agencies, such as the regulatory commissions, are considered more removed from presidential direction. These commissions are even occasionally referred to as "arms of Congress." Congress has historically taken more interest in nominees to these commissions than in other independent agencies. While few nominees to regulatory commissions have been rejected outright, a number have not been confirmed. In 1973, for example, Robert Morris was nominated to be a member of the Federal Power Commission. In effect, he was rejected when a motion to recommit the nomination to the Commerce Committee was carried, 49-44, thus killing it.

The Senate has a record of considerable aggressiveness with regard to Supreme Court appointments. Joseph P. Harris, in his book *The Advice and Consent of the Senate* (1953), reports that through 1953, of the 116 persons nominated to the Court, 21, or nearly one-fifth, failed to receive Senate approval. Nine were rejected outright, ten names were not acted upon by the Senate, which is the equivalent to a rejection, and two names were withdrawn. Since 1953, one additional name has been withdrawn, that of Abe Fortas to be chief justice, and two nominees were rejected, Clement Haynsworth and Harrold Carswell. According to Harris, it appears that about half the rejections were based principally on questions of competence while the other half were motivated by political reasons.

As for the lower courts, the degree of presidential discretion in making appointments varies with the court. Presidential discretion is at its broadest with regard to specialized courts, e.g., the Tax Court or the Court of Claims. Discretion is also substantial in the naming of judges for seats on the circuit courts of appeal. However, as the recent controversy over the nomination of former governor Thomas Meskill of Connecticut to be a judge on the circuit court of appeals suggests, presidential discretion is far from complete.

Federal district court appointments, on the other hand, often raise considerable controversy as many actors attempt to exert influence. Some scholars suggest that the Senate has largely expropriated the president's power to make appointments to local federal district judgeships. The American Bar Association has also entered the fray. The bar vigorously and successfully fought the nomination of Francis X. Morrisey in 1965 to the federal district court bench in Boston, notwithstanding the fact that Senator Kennedy was Morrisey's patron. In this instance the president was merely a bystander.

Two somewhat contradictory trends have emerged in recent years with regard to administrative executive positions requiring confirmation. While it is true that the number of categories of offices requiring confirmation has decreased, the number of confirmation proceedings has increased. This latter trend is largely attributable to three facts. First, there has been a substantial increase in the number of positions at the assistant secretarial and ambassadorial rank. Second, the tenure of administrative executives has become shorter in recent years, thereby increasing the turnover with a consequent increase in the number of formal hearings necessary. Finally, as new agencies have been created, the tendency has been to require confirmation of a number of operating chiefs, positions previously considered exempt from such scrutiny.

It should also be noted that the Senate handles in bloc large numbers of military and foreign service appointments. Only rarely is there any question raised on the names presented. There was, however, some question in 1974 as to whether General Alexander Haig should be required to undergo confirmation proceedings prior to his appointment as military commander of NATO. While most military and foreign service appointments are routine, the Senate retains the residual authority to examine closely specific appointments.

The increasing volume of confirmation hearings raises once again certain basic questions regarding the implementation of this constitutional requirement. Is it proper or wise, for instance, for the Senate to judge presidential appointments on the basis of what policies they intend to pursue when in office? Or is it best to presume that the president should be allowed to appoint whomever he desires if the individual meets reasonable tests of probity and competence? Should the number of nominations submitted to the Senate be reduced? Should an effort be made to limit the number of positions within a given agency subject to confirmation? Is an agency under better congressional oversight because twelve of its top executives require confirmation than an agency like the Social Security Administration, which has only one executive subject to confirmation? Should the submission of mass numbers of nominees, such as foreign service officers, be eliminated or modified when constitutionally permissible? These questions suggest the types of questions Congress faces as it attempts to adjust its constitutional requirement to confirm executive appointments to the changing realities of contemporary politics.

Conclusion

How did the Nixon era, and particularly the Ninety-third Congress experience, modify previous appraisals and generalizations, if at all, regarding Senate confirmation as a check upon the president?

The dominant opinion of the pre-Nixon era regarding the utility and desirable limits of the confirmation power were summed up by Professor Harris in his book, mentioned earlier, *The Advice and Consent of the Senate*, in which he concluded:

A drastic reduction in the number of appointments made by the President and confirmed by the Senate would result in a number of significant improvements in the federal service. It would lead to the extension of the career system to many positions now filled by political appointees and would thus make the federal service more attractive to persons of ability. It would enable the government to utilize better the expertness and experience of its qualified, regular employees by advancing them to higher administrative positions now filled by political appointment. It would establish greater internal responsibility for the operation of executive departments and agencies, for subordinate officials would owe undivided loyalty to their administrative superiors. It would give the President and his department heads a freer hand in the selection of their principal assistants, which is essential if they are to be held responsible for the conduct of the government. Instead of weakening, it would strengthen the role of the President as the leader of his party and would lessen the disputes over patronage, which in the past have often marred his relations with the Senate. It would also strengthen the role of the Senate in passing upon the President's selections for the chief policy-determining offices of the government. Nothing is gained by the routine and purely formal approval by the Senate of thousands of appointments of subordinate officials and employees. The Senate has far greater matters which require its attention.[1]

It is symptomatic of the change in academic opinion, to say nothing of congressional opinion, that a conclusion such as that proffered by Professor Harris in 1953 would probably meet resistance or rejection in 1975. Congress has clearly reasserted its prerogative since 1970 in a number of fields and has involved itself to a much greater degree in administrative oversight. One method it has used to further its oversight objectives has been to extend the confirmation requirement to additional offices and to conduct its confirmation hearings with greater zeal and skepticism than in the recent past.

It is difficult to ascertain to what extent this trend toward reasserting its confirmation prerogatives is the result of the normal antagonisms attendant to having the Congress and the presidency in the hands of opposing parties. No doubt partisan feelings have affected judgments. It is also difficult to ignore the impact of Watergate on this institutional relationship. Nevertheless, statutory change is necessary to extend the confirmation requirement. Hence the current congressional interest in the appointment and confirmation process assumes an institutional rather than a strictly partisan character.

The deliberate ambiguity of the Constitution has ensured that the president must share with Congress his power to appoint officers of the United States. If the Senate's confirmation power has not lived up to the expectations of some of its early supporters, neither has it fallen prey to the dire predictions of those who opposed it. Senatorial confirmation is clearly a fundamental part of the political system not likely to be significantly altered. It may be that the confirmation requirement has not contributed so much to the political system by preventing incompetent appointments as it has in keeping communications open between the two branches of government. At least, it serves to remind administrative executives that in addition to serving the president, they also have obligations to the Congress.

---

[1] Joseph P. Harris, *The Advice and Consent of the Senate* (Berkeley: University of California Press, 1953), p. 398.

Congress and the Intelligence Agencies

HARRY HOWE RANSOM

As this is written, Congress is conducting its most com-
prehensive investigation of the United States intelligence establishment.
This multibillion dollar conglomerate of largely secret organizations in-
cludes the Central Intelligence Agency (CIA), Defense Intelligence Agency (DIA), National Security Agency (NSA), together with elements of the
Secret Service, Federal Bureau of Investigation (FBI), State Department,
Atomic Energy Commission, armed services, and a variety of other units.
These were created to gather, interpret, and selectively to communicate
national security information to decision makers, among other purposes.
Investigations by separate select committees in the Senate and House,
which may take a year or longer, are to cap a shorter study to be com-
pleted by mid-1975 by a special presidential commission headed by
Vice President Rockefeller.

Such inquiries stem both from widely publicized scandals and charges
about the use and abuse of secret intelligence agencies and more fundamentally from a breakdown of consensus about the cold war security requirements of the United States. At the heart of the issue is the division
between the president and Congress of control over, and accountability
for, the intelligence agencies.

After 1947 a perceived threat of "World Communism" fostered a vast
arsenal of foreign policy instruments, including espionage and covert
political operations overseas. The management of this mammoth apparatus, unprecedented in peacetime, required highly centralized executive control and in some cases deception, lying, and deep secrecy. National security decisions were taken in a military spirit, using wartime
procedures. But the world has changed, perceptions of the threat have
sharply altered, and in the mid-1970s the earlier consensus about national security is evaporating. Americans now debate the costs versus the

benefits of secrecy, covert political operations overseas, and other so-called intelligence operations.

A new consensus may be growing that the invisible parts of the cold war apparatus now require more firm and detailed congressional supervision. The legitimacy of many of these activities is also open to serious question. The purpose here is to consider one aspect of this subject: congressional oversight of an inherently executive function—secret intelligence.

In analyzing the problem, three basic factors stand out immediately: the definition of the function; its secrecy; and the complexity and dynamism of the separation of powers, a deliberately ambiguous constitutional system. Behind these is the most perplexing problem, whether any democratic way exists to manage and conduct secret warfare, espionage, and covert political operations.

The definitional problem centers on the word "intelligence," which in its proper sense means *information*. In the present context it perhaps may best be defined as follows: "Intelligence deals with what decision makers need to know before choosing a course of action."

The difficulty is that intelligence as a term in common usage has come to have other meanings, such as espionage, covert political intervention, paramilitary action, and, often, counterintelligence. In fact, the term "intelligence" has, in common usage, lost any precise meaning. This loss has obscured rational discourse on the subject. Presidents (e.g., Ford) and even secretaries of defense (e.g., Schlesinger), and directors of central intelligence (e.g., Colby) have exhibited the common, careless habit of referring to "intelligence" as meaning *both* information and secret political action. "Intelligence" has become a cover word.

This is not just a matter of semantics. The sloppy manner in which the conceptual, and consequently the definitional, problems have been addressed has affected the methods of organizing and managing American intelligence agencies. The ambiguities are compounded in the question of what Congress intended to create in 1947 as a central intelligence agency, as well as in the current question of what Congress is willing to authorize under the heading of "intelligence activities." Perhaps intelligence is a term like "national security" that exists in an "Alice in Wonderland" world where words can mean whatever one capriciously says that they mean. If legitimacy and accountability are the central problems, conceptual confusion about "intelligence" makes solutions difficult.

A second problem, secrecy, pervades this subject and limits its consideration to an inevitably partial view. For example, beyond the National Security Act of 1947 and the 1949 amendments dealing with the CIA, outsiders cannot examine the supersecret National Security Council intelligence directives or the CIA directives that detail the functions, jurisdictions, and operational codes of the various intelligence agencies. Even on Capitol Hill, the matter of how Congress conducts its surveillance role over the intelligence community is a matter not often candidly discussed. Access to internal records is inevitably an obstacle in the way of any such study. Outside scholars and even congressional investigators commonly encounter such obstacles.

The complexity of the American constitutional system is a third problem. The division of powers between the president and Congress is deliberately ambiguous. Moreover, in reality, there is no such thing—except abstractly—as "president" or "Congress." Each is a confederation of numerous subsystems, often working at cross purposes. Indeed, in the executive branch, the State Department, Pentagon, or CIA patently do not always speak with one voice. Just so, the committees and subcommittees of the House and Senate are rarely unified into a coherent and identifiable locus of power that can be called "Congress." If it is hard to focus executive responsibility for the intelligence system, focusing congressional accountability is an even greater challenge.

In the context of these underlying considerations, several questions may be asked about Congress and the intelligence agencies: What did Congress intend and specifically authorize by statute in creating the CIA? How does Congress exercise the oversight function, and does the "watchdog" have either a bark or teeth? Should Congress have equal access with the executive branch to all intelligence estimates and reports? What are the potentialities and limitations of congressional oversight regarding very sensitive clandestine operations, and what structural reforms are needed?

Statutory Authority

The CIA was established in a legal sense by section 102 of the National Security Act of 1947. But just as there was a treasury under the Articles of Confederation before the Treasury Department Act of 1789, so the 1947 statute did not start from scratch. The CIA's predecessor, the Office of Strategic Services (OSS) had existed at least since 1942 when it was established by executive order. During the war the OSS had engaged in covert paramilitary operations as well as in gathering intelligence. The function of the National Security Act in this respect was to specify and so legitimize what were to be the continuing powers and duties of the newly chartered agency. Because legislation is at the heart of the oversight function, it is important to give careful attention to the initial central intelligence statute. So far as the public records show, members of Congress thought they were creating merely an intelligence agency, that is to say, an organization with an information function. Nothing in the 1947 House or Senate published hearings suggests that Congress intended to create, or knew it was creating, an agency for paramilitary operations or foreign political interventions.

Analysis of the Senate hearings on the proposed CIA reveals several major points. First, the testimony made very clear that an agency to gather foreign intelligence, and nothing more, was being proposed. Second, senators were emphatically assured that the statute essentially did nothing more than incorporate functions already assignd to the temporary Central Intelligence Group by presidential directive. No mention was made in the public hearings of covert political operations, psychological warfare, paramilitary operations, or other forms of strategic warfare, though these were activities that the OSS knew well. And, third, Hoyt Vandenberg, an air force general, who was serving as director of central intelligence under the temporary organization, stated flatly that the CIA would have no security functions within the United States. This, he told senators, would guarantee that the CIA could never become a gestapo.

House committee hearings produced somewhat more pointed questions. These included: Was the CIA going to have "operational" activities? Was the assignment of the CIA's functions too vague? Was its purpose to be foreign intelligence only? Should the CIA's authority be more strictly limited? Should the agency be headed by a civilian or military director? Did the creation of the new agency open the door to a potential gestapo?

Witnesses from the government gave reassuring answers to all such questions. In neither House nor Senate committee was there sustained discussion of intelligence policy, organization, or control procedures. It should be noted that primary attention focused during this period on the armed services "unification" aspects of the legislation. Yet Congress was left with the impression that an organization for gathering foreign intelligence, with no domestic intelligence functions, was the limit of the CIA section of the proposed statute. It would coordinate, screen, and evaluate what other agencies gathered. It would work for the president, free of the self-serving bias of a departmental location.

House and Senate reports were cursory. Reacting to some criticisms, the House report undertook to spell out CIA functions, specifically prohibiting any internal security functions. Little analysis, however, was given to the intelligence aspects of the legislation. Debates on the floor of the House and Senate were similarly brief. Virtually without debate the measure was adopted.

Some argue that the 1947 statute creating the CIA was deliberately designed as a flexible charter, permitting the loose interpretations that were to occur later. These phrases are cited: "such additional services as the NSC determines" or "other functions and duties." But it seems clear that the congressional intent was to have all such assigned functions, in the words of the statute, "related to intelligence" or "for the benefit of intelligence agencies." Congress ultimately insisted that the functions of the CIA be specified in the 1947 statute. Speaking in 1974, Senator John Stennis, senior Senate CIA "watchdog," observed that although he came to the Senate soon after the original statute was passed, nothing was clearer than the fact that the CIA was created only for the purpose of foreign intelligence. Stennis was later quoted as disapproving of such missions as "destabilizing" the Allende government in Chile. He was said to favor prohibiting such operations in the future.

When the legislation was amended in 1949 by the Central Intelligence Agency Act, committee hearings were secret. The 1949 legislation expanded the powers of the director of central intelligence, exempted the agency from statutory limits on spending, and authorized the director to spend federal funds for "objects of a confidential, extraordinary, or emergency nature" on his personal voucher. The director's existing authority to protect intelligence sources and methods from disclosure was strengthened. The CIA became expressly exempt from normal legislative requirements for disclosure of details about organization, functions, or number of personnel employed. Its budgeted funds after 1949 were concealed in the general accounts of other agencies, particularly the Department of Defense. The effect of this was to remove CIA operations even further from congressional oversight. The agency had a license to answer only to the president.

The legislative history of the 1949 act, like the 1947 legislation, nevertheless gives no indication that Congress was informed of expanded CIA roles. In a letter to Chan Gurney, chairman of the Senate Armed Services Committee, CIA Director Hillenkoetter referred to the CIA's function as simply "the coordination and production of foreign intelligence pertaining to the national security." He did make clear that the agency would be operating overseas and that this required special secrecy. No hint was given that covert political action was being subsumed under the CIA's original charter.

After secret hearings, House and Senate committee reports stressed the need for confidentiality, noting the sensitivity of intelligence operational details. A few members in each house complained of the secrecy. But House members were assured by the bill's floor manager on two points: the CIA had no internal security functions and it operated only in the field of foreign intelligence. The bill passed in the House 348 to 4 and by voice vote in the Senate.

One view of the matter is summed up in Senator William Proxmire's comments in the Senate in June 1974 (during a discussion of an amendment limiting the CIA's domestic functions): "Senators will notice that nowhere in the 1947 act is the CIA given authority to operate covertly overseas. Nowhere in the language is this spelled out. There is nothing about 'dirty tricks,' nothing about overthrowing governments or sabotage." The same may be said of the 1949 statute.

Yet when William Colby, director of central intelligence, was asked in September 1974 whether he believed that adequate statutory authority existed for the conduct of covert operations, he said yes, that the flexible nature of the legislation coupled with congressional acquiescence (through its intelligence subcommittees) provided adequate authority.

When Congress established the CIA in 1947 and expanded the authority of its director in 1949, other existing government intelligence units were by no means eliminated, though the FBI gave up its extensive World War II intelligence operations in Latin America. After 1947 its activities were confined to counterintelligence within the United States. In the quarter-century of cold war, existing intelligence agencies grew in size, and new ones were created, notably the National Security Agency, created by executive order in 1952, and the Defense Intelligence Agency, created by a Department of Defense directive in 1961. It is worth noting that these two enormous institutions, NSA and DIA, were created by executive fiat rather than congressional statute.

Meanwhile, advancing technology constantly offered new tools for each step in the intelligence process, from collection through evaluation and interpretation to dissemination. And so additional giant bureaucracies arose, such as the air force's National Reconnaissance Office (NRO) for globe encircling surveillance by satellites and the National Photo Interpretation Center (NPIC). These units have remained as much a mystery to most members of Congress as they have to the public. The proliferation of organizations, bureaus, mechanical apparatus, and personnel boosted the annual cost of foreign intelligence to billions of dollars.

Some idea of the size and cost of the intelligence system was disclosed by Senator William Proxmire who inserted the following figures on annual budgets and on personnel strength into the April 10, 1973, *Congressional Record*: Defense Intelligence Agency, $100 million, 5,000 employees; air force, $2.8 billion, 60,000; army, $775 million, 38,500; navy, $775 million, 15,000; State Department, $8 million, 335; and National Security Agency, $1 billion, 20,000. Total personnel of the system was estimated at 150,000 and the overall budget at $6.2 billion.

In theory, the director of central intelligence, as the president's principal intelligence adviser, presides over the allocation of resources of this entire system. Just so, Congress, with the constitutional power of the purse, theoretically oversees the policies, organization, and efficiency of this vast army of intelligence workers. But the reality is considerably short of this. Neither Congress nor the director of central intelligence appears to have meaningful control. Therefore, it is difficult to focus policy or managerial responsibility or accountability on any particular place within the executive or legislative branches. In the absence of such accountability, "oversight" as currently exercised is best defined in the dictionary's other meaning of the word —"overlooking" or the absence of careful attention. The argument is not that congressional attention to the intelligence system has been absent. But such attention has been sporadic, unsystematic, incomplete, and at times casual, as will be detailed below. If this is so, Congress is susceptible to manipulation by the executive branch.

Varieties of Oversight

The 1947 and 1949 legislation set some of the parameters for oversight, marked by delegation and abdication and a posture of self-restraint. Most discussion of oversight centers on the formal committee structure for legislation or appropriations. A realistic evaluation, however, requires attention to the full spectrum of congressional activity. At one end is the legislative and appropriations function, at which Congress operates in its basic constitutional role. At the other end is the individual legislator, operating in a political or partisan context, seeking to gain whatever attention he can to his particular viewpoint. Between these two poles a wide range of activities can occur with a bearing on oversight. Along the most important of these are giving "advice and consent" (in the Senate) on nominations, ad hoc investigations, resolutions or other parliamentary devices aimed at restricting or changing the intelligence system or sometimes designed only for symbolic or publicity impact, accounting and auditing by the General Accounting Office, and the appointment of special commissions or select committees for investigations. This composite activity produces an often overlooked "backdrop" effect, which will be described after a discussion of the formal congressional structure for intelligence oversight.

To the extent that Congress formally monitors the various intelligence agencies, its surveillance emanates from four separate units on Capitol Hill, which control legislation and appropriations. In the Senate and House, the Armed Services and Appropriations committees have designated specific members as intelligence "watchdogs." A total of eleven members in the Senate and nineteen in the House have the formal responsibility for monitoring intelligence. At issue is whether the work of these groups is a sufficiently thorough and detached audit for this multibillion dollar intelligence system.

In their more active years the House subcommittees have met around a half-dozen times annually, spending perhaps as much as fifteen to twenty hours a year on oversight. But the absence of a substantial staff or of a record of the committees' hearings or reports may make even this amount of time ineffective. Exceptions would be special ad hoc investigations, such as Watergate-related matters and the current work of Senate and House select committees.

The Senate Armed Services and the Appropriations intelligence subcommittees have been similarly inactive over the years. Initially, they met separately. In the 1960s, however, because of overlapping membership, the two groups met jointly. The late Senator Richard Russell was chairman of both subcommittees for several years; during this period there was only one Senate subcommittee. Staff assistance for the Senate subcommittees has been minimal much of the time. Over the years, until recently, the Senate subcommittees met no more than two or three times a year.

There have been a number of basic criticisms of the activities of the House and Senate intelligence subcommittees. In order of importance, these are as follows: They tend not so much to control or criticize the system as to protect it from its critics. They meet very infrequently. They have little or no staff, and with rare exceptions publish no hearings or reports, do not keep normal transcripts, and do not communicate their findings to their colleagues in the House or Senate or to the public. They are inhibited in conversations with colleagues by being privy to some state secrets. In a word, they appear to have been co-opted by the intelligence system and do not seem to function as independent critics.

Congress exercises its power of the purse in a limited, secret process for CIA funding. Funds for the CIA are secretly transferred from the appropriations of other agencies. This is managed through the Office of Management and Budget, informed by the chairmen of the House and Senate appropriations committees. Amounts or sources of funds are not disclosed to the full appropriations committees or to Congress generally. House and Senate intelligence subcommittees hold secret meetings to review proposed annual budgets with intelligence officials. In the House, detailed records of these hearings are kept, but the transcripts are held in the CIA's custody. The House appears to have a more careful appropriations scrutiny than the Senate. In 1975 the House substantially increased the number of members active in oversight.

Armed Services intelligence subcommittees also are said to be consulted on the annual intelligence budget by CIA officials. Public statements by various senators assigned as intelligence "watchdogs" raise doubts as to the care with which they have scrutinized intelligence budgets or have been fully informed by CIA officials. Post-Watergate signs point to a more vigorous scrutiny. Yet the process remains a secret one, designed in a wartime rather than peacetime spirit. Congress is doubly deceived, voting blindly on CIA-inflated funds for other agencies, which are then secretly transferred to CIA in amounts unknown to most congressmen. Committees dealing with foreign affairs until recently were frozen out of the process.

Who are these watchdogs? The *Congressional Quarterly* reported that the oversight subcommittees as constituted in 1973 were biased in favor of intelligence agencies. The American Security Council, a private group, "graded" members in terms of their voting for a large defense establishment. In the House, ten of the twelve oversight committee members were given 100 percent favorable ASC ratings, one received 90 percent, and one received zero (House Intelligence Subcommittee Chairman Lucien Nedzi). Of the nine senators, three received 100 percent, four received 80 percent or better, and the remaining two received ratings of 33 and 10 percent (Pastore and Symington).

Defenders of the adequacy of present congressional supervision of intelligence activities point to the existence of the four subcommittees just mentioned. The official stand of the CIA is that the agency keeps the House and Senate subcommittees informed on every aspect of its operations, programs, budget, and personnel strength and provides periodic briefings on world events. The agency also claims to be in almost daily contact with the chairmen and staff members of the four subcommittees. The agency also, on request, briefs a number of other congressional committees on substantive issues.

For the period 1967-72, the agency has said it averaged annually some twenty-three such briefings. Briefings for individual congressmen are also given, averaging some eighty a year. In the same period, there were more than one thousand written communications, and 1,450 personal contacts a year between CIA officials and individual congressmen. In September 1974, CIA Director Colby reported that CIA officials appeared before eighteen committees on twenty-eight occasions during the year (Armed Services, Appropriations, Foreign Affairs, Atomic Energy, and Joint Economic), testifying on numerous subjects. Recent reports and charges of scandals have substantially increased this interaction.

A strong move was made in the Senate in 1956, under the leadership of Mike Mansfield, to create a joint congressional committee on intelligence activities. After a substantial debate on the floor, the Mansfield resolution was defeated by a vote of 59 to 27. Among those voting for it was John F. Kennedy; among those opposing, Lyndon B. Johnson. Apparently, the Senate's "Inner Club" killed the measure, on the assumption that a handful of congressional leaders could know, if they wished, all they need to know about the intelligence system.

The issue was debated again in 1966 when Eugene McCarthy, a member of the Senate Foreign Relations Committee, attempted to have that committee investigate United States intelligence activities abroad. Failing that, McCarthy pushed for a compromise proposal, to include several members of the Foreign Relations Committee on the Senate's intelligence surveillance subcommittee (Armed Services). This mild measure failed in a Senate expression of confidence in the existing structure, by a vote of 61 to 28. Later, senior members of the Foreign Relations Committee were invited to be guest members of the oversight committee.

In debates over such proposals the basic question has been, How thorough is congressional surveillance? Because the existing watchdog committees have had limited staffs, as such, and because for most of their history they have kept no records or minutes, and because committee members are reticent in discussing procedures, it is difficult to judge precisely how careful is the oversight process. The impression is strong, however, that surveillance has been sporadic and timid and the oversight committees have been vulnerable to manipulation by the intelligence establishment.

To summarize: Congress has a committee structure for monitoring the intelligence community. Knowledge of its workings is incomplete; it is currently in a dynamic state with new procedures and jurisdictions still to be tested. Certain types of information apparently are given only to the chairmen and ranking minority members of oversight subcommittees. The other members have appeared to be both complacent and decidedly reticent; they have probably been to some degree uninformed.

Since 1947, more than two hundred bills have been introduced in Congress to expand the system for congressional supervision of the intelligence community. To date, only one has been enacted, although recent changes in procedures foretell more active oversight. Up to 1975, presidents and directors of central intelligence have no doubt manipulated the structure to some extent. The director in 1974 publicly stated his position that how Congress exercises its oversight is for Congress to decide. In the current reexamination of oversight, congressional leaders no doubt will be influenced by the judgments of intelligence professionals as to the dangers of more detailed oversight, as well as by the political advantages and disadvantages of different systems of oversight.

The Congressional "Backdrop"

Those who focus on the formal structure of congressional controls usually find them inadequate. But often overlooked is the congressional "backdrop," or what may be called the "hit and run" role. Congress is a formidable presence always in the minds of leaders of the executive agencies. They know that what Congress gave in the way of discretionary authority to, for example, the director of the CIA in 1947 and 1949, Congress can take back. They know, too, that in the changing temper of the times, Congress can demand information about secret operations that it has been content to let lie hidden in the past, and to judge it now by different standards. And they now know that by leaks or by the acts of disaffected former employees, facts will come to light that may reveal that Congress and the public have been duped, by silence or by half-truths or cover stories. The "top secret" or other higher secret classification labels are no longer guarantees of secrecy. In various ways, then, the existence of Congress with its several roles and ultimate authority exerts real pressures and constraints on the executive.

One feature of the congressional "backdrop" is the Senate role in the confirmation of CIA directors. President Kennedy's nomination of John McCone was opposed on the Senate floor in 1962; similarly, President Nixon's nomination of William Colby stirred opposition in 1973. Floor debate allowed members to put the incoming directors on notice, even though barely a dozen votes were finally cast in opposition in each case. With Colby's nomination, substantial hearings were held that, for the first time, were published. During the hearings the nominee was forced to go on public record with regard to important issues.

Another potential oversight tool is the General Accounting Office, established in 1921 as an independent, nonpartisan investigative arm of Congress, among its other duties, and with a broad charter. Yet the GAO has not performed an effective auditing function with regard to the CIA. Its efforts over the years to investigate the CIA have been effectively rebuffed by the CIA's use of security regulations. Without clearance that the CIA controlled, no one had access to its buildings, let alone to files, records, or people within them. So the CIA has been in a position to thwart comprehensive GAO audits of agency operations. Presumably this could occur only with some congressional acquiesence, since the GAO has stood high in congressional favor.

Additionally, the actions of individual members can have an oversight impact. During the CIA's lifetime various members have individually done battle, proposing CIA or congressional reform, opposing presidential nominations, or releasing information not intended for public consumption. To cite only one recent example: in December 1974 Representative Michael Harrington (Democrat, Massachusetts) sued Messrs. Colby, Kissinger, and Simon, seeking to enjoin the CIA from certain allegedly illegal activities and to force public disclosure of certain CIA expenditures. The congressman claimed "standing" to sue on the basis of his constitutional duties as a member of Congress. The federal courts may dismiss this suit as a "political" rather than a justiciable question, and the congressman, first selected in 1969, has been a maverick activist, outside the centers of influence in his party. But so was Senator Proxmire when he started criticizing the military. In 1975 Harrington was appointed to Congressman Nedzi's Select Committee on Intelligence.

Without going into detail, other examples of "hit and run" congressional activity are as follows:

- The Cuban missile crisis, 1962, in which the Senate Preparedness Investigating Subcommittee found that intelligence agencies had performed poorly and were guilty of substantial errors of information and judgment.
- The Pueblo incident, 1968, in which a House Armed Services sub-

committee noted serious shortcomings in intelligence policy, organization, and control.

• The Symington investigation of the secret war in Laos, 1970–71, in which a Senate Foreign Relations subcommittee revealed that the United States was participating in a CIA-managed "secret war" in Laos, without congressional authorization or knowledge.

• Secret funding of Radio Free Europe, in which the Senate, starting in 1971 under the initiative of Senator Clifford Case and others, forced the end of the secret CIA subsidy to RFE and Radio Liberty, which had been initiated in 1950. Congressional opposition earlier had influenced the cessation of secret CIA subsidies to dozens of private American groups, including the National Students Association. Such disclosures made the CIA a special target of a college-age generation already on the rampage.

• Restraints on the foreign aid bill, in which Congress, in early 1972, passed a foreign aid authorization bill placing new and unprecedented controls on the cost, operations, and personnel of the CIA, prohibiting the transfer of funds from the Pentagon. The purpose was to prevent secret warfare from developing in Cambodia as it had in Laos. Far more restrictive legislation was passed in late 1974, limiting the CIA to foreign information gathering only, unless the president certified to appropriate congressional committees (including the Foreign Relations and International Relations committees) that covert political action is a vital national necessity.

• Investigation of the CIA role in Watergate-related matters, in which the House Armed Services Subcommittee on Intelligence under Chairman Lucien Nedzi investigated, in 1973, the improper use of the CIA by the White House in domestic political action. Revision of the 1947 CIA legislation to prevent future abuses was recommended.

Other examples of this sort could be cited, such as congressional investigations and public reports on the U-2 incident in 1960, the Bay of Pigs in 1961, Senator Howard Baker's special investigation, as part of the Ervin committee probe, of the CIA's involvement in Watergate, Senator Frank Church's investigation of CIA-ITT cooperation in Chile, and other intelligence scandals, including still unfolding Watergate-related matters.

All such events are part of an interactive and dynamic political process in which Congress and the executive are perenially engaged. One may be certain, too, that leaders of the intelligence community seek opportunities for quiet lobbying with Congress. For example, the CIA grants discreet favors to individual legislators from time to time, such as providing material for speeches or special favors overseas, or gives them confidential briefings. Hard evidence about these assumed "interactions" is seldom available, but surely they are part of the system.

Conclusion

Political science offers no conclusive theory that precisely prescribes the role of Congress in the formulation of foreign and defense policy. Problems of policy, organization, and control of secret intelligence agencies pose perhaps the sharpest dilemmas in this regard. Secret operations by definition require secrecy. Democratic government by definition requires accountability with full disclosure at least to representative groups in Congress. And democratic government also requires respect for law and adherence to constitutional principles.

The CIA and the related vast apparatus for secret intelligence face a crisis of legitimacy and accountability. Congress did not, on the record, intend to create what the intelligence system has become. And Congress has played a minor and casual role in the evolution of the intelligence establishment. It is an executive creation, perhaps largely self-generated, that has until lately lived and grown in the shadow of congressional acquiescence. The system for congressional oversight has operated within a wartime ethos. Watchdog committees have been created, but they have assumed that it is too dangerous to ask certain questions. So the tendency has been to accept the leadership of the intelligence system on faith. In recent times, as perceptions of the world order have changed, the legitimacy of the intelligence structure has become debatable.

Furthermore, Congress has uneven access to the product of the intelligence system. So legislators, when consulted, may not be informed participants in the formation of national security policy. More dangerously, members of Congress are individually and collectively subject to the manipulation of an executive that holds a monopoly on important elements of foreign information. Conversely, when they doubt executive credibility, they may be a prey to unfounded rumors and plants from unofficial and unfriendly sources.

A different problem relates to the other type of function that is carried out under the CIA roof, covert political operations overseas. These represent, in most cases, acts of extreme coercion, indeed, acts of war. The Constitution, however, assigns to Congress the authority to declare war. And so the legitimacy of covert operations has also become an issue.

Accountability in a democratic government applies not only to the executive. It should also apply to Congress. If it is difficult to focus accountability on a vast executive bureaucracy, and perhaps unrealistic to expect accountability from secret agents, it is infinitely more difficult to hold Congress accountable. But one should not overlook the extensive "backdrop" role played by segments of Congress. It goes some distance in meeting congressional responsibilities while enforcing executive accountability.

Congress has recently reasserted itself with regard to the intelligence agencies. No attempt has been made in this essay to detail the various current changes in procedure and jurisdiction that may have profound impact on future oversight and on intelligence operations. Perhaps most significant are a major investigation by a Senate select committee with a large and talented investigative staff and a less extensive inquiry by a House select committee, both just beginning in mid-1975. These promise the most intensive investigation of the past quarter-century and offer an opportunity to analyze the problems and to reform the structure.

Major structural reform of the intelligence system and the congressional oversight process is needed and will likely result from these inquiries. The basic statute needs rewriting, Congress needs guaranteed access to the intelligence product, and a joint congressional committee on intelligence is a must. If these solutions are chosen, they will not ensure perfect executive-legislative balance. Pragmatic rather than doctrinaire solutions are preferable, and the system must remain adaptable to fluctuations in international politics and shifting assessments of the national interest. America has always used a sliding scale with markers between peace and war by which it judges the legitimacy of governmental functions.

A newly legitimized intelligence system is now an urgent need. For never before has the American polity had a greater requirement for intelligence in government. But intelligence (knowledge) is power, and since power corrupts, it must be counterbalanced. And that is the role of Congress.

Congress and Foreign Policy: The Nixon Years

EDWARD A. KOLODZIEJ

Henry Kissinger, like the two presidents he has served, has criticized "the growing tendency of Congress to legislate in detail the day-to-day or week-to-week conduct of our foreign affairs." "American policy," argued the secretary of state, "given the wide range of our interests and responsibilities—must be a coherent and purposeful whole."[1] The secretary implied that Congress's participation in foreign affairs lacked the "coherence and purpose" that only the executive branch and the president could provide.

This view can hardly be dismissed as peculiar to the secretary of state. Most students of American politics since the Great Depression and World War II have leaned toward this view, assigning Congress a limited role in foreign affairs. As one eminent analyst has noted, "Congress has, like Bagehot's queen, 'the right to be consulted, the right to encourage, the right to warn.' "[2] Those who have argued for an enlarged role for Congress have despaired over the capacity of the legislative branch to discharge it in the absence of reform.[3] Even those who have become disenchanted with presidential leadership in foreign affairs, especially since the Vietnam war, have looked elsewhere than to Congress, which has been considered impotent or distracted, for institutional mechanisms to oversee American interests abroad.[4]

A look at the Nixon years suggests that there may be a greater coher-

---

[1] U.S., *Department of State Bulletin*, 72, No. 1860 (February 17, 1975), p. 203.

[2] Samuel P. Huntington, "Strategic Planning and the Political Process," *Foreign Affairs* 38 (January 1960), 287.

[3] See, for example, Joseph S. Clark, *Congress: The Sapless Branch*, rev. ed. (New York: Harper & Row, 1965).

[4] Arthur M. Schlesinger, Jr., "Presidential War: 'See If You Can Fix Any Limit to His Power," *New York Times Magazine*, February 15, 1974, p. 12ff.

ence and purpose to congressional behavior in security and foreign policy than the secretary's view—or the view of many congressional experts—will admit.[5] First, Congress has again accepted the invitation of the Constitution "to struggle," in the words of Edward S. Corwin, "for the privilege of directing American foreign policy."[6] Congress's impact on foreign and security policy, discussed in more detail below, has been felt principally in its passage of the War Powers Act and in its unilateral limitation of the United States commitment to Southeast Asia. Congress has also curtailed appropriations for economic and military assistance abroad, motivated by perceptions of limited American capacity to shape international developments abroad, especially in the Third World, of the flawed experience of United States interventions in the internal and external affairs of other states, and of growing opposition and economic troubles at home. In close conjunction with these trends, Congress has moved on a number of fronts to focus public attention on previously overlooked aspects of American foreign policy operations, whose continuation ignored congressional prerogatives in foreign policy decision making, overextended American commitments and resources, or threatened domestic institutions and freedoms.

Second, increased congressional influence on American foreign policy has led to the amendment but by no means the abandonment of the United States global role in world politics. American military-political obligations, other than those in Southeast Asia, have received sustained congressional support despite vocal opposition to some of them (e.g., troops in Europe) expressed in both houses. In the case of Israel, American commitments have been reinforced through sizeable military and economic assistance and diplomatic support. Congress continued to underwrite administration requests for increased defense spending while evidencing an interest, through its budgetary decisions, in defining weapons systems, force levels, and troop deployments. The concept of "Fortress America" had little appeal in congressional debates or decisions during the Nixon years. Neither did the role of world policeman, based on the assumption that security was indivisible, command the adherence of a majority of legislators.

Third, and at the broadest level of generalization, congressional action in foreign policy during the Nixon years served to raise serious doubts about the applicability of the cold war thesis, embodied initially in the Truman Doctrine, that the preservation of American security,

[5] The forthcoming book by Alton Frey, *A Responsible Congress: The Politics of National Security*, is an exception.

[6] Edward S. Corwin, *The President: Office and Powers, 1787-1957* (New York: New York University Press, 1957), p. 200. For recent discussions see Louis Fisher, *President and Congress: Power and Policy* (New York: The Free Press, 1972) and Arthur M. Schlesinger, Jr., *The Imperial Presidency* (Boston: Houghton Mifflin, 1973).

democratic institutions, and social and economic welfare was inextricably bound up with their realization abroad. The trend of recent congressional thinking swelled support for the proposition that national and international problems do not always admit to universal solutions. What works for Americans may not work for others. For those problems requiring global solutions (say, in keeping the environment clean), it is not necessarily the sole, nor primary, responsibility of the United States to effect the required changes in the habits of other peoples or in the policies of their governments. It is possible, however regrettable, that Americans may be able to enjoy the benefits of physical security, free institutions, and social and economic well-being without their having been accepted by or extended to other nations. Indeed, efforts to assure their possessions by all peoples, suggested by the lamentable experience of the Vietnam war, transgress the limits of American will, resources, interest, or obligation, and threaten their preservation at home.

I

The power of Congress to declare war and to influence decisions before and after the outbreak of hostilities has been, until very recently, a casualty of historical precedent and of the exigencies of modern warfare. A large and substantial body of precedents has accumulated and underwritten the president's authority to use force without prior congressional approval. Lincoln justified his violation of the Constitution in calling up troops without prior legislative authorization by relying on his oath of office to defend the Constitution and his authority as commander in chief. Drawing on reasoning most eloquently developed in rationalizing his suspension of habeas corpus, Lincoln asked: "Are all the laws *but one* to go unexecuted and the Government itself go to pieces lest that one be violate?"[7]

Since then chief executives have buttressed the president's right to use American armed forces against foreign people. McKinley acted with questionable authority in consenting to orders of subordinates who sent Dewey to Manila and, later, in dispatching occupation forces to the Philippines. Wilson armed American merchant ships and Roosevelt exchanged American destroyers for English bases without congressional consent. These actions staged America's entry into World Wars I and II. Truman justified American intervention in the Korean war as a police action, not as a war declared by Congress. Kennedy similarly acted on his own authority in the Cuban crises of 1961 and 1962. When Johnson led the United States into the Vietnam war and when Nixon continued American involvement, they called upon long established

[7] Corwin, p. 64.

precedents of presidential initiative and congressional acquiescence to justify their actions. Precedent combined with the needs of modern warfare and America's containment strategy to augment presidential claims. The responsibility of the president to repel attack and to protect American lives and property was recognized from the inception of the Constitution when Congress was given the power to "declare," not "make," war. The concept of defensive war enlarged these responsibilities. Since American containment policy posited a global military network, United States security became identified with its foreign commitments and military deployments. Defending this structure of obligations and protecting American troops overseas became sufficient justifications for Presidents Johnson and Nixon to use additional force (bombing of North Vietnam and mining of Haiphong harbor) and to extend the field of American military operations across national frontiers without congressional consent (Cambodia).

Serious congressional efforts to restrict the president's power, on his own authority, to commit the government to the use of American forces began with the Senate's passage by a vote of 70–16 of a "national commitments" resolution in 1969. It stated "that a national commitment . . . means the use of the armed forces on foreign territory, or a promise to assist a foreign country, government, or people by the use of armed forces or financial resources of the United States . . . and . . . a national commitment . . . results only from the affirmative action taken by the Legislative and Executive Branches . . . by means of a treaty, statute, or concurrent resolution of both Houses of Congress. . . ."[8]

Meanwhile, efforts continued to restrict the president's discretion in committing the United States in Southeast Asia or in employing American forces in the area. In December 1969, an amendment to the defense appropriations bill prohibited the president from introducing ground troops in Laos and Thailand. This restriction did not hinder the president from ordering a military incursion into Cambodia in the spring of 1970. The president's action made Cambodia a charge of the United States, enlarged civil strife, and threw American support behind the now defunct Lon Nol regime at the expense of other competing groups, including the ultimately victorious Khmer Rouge.

The American military action was taken with the cooperation of the Cambodian and South Vietnamese governments, but in the absence of preceding congressional knowledge or approval. A six month debate subsequently ensued in Congress, centered in the Senate, to limit American involvement in Cambodia. A modification of an amendment, introduced by Senators John Sherman Cooper and Frank Church, to the 1970 for-

[8] *Congressional Quarterly Almanac*, 1973, p. 177.

eign military sales bill was finally accepted by President Nixon and incorporated into the supplemental foreign aid law for FY 1971. It prohibited funds for United States ground combat troops or advisers in Cambodia and denied that United States aid to Cambodia committed the United States to defend the country. These restrictions were later broadened and extended in 1973 and 1974 to forbid "the use of any past or present appropriations for financing directly or indirectly United States combat activities in or over or from off the shores of North Vietnam, South Vietnam, Laos, or Cambodia."[9] Impetus for congressional action came after it was disclosed that the United States had been carrying on bombing runs over Cambodia and had utilized helicopter gun ships in circumvention of legislative intent in banning ground troops. As these legislative maneuvers unfolded, an estimated $890.5 million in military and $503 million in economic aid flowed into Cambodia between 1971 and 1974. It had been less than $50,000 in 1969.

Repeated failures to constrain presidential war-making powers led Congress, over President Nixon's veto, to pass the War Powers Act of 1973. It reasserted congressional authority in making war and provided a legislative standard for constitutional prescription. Under the act, the president is exhorted to consult Congress before using armed forces. The president can commit troops only under defined circumstances: a congressional declaration of war, specific legislative authorization, or a defensive reaction to protect armed forces under direct or imminent attack. The president is permitted to commit troops for sixty days with a possible extension for thirty days. Beyond this period, Congress must authorize the commitment of forces. No action by Congress is tantamount to a withdrawal of congressional approval. A concurrent resolution, however, can be passed at any time to disengage American troops from hostilities, and this action is not subject to presidential veto.

That this legislation, when combined with the power of the purse, has had effect was suggested by President Ford's remarks at his news conference of April 3, 1975, reported in press dispatches the next day, and his meeting with television reporters on April 21. In both appearances he blamed Congress for restricting his discretion to aid South Vietnam and for its failure to provide adequate military and economic aid to defend that country. Congress cut the administration's $1.45 billion request for aid in 1974 to $700 million. Additional requests amounting to $522 million in 1975 were not acted upon. The president's request for $725 million in military assistance on April 10 in the wake of the military collapse in South Vietnam was rejected by Congress. Only his recommendation for more humanitarian aid was considered. The president was granted authority, however, to use armed forces to protect Americans

<hr>

[9] Ibid., p. 792.

and Vietnamese being evacuated from South Vietnam. In extending this limited authority to the president, Congress implicitly asserted its right to withdraw even that much if changed conditions so warranted.

Congress has moved in other areas to assert its authority over foreign and security affairs. The Tonkin and Formosa resolutions were repealed. Ceilings on aid spending, especially for Southeast Asia, were set. One-year authorizations for State Department, Peace Corps, and USIA money bills were instituted to permit closer scrutiny of agency activities rather than continuing the practice of long-term authorizations. (The Armed Services committees, which pass on defense procurement and research and development authorizations, had reestablished their right to annual reviews over a decade earlier.) After President Nixon's offer of civilian nuclear aid to Egypt, Congress strengthened its control over nuclear policy, requiring prior approval by the legislative branch of the sale of military or civilian nuclear equipment and facilities.

President Ford and Secretary of State Kissinger also experienced congressional displeasure in the administration's management of the economic and military aid program. A majority in Congress objected to assistance to the Ankara regime in the face of its invasion of Cyprus. The Turkish action violated legislative restrictions on the use of United States military equipment. The Ford administration's refusal to accede to congressional demands to conform to assistance laws prompted Congress to reject military aid requests of $80 million and $90 million in credits and to impose a February 5, 1975, cutoff on aid until Turkey observed the cease-fire, stopped increasing its troops on Cyprus, and ceased shipping war materials to the island. The overthrow of the Athens junta and the installation of a more democratic government also swayed some congressional sentiment to favor Greece.

Similarly, Congress attached conditions to trade with the Soviet Union on a most-favored-nation status until it relaxed emigration restrictions on its nationals. Moscow responded by renouncing the trade accords reached between President Nixon and Premier Brezhnev in 1972. Moving further, trade concessions were denied OPEC nations (Organization of Petroleum Exporting Countries) whether they participated in the 1973–74 oil embargo or not. These actions earned presidential condemnation as detrimental to American relations with the Soviet Union, Ecuador, Venezuela, Nigeria, and Indonesia. Additional limitations were placed on military aid to Chile, South Korea, and the use of the Food for Peace program for political purposes. What is striking about these varied congressional restrictions is the broad base of congressional support that they enjoyed. The Turkish, Soviet, and OPEC measures, for example, were voted by a bipartisan majority of Democratic and Republican legislators.[10]

[10] *Congressional Quarterly Weekly Review*, March 8, 1975, pp. 479-81.

These varied congressional attempts to define American commitments and to restrain presidential discretion in engaging American power do not necessarily signify a withdrawal from all American foreign obligations or a weakening of those already established. In the Middle East, the United States commitment to Israel, measured by military and economic asistance and diplomatic support, increased after the Yom Kippur War. Requests for aid won overwhelming approval in Congress, and on several occasions Congress increased administration assistance for Israel in direct grants and credits. A published letter signed by seventy-six senators in May 1975 asked President Ford to be "responsive to Israel's urgent needs" for such help. American diplomacy in the region meanwhile received tangible congressional bolstering in an authorization of $250 million for economic assistance to Egypt, pending progress toward a Middle East settlement. Repeated attempts to decrease American troop levels in Europe largely failed. The FY 1975 defense authorization called for an overall 18,000 troop cutback in Europe, but allowed this number to be offset by an increase in the component of combat troops there. The United States position in Europe remained basically stable. Whatever doubts may be raised about the liquidation of American obligations in Southeast Asia, a posture of armed détente was at the base of the American regional presence in Europe and the Middle East.

Congressional approval of increasingly larger defense expenditures represented continued congressional support for détente negotiations with the Soviet Union from a position of strength and for a hedge against the failure of those talks as they proceed in several arenas, including SALT (Strategic Arms Limitation Talks), MBFR (Mutual Balanced Force Reductions in Europe), ECSC (European Conference on Security and Cooperation), the Middle East, and Southeast Asia.

Congressional commitment to high defense spending continued throughout the Nixon years. Defense appropriations passed by Congress increased in total each year since 1970, rising from $66.6 billion in FY 1971 to $82.6 billion in FY 1975. (The FY 1976 request of the administration was even higher at $104.7 billion.) The FY 1975 bill was the largest appropriation bill ever passed by Congress and envisaged in magnitude the spending levels at the height of World War II. The gradual American withdrawal from Vietnam had no appreciable effect on Defense Department requests or on congressional willingness to sustain heavy military spending. Congress accepted the volunteer army and the increased cost of attracting and retaining personnel. Keen congressional interest in modernizing the nation's strategic military forces was also characteristic of the Nixon period. Secretary of Defense James Schlesinger's stress on a modified counterforce strategic posture gained ground in legislative decisions. Money was included in the FY 1975 defense bill for superpowerful missiles of increased accuracy. Additional strategic striking power was approved at a future expenditure in excess of $15 billion for the navy's Trident program, designed to supplant the present Polaris fleet. These submarines, with their missiles, were estimated to cost approximately $1.5 billion apiece. Each submarine of a planned fleet of ten was designed to fire twenty-four missiles. Each missile was expected to be armed with from seventeen to twenty-four warheads, and each warhead was estimated to be of sixty kiloton strength, or three times the Hiroshima explosion.

The air force's demand for a follow-on manned bomber for the B-52 received congressional aid, although more questions were raised about the B-1 bomber than the less vulnerable Trident. It has been kept at a research and development stage while Trident was approved for production.

Sentiment favoring a crude equality with the Soviet Union in intercontinental strategic forces had perceptible congressional foundations. Less clearly developed were legislative measures for determining nuclear equality. Most legislators welcomed the 1972 SALT agreement but agreed with Senator Henry Jackson that congressional guidelines should be set for the direction of future negotiations. Senator Jackson's amendment to the accord, passed by a comfortable 56–36 margin in the upper chamber, advised that discussions proceed on "the principle of equality" between the United States and the Soviet Union, that a "vigorous" research and development and modernization program go forward in strategic arms, and that failure to reach a satisfactory treaty limiting offensive weapons would be sufficient grounds for abrogating the ABM accord.[11] Concerns about Soviet expansion and improvement of missile forces, particularly through MIRV (Multiple Independently Targetable Reentry Vehicles), motored congressional pressures to keep the United States in step, although no conclusive legislative definition of "equality" was attempted.

Congress showed more discrimination, however, in critically evaluating and amending the Nixon administration's Safeguard proposal. Legislators displayed considerable skill in revealing the contradictions within the administration's ABM plans, which were alternately justified as a response to Communist China, the Soviet Union, the possibility of irrational or accidental attacks, and as a bargaining in SALT negotiations. Legislative leaders disputed Defense Department contentions that the Soviet Union was seriously embarked on building a first-strike capability because the larger, more powerful rockets it was developing could be used against hardened sites. Congressmen evaluating Safeguard countered that the other segments of the American deterrent posture, especially missile-firing submarines, still remained invulnerable to a Soviet first-strike.

[11] *Congressional Quarterly Almanac*, 1972, pp. 622-25.

Congress also rejected the thesis that Safeguard was a down payment on a thick ABM system to cover cities. The weight of expert opinion in Congress tipped a majority against investing in the ambitious administration plan for multiple sites. The program was authorized, but deployment was limited to only the missile complex at Grand Forks, North Dakota. This modest package essentially kept the ABM program at a research and development level, provided some bargaining leverage for the Nixon administration in the SALT talks, and slowed the arms race. Congressional hesitancy about buying more of the Safeguard program suggested that concern about Soviet aims did not necessarily translate itself into unquestioning congressional acceptance of an expanded ABM program as an answer to growing Russian missile power. Stress continued to be placed on an offensive stance capable of riding out a Soviet strike and of delivering an intolerable second strike.

Foreign military and economic aid proposals from the administration were less favorably received in Congress than defense appropriation requests, particularly after the American troop withdrawal in 1973. As noted above, Congress turned an increasingly deaf ear to American military aid to the region. Between 1962 and 1974, South Vietnam received an estimated $15 billion in direct military assistance and $5 billion in economic aid, out of a total aid package of $25.5 billion for the former French dependencies of Southeast Asia.[12] Table 1 shows the cuts made by

TABLE 1

Congressional Reductions in Foreign Aid Budget Requests, 1969-74
(in billions of dollars)

Fiscal Year	Administration Request	Congressional Approval	Difference	Percentage Reduction
1969	2.92	1.76	-1.16	39.7
1970	2.71	1.81	-0.90	33.1
1971	2.20	1.94	-0.26	11.8
1972	4.34	3.19	-1.15	26.5
1973	5.16	3.65	-1.51	29.3[a]
1974	6.99	5.78	-1.21	17.3
1975	5.95	3.67	-2.28	38.3

Source: Congressional Quarterly Almanac, 1969-73, passim., and Weekly Reports.

Note: The figures reflect gross totals and do not show variations in specific programs from year to year.

[a]The FY 1973 foreign aid appropriations bill was never passed. Funds were continued through successive interim resolutions allowing spending at the rate of the previous year's allowances. In the period 1969-73 Congress failed each year to pass either the annual authorization or appropriation bill for foreign aid for the succeeding year because of sharp differences between both branches over the size and especially many of the military aid features of the program.

[12] Congressional Quarterly Weekly Review, February 1, 1975, p. 229.

Congress in the annual economic and military aid bills from FY 1969 to FY 1975. In three of the six years, the reduction was 33.1 percent or more, reaching heights of 39.9 percent in FY 1969 and 38 percent in FY 1975. If Middle East assistance, earmarked largely for Israel, is subtracted from administration recommendations, the percentage of the annual congressional cut in foreign aid would appear larger, approximating 50 percent in FY 1975.

The authorizing process in Congress also reflected a distinction between American aid to Southeast Asia and to the Middle East. The FY 1975 foreign aid authorization bill approved $2.7 billion for future appropriations. Approximately 40 percent of this total was scheduled for the Middle East. Meanwhile, ceilings were set on assistance to Southeast Asian countries and South Korea. Over 80 percent of the FY 1975 authorization aid bill was concentrated on these two regions, suggesting how narrow the American aid program had become not only regionally, but also functionally in its emphasis on military assistance.

As the aid program narrowed, so did political support in Congress. The final version of the FY 1975 foreign aid authorization passed the Senate (49–43) and the House (209–189) by small margins. The appropriations measure for FY 1975 came close to being defeated. The Senate passed the conference report by a voice vote after an initially favorable 57–40 vote, but the House barely approved the measure (193–185). A majority of the legislators of the president's party voted against the bill as they had a year earlier when the FY 1974 foreign aid appropriations measure became law. In both cases the president had to rely on Democratic majorities to counterbalance the defections of most of his fellow Republicans.

Much of the animus in Congress for lowered foreign aid spending grew out of the poor record of the past and growing demands to concentrate on social and economic problems at home, marked by a severe economic downturn and persistent inflation. An increasing body of legislators questioned aid for political regimes which depended on continuing transfusions of American aid. The aid programs proved economically wasteful and the political and military results were often counterproductive.

Public exposure, partly to inform and partly to discourage executive initiative without prior congressional review and consent, was used to increase legislative control over the making and minding of foreign commitments. Senator Stuart Symington's Foreign Relations Subcommittee on U.S. Security Agreements and Commitments Abroad conducted extensive hearings over two years to learn how the United States acquired its commitments abroad and to define their present structure and rationale. Foreign bases alone totaled 2,200 in thirty-three countries. The Symington study discovered a wide number of problems that had been ignored. The CIA, for example, sustained a 30,000-man Laotian force under the cover of an intelligence operation; Defense Department documents, like those surrounding United States negotiations over bases in the Azores and Spain, were withheld from congressional scrutiny; and the deployment, command, and political control arrangements for nuclear weapons stationed on foreign territory were shrouded in secrecy.

The Symington hearings served as the background for other congressional attempts to widen public and legislative knowledge of executive branch activities in foreign affairs. The practice of secret accords secretly arrived at, often by subordinate officials, in the executive branch (e.g., an air force general negotiated on bases in Spain) was proscribed by legislation. In 1972, Congress approved a measure requiring the secretary of state to transmit to Congress within sixty days the text of any agreement with another nation. In cases involving national security, these communications with Congress could be confidential. The impractical requirements of the Bricker amendment of a generation earlier were avoided since Congress did not assert a right to pass on each agreement but merely insisted on being kept informed.

In keeping with this movement toward greater exposure, arms sales received increasing congressional attention. Data about such sales that the executive branch had kept confidential were ordered published in an amendment to an Arms Control and Disarmament Agency authorizing bill. The United States was shown to be the world's largest supplier of arms. Sales in 1974 totaled $8.26 billion. Approximately 30 percent of the $29.29 billion total of all sales between 1950 and 1974. The top six purchasers in 1974 were Iran ($3.78 billion), Israel ($2.2 billion), Saudi Arabia ($587.7 million), Greece ($434.9 million), Germany ($218.6 million), and Spain ($147.8 million). These sales sparked several, still inconclusive, congressional debates over increasing United States arms sales and their impact on American commitments. Criticism arose that they spurred arms races, promoted international instability, afforded little or no control over their use by recipients (e.g., Pakistan and Turkey), deflected the United States from meeting more pressing socioeconomic needs at home and abroad, saddled the United States with the dubious reputation as the world's leading arms merchant, and underwrote dictatorial regimes whose dependency on the United States hampered its relations with the Third World. Since 1974, Congress has requested the executive branch to give advance notice of any sale in excess of $25 million, and a proposal for a moratorium on arms sales has been seriously discussed in the Senate.

Congressional exposure of executive branch activities has spread to the sensitive operations of the CIA. Disclosure of CIA support of opposition groups in Chile led to a congressional investigation. The probe included an examination of ITT contributions to these undercover activities to block the election of Chilean President Allende, who was later deposed in a coup d'etat. Rumors of illicit CIA operations in the United States and abroad prompted further investigations in 1975. In separate actions, both houses began special investigations, paralleling the blue ribbon panel appointed by President Ford to review the work of the foreign intelligence community. These various CIA investigations were part of the larger congressional interest in disseminating information about governmental activities in foreign countries as a check on excesses and as a guide for instituting additional legislative controls on foreign policy. These aims were also present in Congress's establishment of a commission, headed by Robert Murphy, to review the government's organization for the conduct of all United States foreign relations.

II

This *tour d'horizon* of congressional security and policy making during the Nixon years has been necessarily brief and elliptical. Conclusions about the period must remain tentative until more information and hindsight are available. What appears clear, however, is that Congress has again become a formidable force in the development and execution of American security and foreign policy. Congress has amended, if not discarded, the proposition that the achievement of American security, democratic institutions, and welfare are indivisible at home and abroad. Neither the isolationistic thesis of the prewar period nor the universalist postulates of the postwar era held sway in Congress during the Nixon years or in the first year of the Ford administration. If the congressional record of the past seven years is any guide, Congress's contribution to the definition of America's new role in world politics will emerge slowly out of a pragmatic, case-by-case testing process, and debate will be guided by an ongoing assessment of the limits of American economic and military power, of the prospects of long-term public support for varied international positions, of changing conceptions of adversary political aims and military and economic capabilities, and of the validity of allied and client claims. In any event, foreign policy will have to rest on a broader and more solid congressional foundation than that which characterized the Nixon years if current legislative demands for increased influence and specific controls in these areas are to be satisfied.

That increased congressional participation in foreign policy will be responsive to national needs cannot be predicted with certainty. Meeting constitutional tests for Congress's role in defining the terms of peace and war is a necessary, but in itself an insufficient, condition for the survival and well-being of the nation or its institutions. Legislative control of foreign policy, as the French Third Republic learned, is no guarantee that adversaries will be contained. On the other hand, recent American experience suggests that too great a reliance on executive branch and presidential leadership in foreign affairs has prompted serious doubts about the effectiveness of American policy abroad and its credibility at home. In having moved to correct imbalances in the congressional-presidential relationship during the Nixon period, Congress also contributed to a redefinition of American commitments. Its action, while susceptible to criticism and cavil, rested on a rationale which appeared as compelling as that advanced by the executive branch and which, in the short run at least, appeared more politically viable at home and realistic abroad. This outcome of the "struggle for the privilege of directing American foreign policy" during the Nixon era is not without irony in light of the claims of realpolitik that characterized Secretary of State Kissinger's stewardship of foreign affairs.

After Vietnam and Watergate, Congress moved slowly to get its own house in order. It made discernible progress in disciplining the president and executive agencies to conform to its still evolving collective understanding of its part in defining the nation's role in security and foreign affairs. If a cooperative relationship between the presidency and Congress cannot assure success in foreign affairs, little can be done in its absence without damage to national security, free governmental institutions, or economic and social development. In the words of Congressman Dante Fascell, "consultation, common counsel and continuing accountability (between the President and Congress) are essential to viable foreign and defense policies."[13]

---

[13] Quoted in Frey, Chapter 8 (forthcoming).

Control of Presidential
Campaign Financing

SUSAN B. KING
ROBERT L. PEABODY

Late in the afternoon of October 15, 1974, President Gerald Ford signed into law the Federal Election Campaign Act Amendments of 1974, the most sweeping electoral reform legislation in the history of the United States. P.L. 93–443 established a public financing
program for all phases of the presidential campaign—primaries, party
conventions, and the general election. Overall limits were imposed upon
the amounts that candidates could spend in competition for federal offices
—the House and Senate as well as the presidency. The money and services that individuals and organizations can contribute to candidates
were also strictly curtailed. Reporting and disclosure requirements were
strengthened. A new and independent enforcement agency, the Federal
Elections Commission, was created. Although the full implications of
this campaign reform legislation are still being tested, President Ford
summed up its potential: "By removing whatever influence big money
and special interests may have on our federal election process, this bill
should stand as a landmark of campaign reform legislation."[1]

The occasion was more than the perfunctory White House bill signing
ceremony, where a handful of congressional sponsors pose with the chief
executive for picture-taking and publicity. Present were many of the
principal congressional actors who had struggled over the major provisions of the bill—Senators Cannon, Pastore, and Mathias; Representatives Hays, Frenzel, Udall, and Anderson, joined by some thirty others
from Capitol Hill. Also invited, in an unusual gesture of camaraderie,
were the chairpersons of the Democratic and Republican parties and the
leaders of a broad coalition of interest groups backing election reform—
the Center for Public Financing of Elections, Common Cause, the
League of Women Voters, and the National Committee for an Effective

[1] *Washington Post*, October 16, 1974.

The views expressed here are those of the authors and do not reflect the opinion of
the Center for Public Financing of Elections or any other organization.

Congress. Later, every member of Congress would receive a presidential pen and letter symbolizing the historic occasion.

In the bright glare of the television lights, President Ford openly acknowledged the traumatic events and the lengthy legislative battle that had produced such sweeping legislation. Questions about the sources and uses of political money had prompted Congress to pass a campaign disclosure bill just two years earlier. But it was the massive abuse of campaign funds by the Committee to Reelect the President in 1972 and revelations leading up to the threatened impeachment of Richard M. Nixon that provided the impetus for this new law. Only a few members of Congress had actively supported campaign reforms before, but now the vast majority were on record as trying in this way to restore some measure of confidence in government and its elected leaders. Reflecting this same sensitivity to public pressures, newly appointed President Ford observed: "The American people want this legislation." Noting that his mail had been filled with demands for reform, Ford concluded, "This is a good day for 213 million Americans."[2]

At the conclusion of the signing ceremony, President Ford paused briefly to shake hands with those at the podium, then left to board a helicopter waiting outside on the south lawn of the White House. The irony of his mode of departure was not lost on some who watched. The reform bill that he had just signed into law had passed the House of Representatives on August 8, 1974. Two hours after that vote, Richard M. Nixon, who was then president, had gone on television to announce his resignation. Two days later the nation had watched Mr. Ford's predecessor take his last ride in a White House helicopter.

It would serve little purpose here to review Watergate-related or other campaign financing excesses that obviously played a major role in fueling the forces leading to campaign reform. Nor is there any point in chronicling here the maneuvering and compromises built into P. L. 93–433 and related legislation. Campaign reform will be briefly placed in a more historical context, however, if only to point up with what regularity such legislation has been linked to prior scandals or electoral abuses. Next the principal features of the current laws will be described, and, finally, their ongoing and future implications for presidential electioneering and the two-party system will be considered.

An Overview of Campaign Finance Reform

When [George Washington] ran for the Virginia House of Burgesses from Fairfax County in 1757, he provided his friends with the "customary means of winning votes": namely 28 gallons of rum, 50 gallons of rum punch, 34

[2] "Remarks of the President Upon Signing the Federal Campaign Act Amendmendments of 1974," Office of the White House Press Secretary, October 15, 1974, pp. 1–2.

gallons of wine, 46 gallons of beer, and 2 gallons of cider royal. Even in those days this was considered a large campaign expenditure, because there were only 391 voters in his district, for an average outlay of more than a quart and a half per person.

In 1846 [Abraham Lincoln] was supposedly given $200 by friends in Illinois to pay for his expenses while running for Congress as a Whig. Lincoln claimed his total expenses were 75 cents for a barrel of cider, and that he returned the remaining $199.25 with thanks.

—George Thayer, *Who Shakes the Money Tree*

Contributions for funding American political campaigns have traditionally come from private sources—the candidates' own money; gifts from other individuals, often close friends and relatives; support from organizations ranging from citizens' "good government" groups through political parties to "vested interests." Low funded campaigns, such as those attributed to Washington and Lincoln, were the rule rather than the exception. But what was once a relatively inexpensive, largely candidate-financed system in the early days became a costly, interest-dominated process. This "laissez-faire" campaign funding led to practices inconsistent with traditional democratic principles of fairness and the right to compete freely for public offices.

The central question of campaign finance regulation has been and remains, How to distinguish proper, legitimate efforts to influence elections from those considered unfair or illegitimate? Put in practical terms, How is it possible to uncover, discourage, and, when necessary, punish those who abuse the electoral and governing processes? What positive encouragements can properly be given to desirable courses of campaign conduct? Drawing a fine line between proper and improper activities in the vastly complex, highly competitive American political arena has never been easy. To instigate proper regulation without strangling the process itself has become even more difficult as the role of government has become more pervasive and divisions between the public and private sectors have become increasingly blurred.

The task of regulating campaign practices is complicated further by a unique "conflict of interest" situation. The very men and women who write the electoral laws must also live—and possibly die—by them. And these legislators have often demonstrated an all too human tendency to place their own electoral survival uppermost. This natural political reluctance to tamper with the sensitive and complex questions of campaign financing and regulation is a major reason why reform has often been rather ineffective and late in coming.

Another reason for the shortcomings of prior attempts at campaign regulation stems from the precipitating forces behind their enactment. Most of the laws that found their way into the statute books represented the response of Congress to major political scandals of the time. Once the immediate demand for action was met and the public outcry largely stilled, these earlier laws were generally ignored and have been almost totally unenforced.

Under the pressures of an expanding electorate, increased urbanization, and the growth in the importance of political parties in the latter half of the nineteenth century, election expenditures began to mount and campaign abuses became more widespread. Not until 1883 did Congress attempt to regulate campaign funding, and then the target was the "spoils system." Although the Pendleton Act prohibited political contributions by civil servants, it did nothing to curb the expanding influence of business interests on campaign giving.

The McKinley-Bryan presidential election of 1896 marked a turning point both in styles of campaigning and in overall expenditures. It was perhaps the first "modern advertising campaign," replete with telephone appeals, campaign buttons, literature, posters and billboards. The Republican candidate, McKinley, spent between $6 and $7 million, a record that was not surpassed until after World War I.[3] Revelations of highly questionable contributions by New York insurance firms, dating back to the McKinley campaign, led Congress to pass the Tillman Act in 1907. Prohibiting election contributions from corporations and banks, this legislation was further amended in 1910 and 1911 to require limited disclosure by candidates. More show than substance, it proved largely unenforceable, a pattern that was to repeat itself through the 1960s.

President Theodore Roosevelt and William Jennings Bryan, the defeated Democratic presidential candidate in 1896, 1900, and 1908, were the first major political figures to propose public financing of federal elections. Their proposals to pay for national elections out of the treasury were ignored by Congress. After holding additional investigations into various forms of influence peddling and vote buying, successive Congresses have pursued half-hearted policies of campaign control and regulation. The Federal Corrupt Practices Act of 1925 represented an ultimate effort of this negative type, elaborating upon earlier attempts at full campaign disclosures and limits upon contributions and spending. Subsequent legislation expanded the concept of campaign controls: the Hatch Act of 1939 extended political prohibitions to all federal employees and prohibited individuals or firms doing work for the federal government under contract from making political contributions; the 1943 Smith-Connally Act and the 1947 Taft-Hartley Act prohibited unions from making contributions to political candidates out of general funds.

If measured against what they were designed to prevent, all of these laws would have to be judged failures. Their provisions failed to cover much of the actual political process, for example, primaries and intrastate

[3] George Thayer, *Who Shakes the Money Tree?* (New York: Simon and Schuster, 1973), pp. 48–50.

activities. What was covered could be avoided by devices that eventually came to be standard campaign features: the innumerable fictitious committees, the testimonial dinners, the corporate slush fund, the union political education committees, and the contributions disguised as speakers' honorariums. The almost total failure to enforce even the limited provisions of the existing legislation contributed further to the evasions and reinforced attitudes of general cynicism and hypocrisy about campaign regulations specifically and politics in general.

Against this all too familiar background of noncompliance and nonenforcement, a dramatic escalation of campaign expenditures began in the 1950s. Many factors contributed to the substantial increases—the introduction of television and subsequent media saturation, the emergence of computerized mailing lists and intensive direct-mail solicitation, the hiring of professional managers and full-time staffs, and the use of sophisticated campaign polling practices. Between 1952 and 1972, campaign expenditures for all elective offices more than tripled.[4]

Remembered almost as much for the famed Kennedy-Nixon television debates as for the final outcome of the election, the 1960 presidential campaign ushered in a new era of highly organized campaign techniques, sophisticated mass media appeals to the electorate, and spiraling campaign costs. By temporarily suspending the "equal time" political broadcast requirements of Section 315 of the Communications Act of 1934, Congress made possible the first, and so far only, media confrontation between the two major party contenders (and incidentally, saved Nixon and Kennedy approximately $2 million in television broadcast costs).

Responding to a growing concern about the increasing costs of running for the White House, President Kennedy established a special commission in 1961-62 to study the problem, but no legislation emerged. After President Lyndon Johnson's resounding election victory in 1964, he convened a similar but much less publicized campaign finance study group. As papers from the LBJ Library now reveal, this group extended its exploration well beyond the now accepted ideas of disclosure and tax credits into the relatively unexplored ideas of direct public financing of electoral campaigns.[5]

[4] In 1952 the combined costs of the Eisenhower-Stevenson contest were estimated at less than $12 million. By 1960, Kennedy and Nixon were each spending more than $11 million on their presidential candidacies with an estimated 40 percent of their budgets going for television time. In 1972, President Nixon raised more than $68 million and spent $60 million; the McGovern forces spent almost $40 million. Total campaign outlays for all candidates running in 1952, national, state, and local, have been estimated at $140 million. By 1972, total candidate expenditures ran well over $400 million. The Citizens' Research Foundation of Princeton, New Jersey, under the direction of Dr. Herbert E. Alexander, has been the major source of information on campaign finance statistics for most of this period.

[5] It is mildly ironic that this second quasi-official inquiry into public financing fol-

With the exception of a few reform-oriented congressmen, neither the House nor the Senate became active in the electoral reform arena until the mid-1960s. In the closing days of the Eighty-ninth Congress, Louisiana's Senator Russell Long, chairman of the powerful Senate Finance Committee, managed to secure passage of a measure providing for partial public financing of presidential campaigns. Although P. L. 89-809 was to be suspended in the following Congress, this effort introduced an acceptable mechanism for subsequent legislation, namely, the creation of a special treasury fund to which taxpayers could voluntarily contribute one of their tax dollars to help defray the mounting costs of presidential election campaigns.

Electoral reform legislation was not a major issue in the Nixon-Humphrey presidential race of 1968, but by the congressional campaign of 1970, attempted television blitzes, favor-seeking contributors, and other campaign excesses increasingly brought these concerns to the public's attention. In the closing days of the Ninety-first Congress, public interest groups were able to push through the House and the Senate a bill providing for control of media costs and expenditures and facilitating a second round of presidential television debates in 1972. Claiming that this bill "plugged only one hole in the sieve," President Nixon vetoed the bill in October 1970.[6]

Campaign reform legislation presently on the books is an outgrowth of that 1970 presidential veto. Eager to maintain the reform mantle for itself and to embarrass a Republican president who had refused to make electoral reform a major administration objective, the heavily Democratic Ninety-second Congress finally took action. The process was slow, arduous, and often acrimonious. Without the urgings of a public and press suspicious of politicians and political money, these efforts could have faltered. Nevertheless, with the sponsorship of Senate Majority Leader Mansfield, Commerce Subcommittee Chairman Pastore, and Rules Committee Chairman Cannon, the Senate passed a bill in August 1971, which incorporated the media spending limits of the unsuccessful 1970 bill with a new, comprehensive program of campaign disclosure requirements. Members of the House of Representatives, less electorally secure than their Senate colleagues, were more resistant to change. Still, they endorsed a modified version of the legislation in late November 1971. Following conference committee action, the Federal Election Campaign Act of 1971 was signed into law by President Nixon in February, to become effective

---

lowed a national campaign in which the Democratic nominee received 70 per cent of his funding from donors of $500 or more, while his opponent, Barry Goldwater, made political history's most successful appeal to a broad base of small contributors.

[6] For a case history of this legislation, see Robert L. Peabody, Jeffrey M. Berry, William G. Frasure, and Jerry Goldman, *To Enact a Law: Congress and Campaign Financing* (New York: Praeger Publishers, 1972).

April 7, 1972. After considerable backing and filling, Congress had brought about the first major election reform law in nearly half a century, replacing the Corrupt Practices Act of 1925. It was a sign of the times that administration of its reporting requirements for presidential campaigns was vested in the impartial and universally respected comptroller general.

Almost simultaneously, but with less fanfare, Congress resurrected and passed the earlier "Long proposal" for funding presidential elections out of the public treasury. While it initially called for a $1 checkoff on income tax forms in order to finance the 1972 presidential election, the Nixon administration succeeded in conference committee in postponing the effective date to January 1, 1973. Another rider on the Revenue Act of 1971 (P. L. 92-178) was the old Kennedy commission proposal that tax credits (up to $25 on a joint return) and tax deductions (up to $100 on a joint return) be allowable for political contributions. Thus, the reform movement had added a strategy of public subsidy to the traditional one of financial constraints.

Campaign reform might well have abated had it not been for the revelations flowing from the Watergate break-in, including the discovery of some "laundered" contributions in the possession of the arrested burglars. The rest is recent history: the pattern of big contributors seeking favors, ambassadorships on the auction block, corporations funneling illegal millions into campaigns, the milk-producers' scandal, and the ITT case. Defenders of the old school of political finance were being exposed as admirers of "emperors without clothes." Public opinion polls registered increased cynicism and dismay but also growing popular interest in finding another way to finance politics—out of the public treasury.

After two trial runs, temporarily sidetracked by filibusters, the Senate passed a comprehensive bill in the spring of 1974. S. 3044 set limits on campaign giving and spending for all federal offices, established the independent Federal Elections Commission to monitor and enforce the laws, and provided for public financing of presidential and congressional campaigns in both primary and general elections. The House was slow to respond. Delay in the Committee on House Administration brought forth charges of a spotty hearing record and a seemingly cavalier response to the mushrooming scandal of Watergate. But on the eve of President Nixon's televised resignation, the House reacted to public pressures and adopted a more limited version of the Senate bill. Missing were provisions calling for public financing of congressional contests. After bitter and prolonged wrangles in conference, the Federal Election Campaign Act Amendments of 1974 was finally reported out and approved in early October. President Ford's signing ceremony came one week later, a fortnight before the midterm congressional elections.

In but four years—a dramatically short time for congressional consideration of legislation posing such major issues—more had happened in the electoral reform arena than over the preceding 190 years. It remains to explain what the 1971-74 legislative package contains and to assess its implications for subsequent elections, especially the presidential primaries and general election of 1976.

Campaign Financing Legislation—A Summary

The far-reaching changes made in the campaign laws touch on many aspects of the electoral process and are scattered among various titles of the United States Code.[7] The summary here concentrates on the major provisions of the Revenue Act of 1971 (P. L. 92-178), the Federal Election Campaign Act of 1971 (P. L. 92-225), and the FECA Amendments of 1974 (P. L. 93-443). The total package is still being assessed by participants and observers alike, but the basic framework for conducting the 1976 election is as follows:

CAMPAIGN DISCLOSURE

Registration and reporting. All federal candidates and all political committees and parties supporting candidates for federal office must register with the new Federal Elections Commission and must file full financial reports quarterly, before and after each election, and at the year's end. Duplicate copies are to be filed in the state capitols, and all reports are open and available to the press and the public.

Reports must contain a full statement of financial activities, including loans, transfers, and gifts-in-kind, as well as receipts and expenditures. All contributions over $100 must be fully identified, including date, name, address, and occupation of the contributor, and all expenditures over $100 must be itemized and identified.

Central Campaign Committee. Every federal candidate must designate one committee to serve as his or her "central campaign committee" through which all activities on behalf of that candidate are reported. In addition, candidates must designate specific bank depositories for campaign funds.

Funds not reported by the candidate. Any individual who raises or expends more than $100 on behalf of a candidate, which is not reported by the candidate or one of his committees, must personally file such a report to the commission.

Cash contributions. No cash contributions over $100 are permitted.

---

[7] A complete codification of all statutes governing the conduct of federal campaigns, *Federal Election Campaign Laws*, was prepared by the U.S. Senate Library for the Senate Committee on Rules and Administration, 94th Congress (Washington: U.S. Government Printing Office, 1975).

LIMITS ON CONTRIBUTIONS

Individual limits. No individual may contribute more than $1,000 to any one candidate for the presidency, Senate, or House of Representatives in the primary election, and another $1,000 in the general election. (The presidential primary process is treated as one election to which the $1,000 limit applies.) In the case of special elections or primary runoffs, a separate $1,000 limit applies. In addition, no individual may contribute more than $25,000 in aggregate to a federal candidate throughout an entire campaign.

Organization limits. No organization may give more than $5,000 to any candidate for federal office in the primary campaign and another $5,000 in the general election. (The presidential primary process is treated as one election to which the $5,000 organization limit applies.) In the case of special elections or primary runoffs, a separate $5,000 limit applies. There is no limit on the aggregate amount an organization may contribute to all federal candidates. (In order to qualify as a "political committee" eligible to give up to this $5,000 limit, a committee must be registered with the Elections Commission for six months, have received contributions from more than fifty people, and, in the case of nonparty committees, have contributed to at least five candidates. The purpose of this requirement is to discourage the proliferation of nominal committees established solely to evade the $5,000 limit. A committee that does not qualify is subject to the $1,000 limit.)

Limits on candidate contributions to own campaign. Candidates and their immediate families may not make expenditures in their own campaigns in excess of $50,000 for president, $35,000 for the Senate, and $25,000 for the House. This limit applies to the entire campaign period, not to the primary and general election separately.

SPENDING LIMITS

Presidential. Candidates may spend a total of $10 million in the primary process plus an additional 20 percent of this amount for fund raising purposes. In no single state, however, may a candidate spend more than twice what a Senate primary candidate may spend in that state.

In the general election, a presidential candidate may spend up to the basic limit of $20 million. (If a candidate chooses to finance his campaign with private rather than public funds, an additional 20 percent is allowed for fund-raising.) Also, a national party is permitted to spend up to 2 cents times the voting age population (VAP) on behalf of its candidate in the general election.

Senate. Candidates in the primary may spend up to 8 cents times the VAP of that state, or $100,000, whichever is higher, plus an additional 20 percent of that amount for fund-raising purposes. In the general election, a Senate candidate may spend up to 12 cents times the VAP of that state, or $150,000, whichever is higher, plus an added 20 percent for fund-raising. In addition, the national party and the state party may each spend 2 cents times the VAP, or $20,000, whichever is greater, on behalf of its Senate candidate in that state.

House. Candidates in the primary may spend $70,000 plus 20 percent ($14,000) for fund-raising. In the general election, a House candidate may spend another $70,000, plus 20 percent for fund-raising. In addition, the national party and the state party may each spend $10,000 on behalf of each of their House candidates in the general election. (House candidates running in a single-district state may spend in both the primary and general election as much as a Senate candidate in that state.)

Limits on independent expenditures on behalf of a candidate. No individual or organization may expend more than $1,000, independently of a candidate, his committees, and his party, to support or oppose any candidate for federal office. (No limit on independent activity would provide the means for wholesale evasion of contributor limits, while a total prohibition raises serious First Amendment questions. The legislation attempts to balance the issues by permitting some limited independent activity.

PUBLIC FINANCING

Presidential general election. Major party candidates are eligible to receive full funding of $20 million in public financing from the tax dollar checkoff fund; minor party, new, and independent candidates are eligible for a proportion of the full $20 million based on their votes received in the past or current election.

Public financing is optional; if a candidate accepts full funding, no private contributions are permitted. A candidate who receives less than full funding, or rejects it altogether, may raise up to the spending limit in private contributions.

Presidential nominating conventions. Major parties are eligible for full funding of $2 million; minor parties are eligible for a proportion of that amount based on the party's vote in the past or current election.

Presidential primaries. All candidates are eligible to receive federal matching payments for the first $250 of any private contribution, up to a maximum of $5 million in public funds. In order to qualify, a candidate must first raise a threshold of $100,000 ($5,000 in each of twenty states) in matchable contributions; then, this $100,000 is matched from the Presidential Primary Account in the tax checkoff fund, and all subsequent contributions up to $250 are matched. Only those private contributions received after January 1975 qualify for matching, and no payments will actually be made from the fund until January 1976.

ENFORCEMENT

The new six-member, independent Federal Elections Commission is responsible for administering the campaign laws and the public financing program. It is vested with broad administrative, investigative, and arbitrative powers.

The commission is charged with receiving and publicizing campaign reports, making rules and regulations regarding application of the law (subject to review by Congress within thirty days), maintaining a cumulative index of reports received and failures to file, making regular and special reports to Congress and the president, and serving as an election information clearinghouse.

The commission has the power to render advisory opinions, conduct audits and investigations, subpoena witnesses and information, and initiate civil proceedings for relief. Criminal investigations are to be referred to the Justice Department for prosecution, with special provision for advancing election law cases on the docket. Penalties for violation of the campaign laws range up to five years' imprisonment, a fine of $50,000 or both. Federal law preempts state election laws as they apply to federal candidates.

Implementation and Consequences

In its vast overhaul of federal campaign laws, Congress has set in motion a new scenario for politics in general and for the 1976 presidential election in particular. What the legislation means, both immediately and in the long run, is the subject of considerable hope, speculation, controversy, and, to some, genuine alarm.

Theoretically, the integrated body of law was in effect on January 1, 1975. In reality, however, the situation remained in flux well into the year. As a result of presidential and congressional delays, members of the new Election Commission were not sworn in until April 14, 1975.[8] Even then, the agency had to wait several more weeks for an initial $500,000 appropriation. In the interim, candidates and political committees were left with little direction or guidance as to the application of the complex new statutes. Once operative, the FEC was faced with the need for immediate action in interpreting the laws, writing rules and regulations, and issuing advisory opinions in as orderly a fashion as

[8] The president, the Senate, and the House of Representatives each named two members of the Federal Election Commission. The president: Thomas B. Curtis (chairman), R., Mo., and Neil O. Staebler (vice chairman), D., Mich.; the Senate: Joan D. Aikens, R., Pa., and Thomas E. Harris, D., Va.; and the House: Vernon Thomson, R., Wisc., and Robert O. Tiernan, D., R.I. All but the Senate appointees have previously served for one or more terms in the House of Representatives. In addition, the secretary of the Senate, Francis R. Valeo, and the clerk of the House, W. Pat Jennings, serve as ex-officio members of the commission.

possible. The danger was that its tasks, difficult under the best of circumstances, would convert the commission into little more than a crisis response center.

The early uncertainty was further complicated by a lawsuit filed by Senator James Buckley (Conservative-Republican, New York), former Senator Eugene McCarthy, the New York Civil Liberties Union, the conservative weekly, *Human Events*, and a host of others, challenging the consitutionality of virtually every major provision of the new campaign laws.[9]

Never before has the Supreme Court had to address so directly the First Amendment questions raised by disclosure requirements and limitations on campaign contributions and expenditures, and never has it had to rule on the issue of public financing in either broad or narrow terms. Whatever the Burger Court ultimately decides will be a landmark.

While both the 1974 FECA Amendments and the public financing sections of the tax code specifically provide for speedy judicial review, any hope that the case could reach the Supreme Court before fall was dashed with the immediate development of a complex procedural snarl at the lower court level. As of mid-1975, neither the plaintiffs, the government defendants, nor the public interest groups who intervened to help defend the legislation, believed the major issues could be resolved much before the end of the year. Moreover, the Department of Justice brief, though supporting the law generally, left the commission to defend the constitutionality of its own enforcement powers—an anomalous position for the government.

In the meantime, the Federal Elections Commission, the candidates, committees, and the parties must continue to function under the law as it was written. Should the Court strike down any of the major provisions, such as the limitation provisions or the 1976 public financing program, it remains questionable whether Congress will act speedily without Watergate-type pressures.

In any case, the new laws are already having important consequences. Especially as the legislation applies to the forthcoming presidential election, its implications have become a sharp focus of concern at the White House, in congressional cloakrooms, and in the campaign headquarters of the 1976 contenders.

The issue of campaign finance remains a potent one for the candidates. It has had a distinct impact on the style of presidential campaigning and fund raising, as candidates position themselves on the side of "reform" and try to project an image of financial integrity. Even before the 1974 limits went into effect, acknowledged presidential aspirants Henry M. Jackson and Lloyd Bentsen voluntarily adopted $3,000 limits on

---

[9] *Buckley, et al. v. Valeo, et al.,* U.S. Court of Appeals for the District of Columbia, Docket No. 75–1061, January 2, 1975. Oral arguments were heard June 13, 1975.

contributions, and candidates Morris Udall, Terry Sanford, and Jimmy Carter went a step further by refusing anything over $1,000. Campaign coordinators are paying closer attention to the source of funds; they are more wary of accepting any donation that might be questionable or become a source of embarrassment later. Large contributors are more cautious because they not only have seen the demise of free-wheeling campaign giving, but also are sensitive to the unpleasant publicity that has attended the prosecution of illegal contributions and indiscriminate slush funds.

The strict limits on contributions, the need to develop a broad base of small donors, and the potential for federal matching of small contributions have increased the pressure on candidates to begin an organized fund-raising drive as early as possible. In early 1971, only George McGovern was an active candidate for the 1972 Democratic nomination. At a similar time in 1975, at least seven Democrats and one third-party aspirant were announced candidates. Moreover, one Democrat and one Republican had already entered and withdrawn.[10] The campaign for shorter campaigns fizzled.

The limitations on spending in the primaries, coupled with contribution limitations, puts a premium on careful organization and long-range planning in both the raising and spending of funds. Careful, accurate record-keeping is also an obvious need, one requiring the use of professionals rather than the traditional volunteer treasurer.

While the disclosure rules and the central campaign committee requirement will introduce a degree of centralization and financial control heretofore unknown in most political campaigns, candidates will likely find that this is the only rational way they can operate. Although some critics argue that these constraints will destroy a healthy vitality in politics, many others insist that the "spontaneity" of the credit card campaign of recent years had indeed got out of hand, and any reduction in wasteful, unnecessary spending should be welcomed.

Under the new restrictions, candidates can no longer rely on the assistance of one "angel" or a handful of "fat cats" to launch a campaign or rejuvenate it within the last six or eight weeks. All must look to a broad citizen base of small contributors to sustain their efforts. With less time spent courting a few potential big donors, candidates will pay more attention to middle-level contributors and will have to seek to involve many more people in the fund-raising process itself. Within the framework of these limitations, the ability of an organization to contribute $5,000

---

[10] Although several candidates had yet to declare "formally," authorized political committees had filed quarterly reports on fund-raising for Democrats, Bentsen, Carter, Harris, Jackson, Sanford, Udall, and Wallace. In addition, former Senator Eugene McCarthy had announced as a third-party candidate and Senators Mondale (D., Minn.) and Percy (R., Ill.) had withdrawn.

takes on a new importance relative to the individual donor's $1,000 limit. All of this is likely to refocus the fund-raising picture generally, with several predictable results.

The $100-$1,000 a plate dinner, the informal reception, and the local rally as a fund-raising vehicle will increase in importance. Surrogates for the candidate in meeting people, speaking for the candidate, and raising funds will be used more often. There will be a premium on an effective volunteer operation. Candidates will rely less on big direct mail programs to launch a campaign, except those who have the initial seed money to pay the expensive start-up costs. Expensive television advertising in the early days of a campaign will decrease. The number of business, industry, and labor political action committees probably will increase to take advantage of the $5,000 organizational limit. There will be a greater emphasis on gifts-in-kind by multicandidate and party committees, utilizing bulk purchasing wherever possible (in polls, media time, printing, and consultants) to get the greatest value for funds spent. In addition, parties will be more active on behalf of their candidates in the general election.

As of early summer 1975, the Democratic fund-raising advantage clearly lay with those presidential contenders who were best known nationally and who had begun the year with considerable financial reserves. In April, Governor George Wallace became the first candidate to meet the $5,000/twenty-state threshold that would qualify him, if he so chose, to receive the federal matching funds in 1976. Several weeks later, Senator Jackson became the second contender to qualify for the up-to-$5 million in matching funds. Close behind the $1,730,000 that Wallace had raised through 1974 and the first quarter of 1975 were Senators Jackson and Bentsen with $1,137,000 and $675,000.[11] Some of the lesser known entries were more worried about their prospects for obtaining start-up money and exposure without an existing bankroll or the help of a few rich donors. Others, like Morris Udall and Fred Harris, applauded the restrictions on big donors. Noting that it was still early, they seemed optimistic that a serious candidate could indeed finance a viable campaign under the new legislation.

In the Republican camp, campaign financing remained something of a dormant issue. Although President Ford was slow to establish a formal campaign operation, no one questioned the ability of an incumbent chief executive to raise whatever funds would be necessary, even in small amounts. By mid-1975, no open opposition to his renomination had yet surfaced, despite continued rumblings from the right wing of the GOP.

[11] Kent Cooper, former director, Information Center of Political Finance, to authors, April 15, 1975.

A Look to the Future

Much of the campaign finance scenario remains to be played out in the commission, the courts, the Congress, and on the 1976 campaign trail. As the election approaches and involvement intensifies, perspectives on the merits of "reform" may be radically altered by the ways in which the new laws turn out to affect one's favorite candidate or party.

Yet to be determined, for example, is the effect that Congress's veto power over FEC campaign rules and regulations will have on the overall operation of the law and its application to specific presidential contenders. Can or will the heavy Democratic majority in Congress attempt to bend the rules to the advantage of their party? Or, as seems more likely, will internecine battles develop as various Democratic factions attempt to promote their own presidential candidates or hamper others?

And what will happen if the Supreme Court does strike down substantial portions of the law? Will long-range reform objectives or immediate political realities dictate the terms of subsequent legislative efforts?

Perhaps the ultimate irony would be for the congressional liberals of both parties to abandon the reform cause if they see George Wallace or Ronald Reagan as more effective at broad-based fund-raising than candidates of their own persuasion.

The questions raised by the application of the new law in 1976 make it important to consider the impact further in the future. The attempt to reduce the role of big money in campaigns, to open up the political process to all qualified contenders, and to make the entire system more responsive to the public will be felt in other aspects of the political process. Not all the changes will be the product of campaign financing legislation alone, for there are numerous other forces at work, including the general decline in party affiliation, the increase in split-ticket voting, the adoption of new delegate selection rules by the Democrats, the proliferation of presidential primaries, the expanding role of television, and as yet unforeseen technological developments.

Other questions loom large. Chief among them are the long-range impact on the traditional two-party system, and more immediately, the operation of the parties' candidate selection process. Whether a political observer or practitioner commends or criticizes the new law generally depends on his own view of how well the two-party system has served in the past and continues to meet national needs. The public financing provisions as written, with candidates of a major party (over 25 percent of the vote in the last election) automatically qualifying for the full $20 million in general election funding, will likely work to preserve a two-party system. In addition, the parties are permitted to spend and perform other functions on behalf of their nominees that other organizations are not allowed to do.

On the other hand, the availability of matching funds in the primary process could assure a multicandidate field and possibly institutionalize the intraparty factionalism of recent years. Once in, candidates might be encouraged to stay in by the hope for the one big primary victory that would catapult them to the front, by the prospects of a brokered convention out of which a darkhorse could emerge, or by the promise of full treasury funding in the general election should they become the nominee. Perhaps the public financing provisions will lead to a national primary or a series of regional primaries terminating the present seven-month primary marathon so arduous and demanding of candidates.

The limitations on contributions and expenditures pose Catch-22 problems similar to those in the public financing provisions. Does the effort to end big-money dominance by forcing candidates to reach out for many smaller backers really mean, in practice, that only the already nationally visible contenders have a chance? It has been estimated that less than 10 percent of the public have ever contributed money to a candidate and that only 30 percent have ever been asked for a political donation. An increased sense of relevance in the political process and better understanding of the importance of small contributions, reinforced by tax credits and the income tax checkoff opportunity, could dramatically alter the situation. The increase in the checkoff rate from 3 percent in 1972 to over 23 percent of 1974 taxpayers seems encouraging, especially compared to the low turnout rate of 38 percent in the 1974 congressional elections.

Experience with other provisions of the new laws must also be carefully monitored. It is important, for example, to be sure that spending limitations are not set so low as to inhibit competition at the presidential or congressional level. It would seem that $10 million is presently adequate for launching even a relatively obscure candidate toward the presidency, particularly when some of the funding comes from the treasury. There is disagreement, however, about whether $84,000 is enough to oust an entrenched incumbent in a House primary when there is no public financing available and all money must be raised privately.

The importance of money in the political process has not been diminished. Rather, it has been redirected in what, one hopes, is a more healthy and open fashion. No reform bill is ever an end in itself, nor can it be an ultimate answer. Even as these laws are being challenged in the courts, fund-raising experts were holding seminars around the country to advise large donors how they might stretch the present $1,000 limit on contributions to individual candidates. Adaptation to change has always been part of the American political genius. The age-old tensions of Republicans vs. Democrats, the White House vs. Congress, and probably, most important, the "ins" vs. the "outs" at all levels of government will continue to operate. Indeed, these tensions are part of a free, competitive democracy. Most important now is to ensure that as the 1976 and subsequent elections are played out, the new campaign structure will enhance the competitive process and bring about greater public participation in it.

Index